Junior Cycle English - First Year

GW00357138

GREAT EXPECTATIONS 1

Catherine Leddin

educate.ie

educate.ie

PUBLISHED BY:
Educate.ie
Walsh Educational Books Ltd
Castleisland, Co. Kerry, Ireland
www.educate.ie

DESIGN & LAYOUT:
Kieran O'Donoghue

COVER DESIGN:
Kieran O'Donoghue

PRINTED AND BOUND BY:
Walsh Colour Print, Castleisland

ISBN: 978-1-909376-99-1

Acknowledgements

I would like to thank the following people for their help, advice and support with this book: my students and colleagues at work, in particular, Carmel Browne for fantastic advice, my daughters Aoife, Jennifer and Niamh for advice on teenage fiction, my husband Gerry for his insight and patience, and finally the team at Educate.ie for their guidance and sheer hard work.

Catherine Leddin

Table of Contents

Chapter 3: Songs and Poems: Storytelling 82

Chapter 4: Non-literary Texts: What's Your Point?

Chapter 5
Drama, Short Story and Film: A Story to Tell 214

Podcasts

Introduction

For the Student

Welcome to first year and your new English textbook, *Great Expectations 1*. Your textbook comes with:

- A **Student Portfolio** (hard copy and online copy)
- A free **eBook** and **digital resources** (use the code on the inside back cover of your textbook to access these)

The material and tasks in this book are designed to help you foster a love of reading and to give you lots of opportunity for enjoyment in your English class. You will learn by 'doing' and build your confidence in speaking up for yourself and giving your opinions. As you progress through the book you will assess yourself and learn from your fellow students, as well as from your teacher. You have your own personal Portfolio, where you record your writing and see how you improve and change over time.

Have fun and enjoy the year!
Catherine Leddin

For the Teacher

Great Expectations 1 is a first-year textbook for the new English course leading to the Junior Cycle Student Award (JCSA). *Great Expectations 2* will complete the course. The student receives a textbook and Portfolio, as well as a free eBook and digital resources. In addition to this the teacher is provided with the following:

- Teacher's Resource Book + 2 CDs
- ICT Handbook

This complete package follows the new Junior Cycle English Specification and makes teaching and learning active and fun, ensuring that your students learn by 'doing' and by enjoying their tasks. The material links the 6th Class primary curriculum and students' experiences in primary school with their first year at second level. Therefore, students continue to create and display their own work, learn collaboratively, write poems and stories, complete projects, give oral talks and presentations, etc.

Chapter 1	Welcomes the student and focuses on the individual and **Personal Writing** using 'I' sentences/statements found in biographies, autobiographies, memoirs and diaries.
Chapter 2	Focuses on **Fiction**, encourages reading, and develops descriptive writing.
Chapter 3	Provides a rich and diverse selection of **Poetry** to encourage creativity.
Chapter 4	Presents a wide variety of **Non-literary texts** with opportunities to improve both formal and informal writing skills.
Chapter 5	Looks at **Drama**, **Short Stories** and **Film** and encourages the student to further explore their creative skills.

Features of *Great Expectations 1*

Learning Expectations are stated at the beginning of each chapter

Tasks throughout the chapters are **clearly laid out** under recognisable headings (literacy, numeracy, drawing, research, writing, reading, etc.)

Differentiation is at the core of the choice of material and accompanying tasks

Checklists and **self-assessment** tasks encourage **assessment for learning**

Grammar is integrated in each chapter and reinforced in the topics and tasks

Assessment is integrated within each chapter culminating in an end-of-chapter assessment

Pairwork and **Groupwork** are encouraged regularly and where appropriate

Peer assessment is encouraged with the 'swap copies' signal

Oral Language tasks are integrated in a natural way in each chapter

A Note on Differentiation

Differentiation is important in mixed ability classrooms and so the material in this book has been carefully selected to suit a range of abilities. The language is straightforward and direct, the explanations are short and clear and the questions move from lower order to higher order. Tasks have been set, in each case, to suit all abilities, for example, with a 'challenging' poem an easy task might be to simply 'pick out the rhyme in the poem' or 'pick out a word/phrase that you like'. The more able students may work on the imagery/language/theme. You can choose the materials/tasks which most suit your students.

Readability scales throughout the book help both teacher and student to assess progress. Where a student reads a story with some difficult words in it, they need to get the gist of the story and be able to identify characters, setting, conflict/problems in the plot/story. 'Getting the Gist' is a learning outcome. Students can then use dictionaries and work in pairs to develop their understanding and get more than just 'the gist'.

Student Portfolio

The Student Portfolio is a hard copy or e-copy where students build up a collection of their work and store it safely. Portfolio tasks are identified clearly in each chapter of the textbook so students know when to record their work in their Portfolio. Portfolio tasks are aimed at developing writing and creation skills. Checklists and end-of-chapter assessments are also provided in the Portfolio so students don't have to write in their textbooks.
Portfolio copies may be stored in the classroom where possible or left in students' lockers. Ordinary copies may be used for other tasks in the book.

Teacher CDs

The teacher CDs contain recordings of poems and drama and fiction extracts, as well as radio podcasts and other material to develop oral language skills and bring this aspect of the course seamlessly into the classroom. The CD icon in the textbook indicates where there is listening/oral material you can incorporate into your lesson.

Teacher's Resource Book

Written in line with the new specification and latest in-service, the Teacher's Resource book provides the following invaluable materials:

- ✓ Lesson Plans
- ✓ Planning Templates
- ✓ Learning Outcomes identified beside tasks
- ✓ Checklist for Learning Outcomes
- ✓ Assessment Templates
- ✓ Graphic Organisers
- ✓ Extra Activities for you to photocopy
- ✓ Crosswords & Wordsearches
- ✓ Tips for Assessment
- ✓ Tips for Questioning

The active learning tasks in the textbook, resource book and student portfolio work towards the achievement of the 22 learning outcomes for first year.

ICT Handbook

Eoghan Evesson is an English teacher and the creator of NewEnglishBlog. He has written a handbook of digital activities for *Great Expectations 1*, allowing the teacher to achieve learning outcomes using ICT if they wish.

There is no necessity to use ICT in your classroom but the new specification allows for teachers to use as much ICT in their course delivery as they are comfortable with.

This ICT Handbook:

- ✓ Is divided into 5 companion chapters to match your textbook
- ✓ Features at least 3 lesson plans per chapter covering primary and secondary learning outcomes
- ✓ Guides teachers with general advice on using ICT to teach the new course with simple information on topics like e-mail, blogging, AUP and copyright
- ✓ Offers templates which are available for download from EducatePlus.ie and can be adapted by you

Great Expectations 1 has been designed in such a way that these digital activities can be an added extra to a section or a fundamental part of your teaching. It's up to you!

Good luck and enjoy!
Catherine Leddin, April 2014

CHAPTER 1

Me, Myself and I

 *My Learning Expectations*

In this chapter I will:

- **Talk** about myself using 'I' sentences
- **Listen** to the teacher, my classmates/peers and to the CD extracts
- Write into my **PORTFOLIO** to keep a record of my **personal writing**
- **Speak** to my classmates/peers to express my opinion
- Use and recognise **capital letters, full stops, commas, question marks, nouns and adjectives**
- **Write** complete, correct sentences
- Understand the difference between a **biography, autobiography, memoir** and **diary**
- **Analyse, Create and Edit (ACE)** when I write something original

Me, Myself and I

All About Me

'The newness in every stale thing'

Patrick Kavanagh, a famous Irish poet, found beauty, wonder and mystery in ordinary things: 'a green stone lying sideways in a ditch', 'tracks of cattle to a drinking place', 'the winking glitter of a frosty dawn'. Your school is new to you but 'stale', perhaps, to the teachers and students who are well used to it. You are the 'newness' in it, livening it up, creating wonder and mystery. Being in an unfamiliar place is frightening at first, but it's also exciting.

Remember, just as you may not know many people in your new school, they don't know you either. So what kind of person are you?

A. Oral Language

It's good to talk and to develop your confidence in public speaking, so begin by talking to the people beside you.

1. Talk to the person beside you and chat about how you are getting on in your new school, what's good/bad, what your last school was like, etc. Tell him or her about your family and your likes and dislikes.

2. It's good to listen too. Listen to the information that your partner is telling you, then see if you can tell someone else what you have learned about that person.

3. Listen to the conversation on the CD. How would you describe the girl and the boy?

B. Drawing

Draw some pictures of your family, pets, house, etc. Matchstick-type pictures are fine if you are not great at drawing!

C. Personal Writing – Who am I?

1. In your **PORTFOLIO**, fill in the table to show your likes and dislikes under each heading given.

For example:

My likes

Food	Sport	Books/Authors	Music	Places	Celebrities
Curry Goat	Cricket	Songs of Freedom	Reggae	Jamaica	Bob Marley

My dislikes

Food	Sport	Books/Authors	Music	Places	Celebrities
Low fat stuff	Football	Sci-fi	Pop	Discos	Kardashians

2. In your **PORTFOLIO**, write a short paragraph describing your family. For example:

I'm Sarah. I'm twelve, which makes me the eldest child in my family. I have two brothers: Tony is ten and Paul is seven. I have one sister, Jane, who is three. My Mum is a primary school teacher and my Dad is a postman. We have two goldfish, a cat and a dog. Sometimes my brothers and I fight 'like cats and dogs' but usually we get on alright together.

3. In your **PORTFOLIO**, write a short paragraph about your life story so far. Use the example below for ideas.

I was born in London and when I was six we returned to Ireland. I was sad leaving my school friends and my neighbourhood. I was nervous starting in a new school, but I had a nice teacher, Mr Ryan, and I soon made new friends. My first Communion was a day that I really enjoyed. It was a scorching hot day in May. All my cousins were there and I got lots of money. We had great fun on the bouncy castle in the garden. Next day we went to Smyths toy shop and I bought myself a new bike. I was very nervous and excited starting secondary school. I have joined the basketball team and the drama club and made new friends. I'm looking forward to going to my first ever disco this year!

Proofreading

Reading over what you have written is called **proofreading**.
Here is a proofreading checklist.

- Do your **sentences** make sense?
- Have you **left out a word** in any sentence?
- Did you begin with a **capital letter** and have you used capital letters for people's names and for places?
- Did you end each sentence with a **full stop, question mark or exclamation mark**?
- Have you checked your **spellings**?
- Have you used **paragraphs** to separate your points?
- Have you included a **title and a date** at the top of your page?
- Is your work **neat** and well spaced out?

Allways chek for speling erors

 ## A. Reading

Read over what you have written for task C on p. 3 using the proofreading checklist above.

Sentences have to make sense, so you need to think about the order of the words in your sentence. After you have written a sentence or a paragraph, ask yourself 'does it sound right?' and 'should I write it in a different way?'

For example:
Manus is the local headmaster's eldest son.
Manus is the eldest son of the headmaster in the local school.

Manus walks with a lame and so us as an audience gain great sympathy for him.
Manus walks with a limp and so we as an audience feel great sympathy for him.

 ## B. Pairwork

Work with a partner. Pick out the sentences from the following list that do not make sense.

Talk to each other about why some of the sentences do **not** make sense.

1. So she went home early and was delighted that.
2. The heavy rain and wind lashed the tiny fishing village.
3. Matt walked swiftly to the car park because.
4. So he never saw.
5. It was miserable, truly sad.
6. They said that it was simply breath-taking.
7. He dismissed the jury because they were awful.
8. Linda's favourite drink is hot chocolate.
9. The boat bobbed lightly from side.
10. 'It's true; you've made it to the finals!' Jane yelled excitedly.

C. Writing

Can you spot the mistakes in the following sentences? Write the sentences correctly in your copy.

1. Tom and joe Go too hurling Trainin on wenesdays n frideys.
2. They lovd eatin Cake n biskets n Ben n jerry's ice-Creem.
3. She new she Should of brought her fone wit her But she forgot it.
4. Two plus too eequels four And tree plus Tree is six.
5. De most Common misteaks in English are in speling and in usin Capital Letters.
6. Stewdents are Not in de habbit of Reedin bac over there work So dey don't c de misTeaks.
7. Polly thinks she's perfect butt I know there's no such thing, good is good enough for me.
8. There new dog was a st. Bernard, cute wit soft, white, grey and Black fur.
9. The scorching sun melted the tar on the Roads to a Gooey, stikey mess.
10. Halloween and christmiss were her Favourite times of de Year.

Capital Letters

Think about what you learned about grammar in primary school.
What can you remember about capital letters, full stops and commas?

Capital Letters

Capital letters are used for:

- **Beginning a sentence** (**O**nce upon a time…)
- **People's names** (**J**ohn, **A**danna, **F**ryderyk)
- **I** (on its own)
- **Place names** of countries, counties, cities, towns and villages (**I**reland, **K**erry, **T**ralee, **D**unloe)
- **Other names**, such as days, months, rivers, mountains, seas, hills, volcanoes (**M**onday, **J**anuary, **R**iver **L**ee, **C**arrauntoohil, **N**orth **S**ea, **H**ill of **T**ara, **M**ount **F**uji)
- **Titles** of films and books (*Despicable Me*, *Rebecca Rules*)
- **Brand names** (*Toyota*, *Coca-Cola*, *Primark*, *Gucci*)

A. Pairwork

In pairs, make a list of 20 words with capital letters. Make sure you are both happy that your list is correct before handing it up. Double check your 20 words using the above list.

B. Writing

Write out the following sentences, inserting the correct capital letters.

1. tadhg drove his new ford focus home to galway, feeling very pleased indeed.
2. pineapple is delicious and versatile, so the chef included it in ten recipes in his new book, entitled *Fruit for All*.
3. she was disappointed with india but mesmerised by china, japan and the philippines.
4. joan bought new beachwear in penneys, then got shoes in dunnes and a bag in debenhams.
5. most people start their tour of the brazilian amazon from the nearby city of manaus.
6. the german sixth army were led by general von paulus.
7. auntie kate works in tesco, but prefers to shop in supervalu and aldi.
8. nurse reilly climbed croagh patrick, then toured around mayo and sligo.

Full Stops

Full stops are dots that stop your sentences from running on and on and on. Use full stops to end a sentence.

For example:
- The runaway train slammed into the wall and came to a sudden halt.
- Maud chose the strawberry ice-cream.
- Jake swam ten lengths, cycled two miles and strolled home.

You can also end a sentence with a question mark (?) or an exclamation mark (!).

Writing

Insert full stops in the following text:

When Ruth was allowed home, everyone was relieved and happy She had been in hospital for two weeks and was missed at home Ruth was the fun person in the family She was quick-witted, generous and kind Simon missed her crazy dancing and singing during the X Factor Lucy missed the help with homework and she didn't do as well in her tests since Ruth was in hospital Even the dog missed her He whined outside her bedroom door for the first few days but then got used to her absence.

Commas

Commas are small curved marks used to separate word in a sentence.

For example:
- They **separate adjectives:** long, golden, wavy, shiny curls. Notice that there is no comma at the end of your list: …shiny curls.
- They **separate nouns** in a list: butter, eggs, sugar, milk, bun cases, vanilla essence. However, note that there is no comma before the word 'and' in a list: She plays flute, piano, guitar and drums.
- They **indicate a pause** in the sentence: Mary didn't just shout, she roared.

LET'S EAT GRANDMA!

LET'S EAT, GRANDMA!

PUNCTUATION SAVES LIVES!

A. Writing

Insert commas in the following sentences.

1. It was a cold icy bitter morning and Betty felt tired weary sad and lonely.
2. Paul loved chicken broccoli roast potatoes gravy carrots and parsnips for Sunday dinner.
3. Nigel and Norma played tennis golf basketball rounders cricket and football.
4. The Girl Guides brought tents torches rucksacks stools blankets sleeping bags and food to the campsite.
5. Medical supplies of food water and blankets were distributed to the survivors.
6. The tornado ripped up trees plants flowers bins and streetlights.
7. I like to put butter and jam on toast then cut it into small squares then eat it slowly to savour every bite.
8. For Christmas Bob wanted a bike a train set Lego and a surprise.
9. Line-outs are about the calls, the jumpers, the lifters and the thrower.
10. The soft swirling delicate light snowflakes fell swiftly and covered the land.

B. Pairwork

In pairs, rewrite the following text, inserting capital letters, full stops and commas.

Hints:

- Full stops go at the end of a sentence.
- Capital letters go at the start of a sentence.
  (So you need to figure out where each sentence in the following text begins and ends!)
- Use capital letters for people's names and for places.

tony loved visiting the zoo he was wild about animals his first outings were to fota wildlife in cork which he loved but after three annual trips there he longed for somewhere bigger and more exciting the following summer his parents took him to dublin zoo then to edinburgh in dublin they stayed overnight in the maldron hotel and in edinburgh they stayed in the holiday inn hotel tony bought souvenirs from each zoo especially lots of panda bears he hopes next year to go to washington to the smithsonian national zoo so he has started a savings fund his godparents, jane and mark, gave him €50 for his tenth birthday aunt mary pays him €20 a month for maintaining her garden and his parents, tom and kate, give him €10 pocket money every friday how much money will he save in a year do you think if he saves it all?

Peer Assessment – *Swap copies and correct each other's work to help each other to improve. This is collaborative learning – you learn from each other.*

CHECKLIST OF MY SKILLS ☑

Fill in the following checklist in your **PORTFOLIO**.

Target Skills	Can Do	Needs Work
Listen to instruction		
Bring copy and book/PC/tablet to class		
Write the heading and date in my copy		
Read the text in the book		
Understand some of the text		
Understand all of the text		
Understand how to do the tasks in the book		
Ask questions when I don't understand		
Feel confident asking questions		
Write neatly using paragraphs		
Use capital letters correctly		
Spell correctly		
Read over my work to correct mistakes		
Write it out again to get it right		
Share ideas and opinions with other students		
Think about how I learn and how I can improve		

A. Writing

In your copy, describe any two of the following photographs using short sentences.
(Hint: talk about colours, objects, how you feel about the image, etc.)

B. Pairwork

Working with a partner, write a description of your new school in ten sentences.
(Remember to be original and to check your work!)

Question Marks

The question mark is used **at the end of a sentence** to show that it is a **question rather than a statement**.

For example:

'When is your train due in?', enquired Martha.

'How long is the table? Will it seat 12?', Tommy asked.

'Which musical are you performing in?', asked Siobhán.

 ## Writing

Fill in the question marks in the following sentences.

'When is the film starting', asked Julia.

'Where are you going now', enquired the secretary.

'When will dinner be ready', the children chorused.

'How did you do that', Paul asked in wonder.

'Why are you putting up blinds', the salesman asked.

 **Peer Assessment** – *Swap copies to correct each other's work*

CHECKLIST OF MY ENGLISH SKILLS ☑

Fill in the following checklist in your **PORTFOLIO**.

Writing

I like writing. . ...☐
I know how to write good sentences. ....☐
I don't like writing. ....☐
I find writing hard. ....☐
I can write short paragraphs on a range of topics. ☐
I am good at spelling. ....☐
I find spelling hard. ....☐
I am good at using capital letters. ....☐
I find capital letters confusing. ....☐
I am good at using full stops and commas. ....☐
I prefer typing to handwriting. ....☐

Reading

I am a confident reader. ....☐
I like reading. ....☐
I never read. ....☐
I read sometimes. ....☐
I read as much as possible. ....☐
I find reading difficult. ....☐
I find reading boring. ....☐
I like to read (tick each one that you like).
    – Books..☐
    – Magazines ....☐
    – Newspapers ....☐
    – Online material......................................☐
I would like to read more often and
improve my reading skills. ....☐

Listening

I am a good listener. ....☐
I am a listener rather than a talker. ....☐
I like listening to music. ....☐
I like listening to stories on CD. ....☐
I like watching films. ....☐
I find it hard to hear the teacher in class. ....☐
I use a hearing aid to help me. ....☐

Speaking

I like talking to my friends. ....☐
I don't mind talking to teachers and parents. ......☐
I am a confident speaker. ....☐
I am a shy speaker. ....☐
I can stand up and talk confidently to the class. ☐
If asked to do a reading in public I could do it. ...☐
I don't like reading in public. ....☐

My Skills Overall: Reading, Writing, Listening, Speaking

I am good at_____

I would like to improve _____

My Expectations
At the end of this chapter, I hope to improve:

My speaking skills ....☐
My listening skills ....☐
My confidence in asking questions ....☐
My ability to concentrate on tasks ....☐
My ability to offer my opinion ....☐
My ability to finish tasks ....☐
My ability to write full, complete sentences.........☐

My skills in discussing issues ....☐
My IT skills ....☐
My reading skills ....☐
My confidence in speaking to my class...............☐
My writing skills ....☐
My confidence using 'I' sentences ('I think...') ....☐

At the end of this chapter, I hope to _____

Biographies, Autobiographies and Memoirs

A **biography** is a book written about a person's life, usually a famous person, by someone else. The book tells you about where they were born, their early childhood, their family, their education, their career, etc. For example, Bieber J. Smith wrote a biography of the pop star **Bruno Mars**, Richard Aldous wrote about **Tony Ryan** and Walter Isaacson wrote about **Steve Jobs**.

You could decide to write a biography about your favourite singer, band, sportsperson, etc., but you would usually ask their permission first so they could help you to write their life story.

An **autobiography** is a book written by someone about their own life. For example, in 1995, **Nelson Mandela** wrote his autobiography, *Long Walk to Freedom*, detailing his childhood, early adult life and his 27 years in prison. **Morrissey** (a well-known singer in the 1980s) recently wrote his autobiography and simply called it *Autobiography*.

Sometimes a person gets help to write their autobiography, but the story is still told by that person. For example, in 2013 **Malala Yousafzai** wrote her autobiography, entitled *I Am Malala*, with help from Christina Lamb.

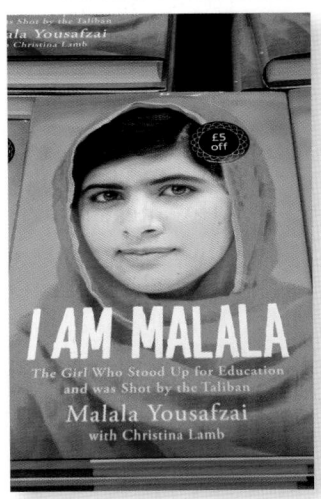

A **memoir** usually focuses on memories or events in a person's life that had a significant impact on them. People like to write about all kinds of memories: of childhood, of growing up, of teenage years, of houses or places they lived in, of successes, of bad times etc. For example, **Alice Taylor**, a popular Irish writer, has written various memoirs, such as *To School Through the Fields*, about her experiences during her childhood and growing up in Ireland. **Seán O'Connor** wrote *Growing Up So High, A Liberties Boyhood* about his childhood in Dublin in the 1940s and 1950s. In 2012, Katie Taylor wrote a memoir of her time at the Olympics entitled *My Olympic Dream*. She was helped by *The Irish Times* sports writer, Johnny Watterson.

Often there can be overlap and it can be hard to distinguish between what is an autobiography, biography or memoir. They all look back to the past and recollect and reflect on past experiences and memories.

A. Oral Language

Have you or your classmates read any autobiographies? If so, discuss these in pairs or groups.

B. Research

Do some research on a person whose autobiography you would like to read. List five pieces of information which you found out.

The Sweet Shop *by Roald Dahl*

Roald Dahl was born in Wales in 1916 and is a popular author of books for children. Many of his books have been turned into films, such as *Charlie and the Chocolate Factory*, *Matilda* and *The Witches*. The following story is from his first autobiography, *Boy*, which tells tales of his childhood. He died in 1990.

On the way to school and on the way back we always passed the sweet shop. No we didn't, we never passed it. We always stopped. We lingered outside its rather small window gazing in at the big glass jars full of Bull's-eyes and Old Fashioned Humbugs and Strawberry Bonbons and Glacier Mints and Acid Drops and Pear Drops and Lemon Drops and all the rest of them. Each of us received sixpence a week for pocket-money and whenever there was any money in our pockets, we would all troop in together to buy a pennyworth of this or that. My own favourites were Sherbet Suckers and Liquorice Bootlaces.

One of the other boys, whose name was Thwaites, told me I should never eat Liquorice Bootlaces. Thwaites's father, who was a doctor, had said that they were made from rats' blood. The father had given his young son a lecture about Liquorice Bootlaces when he had caught him eating one in bed. 'Every ratcatcher in the country,' the father had said, 'takes his rats to the Liquorice Bootlace Factory, and the manager pays tuppence for each rat. Many a ratcatcher has become a millionaire by selling his dead rats to the Factory.'

'But how do they turn the rats into liquorice?' the young Thwaites had asked his father.

'They wait until they've got ten thousand rats,' the father had answered, 'then they dump them all into a huge shiny steel cauldron and boil them up for several hours. Two men stir the bubbling cauldron with long poles and in the end they have a thick steaming rat-stew. After that, a cruncher is lowered into the cauldron to crunch the bones, and what's left is a pulpy substance called rat-mash.'

'Yes, but how do they turn that into Liquorice Bootlaces, Daddy?' the young Thwaites had asked, and this question, according to Thwaites, had caused his father to pause and think for a few moments before he answered it. At last he had said, 'The two men who were doing the stirring with the long poles now put on their wellington boots and climb into the cauldron and shovel the hot rat-mash out on to a concrete floor. Then they run a steam-roller over it several times to flatten it out. What is left looks rather like a gigantic black pancake, and all they have to do after that is to wait for it to cool and to harden so they can cut it up into strips to make the Bootlaces. Don't ever eat them,' the father had said. 'If you do, you'll get ratitis.'

'What is ratitis, Daddy?' young Thwaites had asked.

'All the rats that the ratcatchers catch are poisoned with rat-poison,' the father had said. 'It's the rat-poison that gives you ratitis.'

'Yes, but what happens to you when you catch it?' young Thwaites had asked.

'Your teeth become very sharp and pointed,' the father had answered. 'And a short stumpy tail grows out of your back just above your bottom. There is no cure for ratitis. I ought to know. I'm a doctor.'

We all enjoyed Thwaites's story and we made him tell it to us many times on our walks to and from school. But it didn't stop any of us except Thwaites from buying Liquorice Bootlaces. At two for a penny they were the best value in the shop. A Bootlace, in case you haven't had the pleasure of handling one, is not round. You buy it rolled up in a coil, and in those days it used to be so long that when you unrolled it and held one end at arm's length above your head, the other end touched the ground.

Sherbet Suckers were also two a penny. Each sucker consisted of a yellow cardboard tube filled with sherbet powder, and there was a hollow liquorice straw sticking out of it. (Rats' blood again, young Thwaites would warn us, pointing at the liquorice straw.) You sucked the sherbet up through the straw and when it was finished you ate the liquorice. They were delicious, those Sherbet Suckers. The sherbet fizzed in your mouth, and if you knew how to do it, you could make white froth come out of your nostrils and pretend you were throwing a fit.

Gobstoppers, costing a penny each, were enormous hard round balls the size of small tomatoes. One Gobstopper would provide about an hour's worth of non-stop sucking and if you took it out of your mouth and inspected it every five minutes or so, you would find it had changed colour. There was something fascinating about the way it went from pink to blue to green to yellow. We used to wonder how in the world the Gobstopper Factory managed to achieve this magic.

'How *does* it happen?' we would ask each other. 'How *can* they make it keep changing colour?'

'It's your spit that does it,' young Thwaites proclaimed. As the son of a doctor, he considered himself to be an authority on all things that had to do with the body. He could tell us about scabs and when they were ready to be picked off. He knew why a black eye was blue and why blood was red. 'It's your spit that makes a Gobstopper change colour,' he kept insisting. When we asked him to elaborate on this theory, he answered, 'You wouldn't understand it if I did tell you.'

Pear Drops were exciting because they had a dangerous taste. They smelled of nail varnish and they froze the back of your throat. All of us were warned against eating them, and the result was that we ate them more than ever.

Then there was a hard brown lozenge called the Tonsil Tickler. The Tonsil Tickler tasted and smelled very strongly of chloroform. We had not the slightest doubt that these things were saturated in the dreaded anaesthetic which, as Thwaites had many times pointed out to us, could put you to sleep for hours at a stretch. 'If my father has to saw off somebody's leg,' he said, 'he pours chloroform on to a pad and the person sniffs it and goes to sleep and my father saws his leg off without him even feeling it.'

'But why do they put it into sweets and sell them to us?' we asked him.

You might think a question like this would have baffled Thwaites. But Thwaites was never baffled. 'My father says Tonsil Ticklers were invented for dangerous prisoners in jail,' he said. 'They give them one with each meal and the chloroform makes them sleepy and stops them rioting.'

'Yes,' we said, 'but why sell them to children?'

'It's a plot,' Thwaites said. 'A grown up plot to keep us quiet.'

The sweet-shop in Llandaff in the year 1923 was the very centre of our lives.

GLOSSARY

Chloroform: A liquid used by doctors as an anaesthetic.

Anaesthetic: A substance which makes patients unable to feel pain when they become unconscious.

A. Reading

Rate this text for 'readability'. Write the word/phrase of your choice into your copy.

VERY EASY ☐   EASY ☐   OKAY ☐   HARD ☐   VERY HARD ☐

B. Literacy Questions

1. Can you name ten kinds of sweets sold in the sweet shop?
2. What was rat-mash?
3. What happened if you caught ratitis?
4. What made pear drops exciting?
5. Why were Tonsil Ticklers invented?

Proofread your answers and correct any mistakes.

C. Numeracy Questions

1. How much pocket money did Roald get each week?
2. How many rats were needed to make rat-mash?
3. How much were Liquorice Bootlaces?
4. How long could a Gobstopper last?

D. Personal Writing – My Favourites

In your **PORTFOLIO**, describe **in detail** five of your favourite sweets, chocolate bars, ice-creams, lollipops, etc.

Part 1: Katie Taylor: Journey to Olympic Gold *by Jason O'Toole*

Katie Taylor is the Irish lightweight boxing champion who has repeatedly won gold in Irish, European and world boxing competitions. Her biggest achievement was winning a gold medal in the Olympics in 2012, when she also won the hearts of thousands of proud Irish people. She was born in Bray, Co. Wicklow in 1986 and attended St. Kilian's Community School. This excerpt is taken from Jason O'Toole's biography of Katie entitled *Journey to Olympic Gold*.

No sooner had the bell signalled the end of the unbelievably tense final round than Katie Taylor glanced **tentatively** over to her corner and asked her father for **reassurance**. It appeared that she was mouthing the words, 'Did I do it?'

Peter Taylor nodded confidently and spoke words of encouragement, but – despite the positivity **emanating** from her corner – Katie's **trepidation** was obvious during the seemingly endless seconds before the judges' **verdict** confirmed that her lifelong dream had come true.

A few seconds later Katie was jumping for joy when the ring announcer began declaring the winner with those magic words: 'red corner'.

The entire country **rejoiced** as Katie danced joyfully around the ring after she had won what was only Ireland's ninth gold medal since the **foundation** of the state. She was now in the company of just six Irish gold medallists: Pat O'Callaghan, Bob Tisdall, Ronnie Delany, Michael Carruth and Michelle Smith.

A. Reading

Rate this text for 'readability'. Write the word/phrase of your choice into your copy.

VERY EASY ☐   **EASY** ☐   **OKAY** ☐   **HARD** ☐   **VERY HARD** ☐

B. Literacy Questions

1. What did Katie Taylor win?
2. How did Katie feel before the announcer called out the result?
3. How many gold medals has Ireland won so far in the Olympics?
4. Use your dictionary to find the meaning of the following words from the text: *tentatively, reassurance, emanating, trepidation, verdict, rejoiced, foundation*.

Proofread your answers and correct any mistakes.

C. Research

Do some research into the other five Irish gold medallists listed above. For which sports did they win medals? Which years did they win? Where are they now?

Part 2

From the outside, Katie can appear to be a **contradictory** character. In the ring, she is a tough but elegantly expressive boxer who likes to entertain **punters**, sometimes by **showcasing** with sleek footwork to match her dazzling boxing skills, as during the Olympics. But once she steps out of the ring, Katie is shy and retiring – to such an extent that she is uncomfortable in the **spotlight** and doesn't like doing interviews. 'She's very quiet, but there's a real strength behind her quietness,' Bridget (her mum) once explained to a journalist. 'A lot of people look at her as "Katie Taylor the boxer" – but I always say to her that's not who she is, that's what she does. Katie is very kind-hearted and would take the clothes off her back and give them to you.'

Katie is also
a keen soccer player.

As a born-again Christian, religion plays a vital role in the **psychological** make-up of this Irish boxing hero. She often quotes Psalm 18 to the press, praising God in post-match press conferences for being her 'shield' and her 'strength' when she steps into the ring. She also spoke of her belief that the prayers of a nation willed her on to her Olympic gold.

Prior to every fight, Katie's pre-match **ritual** involves a routine of listening to Christian rock music on her iPod when she is warming up for the fight. She will then pray and recite Bible verses – particularly Psalm 18, which is affectionately known among her church's **congregation** as 'Katie's Psalm' – with her mother, when Bridget is tying back her daughter's hair.

Katie has made **countless** sacrifices with her personal life on the road to gold. The dedication to boxing has been such that her social life is practically non-existent and she's never really had a serious relationship, despite now being 26 years old. 'Katie hasn't had a holiday in about 10 years – neither have my parents,' Katie's brother Peter said before the London Games. A good night out for Katie, her father once stated, is sitting in front of the telly with her 80-year-old grandmother.

A. Reading

Rate this text for 'readability'. Write the word/phrase of your choice into your copy.

VERY EASY ☐   **EASY** ☐   **OKAY** ☐   **HARD** ☐   **VERY HARD** ☐

B. Literacy Questions

1. What does the writer mean when he describes Katie as a 'contradictory' type of person? (Use a dictionary to look up the meaning of 'contradictory'.)
2. How does Katie's mother describe her daughter?
3. What does Katie do when she is warming up for a fight?
4. List the sacrifices Katie has made in order to put her career first.
5. Do you think that you have any of the qualities or personality traits that Katie has?
6. Use a dictionary to find the meaning of the following words from the text: *punter, showcasing, spotlight, psychological, ritual, congregation, countless.*

Proofread your answers and correct any mistakes.

C. Writing

List ten qualities you like about your friends. Write them into your copy.

(Hint: hardworking, funny, kind, pleasant, caring, witty, strong.)

D. Personal Writing – My Autobiography

Fill in the blanks in your **PORTFOLIO**.

1. My name is .... and I was born in .... in the year ....

2. My star sign is .... because my birthday is in ....

3. My family: I have ....

4. Pets: I have/do not have ....

5. My likes/dislikes are: ....

6. One memorable event in my life was ....

7. My favourite singers/bands are: ....

E. Oral Language

Talk to the class about your life so far. If you feel confident enough, stand up, if not, then remain seated, but promise yourself you will try to stand up next time! If you wish, you may start with the sentences you have written in your portfolio and continue on.

CHECKLIST OF MY SKILLS ☑

How are you getting on so far? Have you improved your skills since your first day of English class? Let's see! Fill in this table in your **PORTFOLIO**.

Target Skills	Can Do ✓	Needs Work ✓	My Comment
Reading for understanding	☐	☐	
Writing about myself	☐	☐	
Reading aloud confidently	☐	☐	
Using dictionaries	☐	☐	
Planning my writing	☐	☐	
Checking for mistakes	☐	☐	
Rewriting drafts 2 and 3	☐	☐	
Talking more confidently	☐	☐	
Using 'I' statements	☐	☐	

A Year in the Centre *by Brian O'Driscoll*

This extract is from Brian O'Driscoll's book, *A Year in the Centre*, which is a memoir, written in the form of a diary. It covers the period from December 2004 to July 2005, when Leinster were looking for Heineken Cup glory and Ireland were chasing their first grand slam in 57 years.

Sunday 10 July, airborne – somewhere between Sydney and Singapore

Leaving on a jet plane, don't know when I'll be back again. Don't care either for the time being. Just want to get home to Ireland, the best country in the world despite the weather! Long journey ahead and I'm just wishing the hours away.

We got beaten again last night, very similar to the second Test, pretty good gutsy performance, but flawed as well – and New Zealand were just too good. My new mate Conrad Smith had a terrific match, he looks a very complete player and it will be some competition between him and Aaron Mauger to see who gets the starting spot at inside centre for their big games ahead. The depth New Zealand have in some positions is staggering.

At one stage in the first half we managed to squander a three-man overlap 5 yards from the line. Donncha O'Callaghan went to ground just short of the line, but we should still have scored with men begging on the blindside – except Tana prevented release at the ruck and got a yellow card for his pains. And then, with them down to fourteen men, we let them in for two softish tries. Effectively a twenty-one point swing in ten minutes. No side in the world can give New Zealand twenty-one points. The match was over there and then, although we kept plugging away gamely. I was proud that our heads never dropped, and there were times up front last night when we began to take control and got those powerful rolling mauls going at last. A hint of what might have been. I would like to have seen some more of earlier in the series. Paul O'Connell had a big game – aggressive but disciplined – and Shane Byrne a much happier night at line-out time. He stoically bore the brunt of the criticism after Christchurch, which was, of course, grossly unfair on him. Line-outs are about the calls, the jumpers, the lifters and thrower. Everything has to work in unison to be successful. No one single person is the cause of a nightmare like the one we endured.

A. Reading

Rate this text for 'readability'. Write the word/phrase of your choice into your copy.

VERY EASY ☐   EASY ☐   OKAY ☐   HARD ☐   VERY HARD ☐

B. Literacy Questions

1. This is written as a diary, so it looks back and reflects on events that have already happened. It also looks forward to the future, to what's next. Find one example in the extract that proves that O'Driscoll is looking back at an event that has already happened.

2. The language in the extract is technical – words that apply only to rugby are used. Make a list of the rugby words (rugby terminology) that you can find in the text.

3. Use a dictionary to find the meaning of the following words from the text: *flawed*, *staggering*, *squander*, *unison* and *endured*.

4. Read the final two sentences in the text. What do you think O'Driscoll means here?

Proofread your answers and correct any mistakes.

C. Writing

Think of a time in your life when you or your team suffered a defeat. Write a paragraph about it. Use the same diary style and reflective mood that O'Driscoll has used above.

D. Pairwork

Create a table like the one below in your copy. In pairs or groups, make a list of the words and terminology that are associated with the sports listed.

Golf	Basketball	Horse-riding	Hurling	Football
tee	basket	gymkhana	sliotar	goalpost

Diaries

A **diary** is a personal record of events, experiences or thoughts. Diaries are written using 'I' sentences and can be written on a daily, weekly or monthly basis. Most diaries are written regularly and are in sequence, but there are great variations in the types of diaries people keep. Have you read *The Secret Diary of Adrian Mole Aged 13 ¾* by **Sue Townsend**? It's hilarious.

Diaries were very popular years ago. They were a great way of recording events and feelings and could capture how a person felt at a particular moment in time. People had actual books, called diaries, which they filled in. They were often given as gifts.

The style of writing in diaries is personal and informal. Often only half-sentences are written or quick notes are scribbled down. The words or vocabulary used in diaries varies depending on things like the period in history that the diary was written in, the age and life experiences of the writer and the level of education the writer had at that time.

With the development of technology, diaries can be seen as old-fashioned. Many people now write online blogs as a way of recording their thoughts and feelings, but blogs are very public while diaries are generally private.

Read and enjoy the following examples of diaries.

The Diaries of Evelyn Waugh *edited by Michael Davie*

Evelyn Waugh (1903–1966) was a famous English author and journalist. He kept a diary almost continuously from the age of seven until a year before his death in 1966. Can you find the spelling mistakes in the following extract?

September, 1911; aged 7

My History

My name is Evelyn Waugh I go to Heath Mount school I am in the Vth Form, Our Form Master is Mr Stebbing.

We all hate Mr Cooper, our arith master. It is the 7th day of the Winter Term which is my 4th.

Today is Sunday so I am not at school. We allways have sausages for breakfast on Sundays I have been watching Lucy fry them they do look funny befor their kooked. Daddy is a Publisher he goes to Chapman and Hall office it looks a offely dull plase. I am just going to Church. Alec, my big brother has just gorn to Sherborne. The wind is blowing dreadfully I am afraid that when I go up to Church I shall be blown away. I was not blown away after all.

June, 1912; aged 8

Vol. I.

My history by Evelyn Waugh.
& Diary. Big Print.
Begining at June 10th 1912 at school & at home.
My HISTORY
   BY E. WAUGH
    AT SCHOOL & HOME
     ILASTRATED BY THE AUTHER
      WRITEN AT THE AGE OF EIGHT
    AT SCHOOL & AT HOME & at the seaside CHEEFLY AT HOME.

My name is Evelyn. I live in a house called Underhill. I have been in bed with something wrong with my stomach & have got to stay in bed for the hole of this week it is awful. This morning Maxwell, my great chum, came round to see me It was his birthday & he showed me all his presents. He had a riping pair of pads & a pair of wicket-keeping gloves & bat. In the evening Dady came back from office & brought me a lot of paper to draw on. The next morning I read 'How Heat Travels' in the Childs 'Encyclopaedia' then I had breakfast and read the Boy's Friend.

In the afternoon Miss Hoar came to see me & brought me a dear little hand bag with some soldiers of the regiment of the 'Black Watch'.

Mother read me a article the following morning called 'How To Join the Navy' & I have made up my mind that I am going to be a 'Merry Jack tar', if my eyes will pass Mother dous not think they will. If they do not I shall go board a 'Merchantman' for I must go to sea.

I am just go to make my little elephant a coat.

> If I should be a sailor bold
> I'd stand up on the deck
> I'd lock my prisoners in the hold
> And make their ship a wreck

Chap IV

Next morning Mrs Simmons came to see me & showed me some carvings she had done and Max came to tea with me. On the following morning I found I had the appendicitis & had an operation. Mother had a nurse in. This happened VI days ago for I have not been able to write this till now. I have had IX presants since the operation cheafly soldiers.

June, 1913; aged 9

Volume II

Chapter III

The first lesson this morning was history in which Mr Stebbing 'heard us' our 'notes' on the Peninsular War. Then Latin in which Mr Cooper was in a rotten bate about what Stebbing had set us. Then we had break. After break we had French in which I translated 'Here is the church' into 'Ici est lêglise.' Then Spelling in which I got 13 marks out of 20 (not bad). Then we had Arith. I got the arith 'prep' right and got full marks ($\frac{8}{8}$) 3 for the Prep and 5 for the other sum. Then break and dinner. After dinner I fought Geogan. Then Rep in which we had to say 'Tall are the oacks whos ackorns drop in dark Auserrill, Fat are the stags that champ the boughs of the Ciminian Hill & ect' (it comes in Horatios) for which I got $\frac{19}{20}$. Then Extra Geog for which I got $\frac{18}{20}$. Then Cricket. I was on Roscoe's side and made o (Mr Stebbing's bowling).

A. Reading

Rate this text for 'readability'. Write the word/phrase of your choice into your copy.

VERY EASY ☐   **EASY** ☐   **OKAY** ☐   **HARD** ☐   **VERY HARD** ☐

B. Literacy Questions

1. Read the first diary entry. For a seven-year-old child in 1911, do you think it is good in terms of the spelling? Have you any examples of spontaneous writing that you did yourself at the age of seven, eight or nine?
2. Read the second diary entry. List the kinds of activities the eight-year-old did for fun in 1912.
3. Read the third diary entry. Imagine you are the boy's class tutor and you have been asked to write up a progress report on his results. Choose a format that you feel is suitable and write up a school report based on the information in the diary extract.

Proofread your answers and correct any mistakes.

C. Writing

Use the third diary entry as a template (an example) and write your own real diary entry. Write it about your own experiences on a particular day in your school.

Hilda Murrell's Nature Diaries 1961–1983
edited by Charles Sinker

Hilda Murrell (1906–1984) was a well-known rose grower and a leading authority on old-fashioned roses. She ran her family's rose nursery in Shrewsbury, and during her time as manager it regularly won gold awards at the Chelsea, Shrewsbury and Southport flower shows. Her name became familiar to a different public after her much-publicised murder in March 1984. Her killers have never been found. During her life, Hilda Murrell kept separate sets of personal journals, diaries on botanical and other natural history subjects, planting logs and records of her holiday trips in Britain and Ireland.

6

UNMITIGATED SUPERFLUITY OF H_2O

April–May 1964. Ireland

27 April, Monday

Flew to Cork from Birmingham airport. Left in glorious weather, almost hot. For about twenty minutes looked down on patchwork of green and red, then went into cloud. Climbed until we were out of it, and flew all the rest of the time above the white snowfield. Came down into the murk again at Cork – it was right down on the airfield and the taxi-driver told me it was touch and go whether we landed or were sent off to Shannon!

28 April, Tuesday

Not raining when I looked out of window – and signs of breaks in the clouds. Sun shining by mid-morning. Collected car and left Cork 12.30. Went to Bantry via Bandon and Dunmanway. This is dull. Splendid gorse, but country looked increasingly poverty-stricken the further west. Ardnagashel House proved to be on the edge of better country – Bantry and onwards a scatter of bungalows etc. and as they are of poorer quality than in Wales the effect is even worse. Nor is there the mitigating solid or good-looking cottage that helps in Wales. Was tempted to write off Ireland!

In Ardnagashel grounds there were beautiful slender trees with rich cinnamon bark. I thought they must be *Arbutus* but the leaves were small. These are *Myrtusluma*, which seeds itself here all over the place.

After tea, went up the lane by the Barony river. In the first sheltered corner were handsome plants of *Euphorbia hyberna* (Irish Spurge), just coming into flower.

29 April, Wednesday

10.30 crossed to Garnish Island to see the garden. Conducted round by Mackenzie.
Rhododendronfragrantissimum flourishing in the open, huge leptospermums which seed themselves and provide leg cover. Came away at 1.30 and went along west along the coast road. Found a grassy hollow just over the wall above Seal Bay and lay in the sun for an hour or so. To find such a hollow is not easy – the land is either gorse or bog, without the nice soft heather bush of home. After this explored on along the coast road as far as the east tip of Bere Island. Just after the Tim Healy Pass turn, there was a small saltmarsh, which had Scurvygrass and Thrift in the usual mixture, but by a small stream there was Sea Plantain and *Glauxmaritima*.

30 April, Thursday

Spent the morning in the Barony Valley. The weather turned grey after the usual pattern. Had lunch here then set off for Dereeny. Stopped in Killarney and bought a skirt-length in tabby weave of coral-red and gold. The Kenmare Bay is much less populated than Bantry. Dereeny quite wonderful – a beautiful position, with 100-year-old trees and rhododendrons here and there.

1 May, Friday

Superb early morning – glorious sunshine. No wind. As soon as I stepped out of the door heard a little 'chip-chip' out over the water – the terns had arrived. Got the glass and there was a pair – Common? – with black heads and rather dusky plumage.

A. Reading

Rate this text for 'readability'. Write the word/phrase of your choice into your copy.

VERY EASY ☐   **EASY** ☐   **OKAY** ☐   **HARD** ☐   **VERY HARD** ☐

B. Literacy Questions

1. From the above diary extracts, what do you think Hilda Murrell is most interested in?
2. The names of the flowers and plants are in italics. What language are they in?

Proofread your answers and correct any mistakes.

C. Research

1. Do a little research on terns (birds). Write a short paragraph about them.
2. Examine a map of Munster. See if you can find the places Hilda visited.
   (Try *http://www.osi.ie/Education/Secondary-Schools.aspx*)

D. Writing

What differences in language and in writing style did you notice between Evelyn Waugh's diary and Hilda Murrell's? In your copy, write your own thoughts and observations on the differences in the two styles. See the sample below to get you started.

Diary writer	Viewpoint of...	Topics	Style	Other comments
Evelyn Waugh	A child (7-9 years)	School and friends	Friendly, casual	I related more to this diary
Hilda Murrell	An adult	Plants and flowers	Abrupt, casual	She talks a lot about the weather

The Diaries of Hannah Cullwick, Victorian Maidservant *edited by Liz Stanley*

Hannah Cullwick was never famous, but she wrote diaries which bring home to us with a unique freshness what it meant to live and work as a lower-class woman 'in service' in Victorian England (during the reign of Queen Victoria, 1837-1901). Hannah was born in Shropshire in 1833, the daughter of a housemaid and a saddler.

1841–1843

1. And might glad I was for going to Mrs Phillips, for the living was good & strengthen'd me, as I was growing fast & tall & 'cause Mrs P. was so very kind to me & teach'd me how to do everything properly – to wait at table, to wash up, to clean silver, & indeed everything. So, as she said, there wasn't a job I couldn't do as well as the cook or housemaid could. She always prais'd me after I'd clean'd the red brick floor on my hands & knees & scour'd the big white tables in the kitchen. And I could clean the dining room & the bright long hall, & the door steps & all before breakfast. The Missis always said I sh'd be her servant when I was old enough & I could sew neatly at Irish cloth shirts or shifts, so I did that too. Mrs P. used to take me with her for a ride, or a fishing, & I carried the stool & mind'd the little dog.

2. At last I wasn't wanted & the Master gave me a *sovereign*, & I jump'd for joy, & looked at it as such a prize, but I was going to live at home again getting nothing after I'd once began. It wasn't that I didn't like being at home tho', for then there wasn't a day but I was up to see Mother, if 'twas only for a minute. And when I was sent to the grocer's I'd order the things & run up home & back again afore the man'd finish'd tying 'em up, so as I sh'd n't be no longer gone nor I ought to be.

3. I got a place at the Lion for a shilling a week & stopp'd eight months. There I clean'd the tables & floors & even waited on the farmers dinner of a market day. They gave me always 2^D or a penny each on the plate as I carried round o' purpose, after the cheese, making a curtsy to them as give the most, 'cause I thought they was the biggest farmers. But my father thought it wasn't good for me there at a public house & I was to give warning. I did & met

Mrs Philipps one day with my hair in curl. She said, 'Hollo, miss, what do you mean by wearing your hair in curl? Missis always used to mean contempt with us in Shropshire & its so now I believe,' I said, 'My Missis at the Lion makes me curl it, she says I look better to wait in the parlour – I'm going tho' & I sh'd like to come to you again, ma'am, if you want me,' & I made her another curtsy. She said, 'Well I'll think about it, but you know it's not respectable to have a girl out of a public house,' but however I felt frightened rather at that.

4. She very soon had me back again, off & on, & at last my kind Missis died. I'd bin there entirely twelve months, slept in the house & all. She kept her bed & she had me to wait on her & all I could, & gave me a lot of her things for she was sure of dying. She made Mr P. promise to be a friend to all us children (Martha's Children she call'd us). It was in July 1847 when she died & I'd a suit o' black & follow'd her to the grave. In Sept or early in Oct I got the nurserymaid's place at Ryton & went to it. A month after my mother came to see me, & in December both my father & her was dead. So I never saw them again, for they died of a fever just a fortnight 'twixt each other & my Missis wouldn't let me go. They died on the same day and at the same hour as one another, only a fortnight between – on a Saturday at ten o'clock in the morning.

5. My mother wrote me a letter about Father being so bad, but nobody told me of Mother's being so ill else nothing'd o' kept me away. I sh'd o' run across them fields & all the 3 mile in ½ an hour *I know*. But when Phillip Blud come on the Saturday evening & said she was dead I thought it was no use, tho' I ax'd to go, & all my strength seem'd gone.

6. And when the Missis call'd me out o' the schoolroom from minding the children there in the ½ holiday into the dining room & told me, I fell on the floor & she left me to cry by myself. I pray'd heartily that it mayn't be true or that she'd come to life again.

After a time I got up & came out. I saw Phillip standing in the passage & I said 'Is it true, Phillip?' & he said, 'Yes.' I said, 'Where are the children?' & he said, up at your Uncle Owen's. So I was afraid it was too true.

A. Reading

Rate this text for 'readability'. Write the word/phrase of your choice into your copy.

VERY EASY ☐   **EASY** ☐   **OKAY** ☐   **HARD** ☐   **VERY HARD** ☐

B. Literacy Questions

1. From paragraph 1, list the jobs that Hannah did in Mrs Phillips's house.
2. Read the last sentence in paragraph two. Rewrite it in today's English, with correct spelling and punctuation.
3. List the jobs that Hannah did in the pub, The Lion.
4. What do you think Hannah might have used to curl her hair in the 1840s?
5. Using the information in Hannah's diary above, write a sentence or two about life in rural England in the 1840s using **each** of the following headings: Classes in society (upper, middle, lower), Manual Work, Education, Manners/Courtesy, Forms of transport, Methods of communication, Health, Life expectancy, Money.

Proofread your answers and correct any mistakes.

C. Numeracy Questions

1. Would you enjoy starting full time work at the same age Hannah did?
2. Find out how much a sovereign was worth in the 1850s. What would it be worth in euro today?
3. Find out how many pennies were in a shilling.
4. What month and year did Mrs Phillips die?
5. How soon after Mrs Phillips's death did Hannah's parents die?

D. Writing

What language and writing style did you see in the diary of Hannah Culwick? Copy the following table and write in your thoughts and observations on her style.

Diary writer	Writer's viewpoint	Topics discussed	Style of language	Other comments
Hannah Cullwick				

E. Oral Language

1. Discuss the following questions in pairs or groups.

   - Do people today keep diaries or records of events and feelings in their lives? If yes, explain how they keep records. If no, do you think we have lost anything in today's world by not keeping diaries?

   - People took 'time out' to write their diaries. This allowed them time to think and reflect on events that had happened. Do we take any 'time out' for thinking and reflection in today's world?

   - To what extent (if any) are blogs diaries?

2. Now organise a class debate on the topic: 'Diaries are treasure troves that should be brought back into popular use.'

F. Personal Writing – My Diary

In your **PORTFOLIO**, write three diary entries about real events that have happened recently in your life. Perhaps also mention some future event or occasion that you are looking forward to.

Remember: Diaries must have dates and/or times at the top of the page.

My Diary

Creating Something Original

As a student of English, you are often asked to create/write an original piece of work such as:

- a diary entry
- a poem
- a drama scene
- a radio advertisement

- a personal essay
- a speech
- a video
- a blog

So here are some top tips for creating something original.

Try to ACE Every Task!

ANALYSE

I analyse what has to be done and think about ideas....

- Analyse/think before you create
- RAFT (role of writer/audience/format/topic)
- Brainstorm – list ideas

CREATE

I write/create my task...

- Write/create your task
- Make it specific to the genre required (use RAFT)
- Do a first draft

EDIT

I edit and re-draft.....

- Check for errors (spellings/capitals/punctuation/grammar)
- Teacher/peer/self-assessment
- Fix all mistakes
- Do a Final draft

ANALYSE

With any form of creation/writing you need to consider the purpose of the piece and structure it accordingly. To do this it is useful to consider the RAFT strategy or approach.

RAFT

Role of the writer	Who are you as the writer? A movie star? The President? A novelist?
Audience	To whom are you writing? Your fans? The public? A company?
Format	In what format are you writing? A diary entry? A newspaper? A blog?
Topic	What are you writing about?

Brainstorm

Once you have worked out the answers to these questions, you need to think about what you will write. A good way to think of ideas is by **brainstorming**. This involves writing down a lot of ideas very quickly before considering them more carefully.

When looking through all your ideas, pick out the ones that you think everyone else will have written down and… **bin them!** If you haven't written anything with a different angle/way of looking at the task… **keep thinking until you do!**

CREATE

You are ready to create your work now. Focus on the task and pull together your ideas to create the best work you can.

Paragraphs

For many of your tasks you will need to write in **paragraphs**. Paragraphs can be as short as two or three sentences or as long as half an A4 page.

If you have four points to make then you need to give each one its own paragraph.

Paragraph 1

Start with an introduction.

You might use a question or a quote to begin with.

Introduce your ideas, discuss them briefly.

Paragraph 2

Choose the most interesting/exciting/wild/unusual point for this paragraph in order to grab the reader's attention.

Paragraphs 3, 4, 5

Give each of your other points a paragraph of their own.

Paragraph 6

This is your conclusion.

How will you finish your essay? Think about your introduction, can you tie it in to your conclusion? Have you set up a link between the two which can be rounded off at the end?

Think about ending with a question or a quote or a dramatic statement.

You have created draft 1

EDIT

Editing your work means making sure that you are happy with the content and accuracy of your material.

Self-Assessment

Look/read through your work again, making changes to improve what you think is necessary.

Peer Assessment

Ask another student to look at/read your work and to give you feedback on the content or errors.

You have created draft 2/3

Proofreading

Proofread your work and correct any mistakes.

You have created your final draft

An ACE Example

Write a Personal Essay on *Things which are indispensable in my life.* (These are things which you cannot live without.) You have already worked on personal texts in this chapter, writing sentences and paragraphs using 'I', so now let's see an 'I' essay. Then you can try it yourself.

ANALYSE

Use the raft strategy to decide on your structure.

Role: A student writing an essay
Audience: My teacher and my class
Format: Essay form in paragraphs
Topic: Why I couldn't live without certain things in my life

Brainstorm some ideas. Your first thoughts might be:

iPhone/ iPad

Money

Friends

TV

Do you think everyone else has thought of those ideas? Probably! So bin them. Make the choices **personal to you.** Choose a variety of your own personal, indispensable items so that you have an interesting essay that could only have been written by you.

HURLEY	**Crosswords**	**OREO BISCUITS**	*Cuddly teddies*
Hockey stick	MILKSHAKES	*Pringles*	**FOOTBALL BOOTS**
Cricket bat	*Hot chocolate*	Tayto	HAIR GEL
Sudoku	**TEA**	Hot water bottle	Pen

Then choose the ones that give your piece a different angle, perhaps small but vital necessities for daily living which keep you sane:

Think about how you will write about these items in a way that will entertain the reader and keep their interest. You might exaggerate, be funny, sentimental, over the top, etc. as long as you **try to be interesting**.

Things which are indispensable in my life

Indispensable things in my life...hmmmm...I suppose I'll have to own up and admit it...hmmm...well yes, what's really, truly, without a doubt indispensable in my life is my family. Yes, seriously, I couldn't survive without my family.

No, not my actual family, doh! Never! (nagging parents and annoying siblings), my own little family, my 'toasties' and 'mosties'. They are a large, warm loving family who really take great care of me especially in winter. There's at least six in the family, but it can expand from time to time depending on the seasons and on my moods. Head of the family is Sleep, next in kinship come fleecy PJs, a hot water bottle, my tatty teddy (so cute and adorable) a mug of steaming hot chocolate (with marshmallows), Oreo biscuits and finally chocolate. Yum! My truly indispensable family.

'Sleep no more, Macbeth hath murdered sleep'. You may have heard of this famous line from Shakespeare's play *Macbeth* in which the main character, Macbeth, commits murder and initially suffers from a guilty conscience; hence he says he has murdered sleep. Well, more fool he! Sleep is the balm of the body and mind, most soothing and rejuvenating. There's nothing as satisfying for me as laying my weary head down on my cool soft pillow, snuggling under the warm enveloping duvet and finally closing 'tired eyelids upon tired eyes' ('The Lotus Eaters', Tennyson – check it out, great poem). So naturally head of my 'toastie mostie' family is sleep.

Bet you won't learn in science class how to *instantly* (well in less than 7 seconds) transform a cold, shivering, miserable, 12-year-old 'almost human' into a warm, cosy, happy person. So here's the lesson – I come home from school on a bitter December evening, exhausted, mentally drained from irregular Irish verbs, algebra, reams of French vocabulary, and boring history. I'm physically drained from dragging a forty tonne bag around all day and from the punch up on the pitch at lunch-time, and I'm absolutely freezing since it lashed rain as I trudged wearily home minus a jacket 'cos it's simply not cool to wear one. Dumping the forty tonnes in the hall, I head upstairs, whip off the itchy, uncomfortable, horrible, nylon/polyester uniform and quickly throw on my soft, soothing, fleecy PJs and slipper socks. The miserable, perished, grumpy monster dissolves revealing a warm, thawed out, calm, happy human. Oh such bliss! My truly indispensable PJs.

My hot water bottles; I have quite a selection you know! There's the one I got in Disneyland (of the seven dwarfs) at a rip-off price so I don't actually use that one, it's an ornament alongside my prized Harry Potter collection. There's my zebra print one with the matching dressing gown, slippers, mug and jewellery box. Yeah, I only went in to Argos to get a hot water bottle, nothing else, but of course the marketing people will hoover every last euro out of you. They'll sell you a simple plain boring beige bottle, granny style, all on its own, no strings attached, but if you want *panache* you have to buy the whole package, another 'family' of 'must have' accessories. Anyway, I got one winter out of zebra toasting my tootsies, and then went dotty for dots so the red polka dot family took up residence next. It started with the red polka dot hot water bottle, then the beanbag, handbag, wallet, duvet cover, lampshade, matching underwear, etc. etc. etc.

I could go on but hey, enough about hot water bottles; they're only functional, seasonal, part-time family members. Let's move on to the loving, permanent, 'can't live without' family members. I snuggle in to about thirty assorted cuddlies every night ranging from the golden, honey coloured Lindt Easter bunny to my penguin from Dublin zoo, my big fat fluffy chick, a myriad of cheapies won at funfairs and my cradle friends Peter Rabbit and Jemima Puddle-Duck. The cutest, most adorable one in my family who is utterly indispensable in my life is my large, grey, gorgeous tatty teddy (the bear with the blue nose, for those of you who don't know your teddies.) This little family welcome me home every day, and put up with my grumbling and complaining. Just the sight of them all, so sweet and so familiar lounging in disarray on my bed, soothes my teenage soul. Aaaahh! My indispensable family!

Is that a key I hear clicking open the front door? Yes, a glance outside at an open car boot confirms the replenishment of my family. Mum's just arrived home with the weekly shopping, I'm off to meet and greet my family favourites again, hello Oreos, hiya chocolate and now it's time for a few squishy marshmallows. Yum. My truly indispensable family.

EDIT

Read over your essay and change it here and there if you think it will make it better/more interesting. Think about using more/different adjectives to make the text more appealing to the reader.

Ask a fellow student, or a family member to read it and tell you what they think. Take their advice on board if you feel it will help and correct any mistakes that they point out.

Proofread your essay and correct any final mistakes.
Use the Proofreading Checklist on p. 4.

Personal Writing – My Essay

Now it's your turn! Write an essay on 'Things that are indispensable in my life' and remember to ACE the task!

Nouns and Adjectives

Nouns

A noun is a person, a place or a thing. Lots of the ordinary things around you are nouns, such as tables, chairs, pens, lights, books and doors.

A. Writing

Rewrite the following sentences in your copy, highlighting the nouns. The first one has been done for you.

1. A pair of legs dangled over the edge of the bunk beds.
2. The moon went behind a cloud and the house was in complete darkness.
3. Joan painted the door and scrubbed her hands clean.
4. Suddenly a ghost loomed out of the mist.
5. His teeth were sharp but his paws were soft.
6. The flowers bloomed in the window box.
7. Margery was born in London but she grew up in Cork.
8. The nurse wrapped the newborn baby in soft blankets.
9. Across the bridge lay the thatched cottage and small stream.
10. The children bought sweets, books, crayons and toys with their birthday money.

Nouns are sorted into groups

Common nouns: Ordinary, everyday nouns, for example **box, milk, teacher, car, dog** and **biro**.

Collective nouns: Collections of things, such as a **swarm** of bees, a **herd** of cattle and a **gaggle** of geese.

Proper nouns: A bit formal, serious and 'proper'. They are people's names, place names, the months, days of the week, etc. Examples would be **Michael D. Higgins, Ireland, December** and **Thursday**.

Abstract nouns: You can't see, touch, smell, taste or hear these nouns. They are feelings and qualities, for example **love, beauty, bravery, kindness, greed** and **sympathy**.

B. Personal Writing – My Nouns

In your **PORTFOLIO**, draw two columns, as shown in the example below, for common nouns and proper nouns. Fill in nouns as they apply and relate to you personally. For example, under common nouns you could list the objects/nouns in your bedroom and for proper nouns you might list the names of your family, places you have been, your favourite months of the year or brand names in your house. You choose the nouns, but make them personal to you.

Common Nouns	Proper Nouns
Things in my bedroom: Xbox Harry Potter books Weird lamp *Match* magazines Desk Radio/alarm clock Cobwebs Dust Bin Sweets (hidden!) Sweet wrappers Cuddly toys Money (hidden!)	**Names of my family, friends, relations:** Isobel, James, Sophie, Seán, Claire, Emma, Declan, Colin, Aoife, Jennifer, Niamh, Joseph **Places I've been to:** Kilkee, Portugal, Belfast, Cork, France **My favourite months of the year**: December and June **Names of brands in my house:** Volkswagen car, Puma runners, Canterbury tracksuits, Kellogg's cereal

Adjectives

Adjectives are words that describe nouns: the **big** table, the **blue** chair, the **red** pen, the **heavy** book, the **broken** door.

A. Writing

1. Rewrite the following sentences in your copy, highlighting the adjectives.

   i. The small, round tower had narrow windows.

   ii. Dead Cat Alley was noisy, cold, grey and scary.

   iii. In the darkness, the great towering cliffs looked menacingly over the seafront.

   iv. Tony chose the blue paper with silver stripes and a green border.

   v. The fat, golden cat snoozed happily in front of the warm fire.

   vi. Bitter lemon is delicious on sweet, sugary, fluffy pancakes.

   vii. Linda's croaky voice sounded cracked and broken.

   viii. The gasping flowers wilted in the hot sun.

   ix. A gorgeous golden Labrador bounded up the huge steps.

   x. In summer Sarah loves the cool, blue sea and strawberry ice-cream.

2. Match up the adjectives with the nouns. You can use the same adjective for more than one noun. See how many adjectives you can use for each noun, e.g. *sweet*, *fresh* bread.

Adjectives	Nouns
sweet	bread
hard	swan
noisy	cinema
ferocious	apple
calm	nurse
rotten	lion
dry	London
fresh	hair
graceful	nail
empty	juice

3. In the following text, the adjectives are coloured blue and the nouns are green.
The **raw wind** reached **gale force** as it swept down from the **mountains** and hit the **wide valley**. It whipped up the **surface** of the **snow** and made it swirl into **drifts** that formed **craggy ridges**, almost like **waves** on a **frozen sea**.

Rewrite this paragraph into your copy and highlight the nouns and adjectives. Use one colour for nouns and another for adjectives.

For example, this morning for breakfast I had Ready Brek and some hot raspberry milkshake. But if I say that I actually had Shreddies and a mug of tea I start thinking about Coco-Pops and lemonade and porridge and Dr. Pepper and how I wasn't eating my breakfast in Egypt and there wasn't a rhinoceros in the room and Father wasn't wearing a diving suit and so on and even writing this makes me feel shaky and scared, like I do when I'm standing on the top of a very tall building and there are thousands of houses and cars and people below me and my head is so full of all these things that I'm afraid that I'm going to forget to stand up straight and hang on to the rail and I'm going to fall over and be killed. (*The Curious Incident of the Dog in the Night-Time* by Mark Haddon)

Peer Assessment – *Swap copies to correct each other's work.*

B. Research

Try the adjectives and nouns games at *www.britishcouncil.org*.

Oral Language

When you talk you communicate **verbally** (oral/spoken) and **non-verbally** (action).

The listener hears your verbal sounds, your voice, your words, your tone of voice, while also 'reading' your non-verbal signs, your **facial expressions**, your **hand gestures**, your **body language**. Even your **posture** (how you position your body) communicates a message to the listener/audience.

Features of Informal Talks/Chats

The kind of language you use and the way you say it tells the listener a lot. Sometimes you need to speak in an informal manner, at other times you may have to speak in a formal way.

Verbal – What you say and how you say it

Here are some verbal features of informal talks/chats:

- **Casual**, colloquial (everyday), conversational language (makes the listener feel relaxed)
- Personal **anecdote** (I remember…when I was….)
- **Humorous language** (jokes, quips)
- Tone of voice (light-hearted, confident, strong, convincing, sincere, angry, happy, sad)
- Volume of speech (loud, normal, soft, mumbling, muttering)
- **Emotive** words/language (brings out emotions in others)
- **Inclusive** language (includes everyone: we, we all, our society, our feelings)

Non-verbal – Your silent signals

Here are some non-verbal features of informal talks/chats:

- **Posture** (the way you stand/sit, etc.).
- **Body language** (your body can express how you feel, for example crossing your legs away from someone or folding your arms can mean that you are not going to co-operate; putting your hand under your chin can mean you are fed-up or bored).
- Making **eye contact**/avoiding eye contact (making eye contact makes you seem more confident).
- **Smiling**/not smiling.
- **Facial gestures** (eyebrows raised, eyes scrunched, etc.).
- **Hand gestures** (pointing, fist thumping, open hands, etc.).

A. Pairwork

In pairs do one of the following tasks:

- Write and deliver a one-minute Talk to your class about the latest and greatest app/game/website/book/film/funfair, etc. that you have seen.
- Write and deliver a one-minute Talk on your favourite pet/hobby/food/subject, etc. Talk about something you feel strongly about or passionate about.
- Write and deliver a one-minute, informal Welcome Talk to a guest visitor who has come to talk to your class (a poet/novelist/sportsperson/guard/fireman/nurse, etc.).
- Write and deliver a one minute Thank You Talk to your teacher who has coached your team to victory. (Sporting victory or victory in any type of competition).

B. Research Project

Think about tone of voice as you read the fiction extracts in the next few pages. Imagine how the characters would say their lines. Think about the facial gestures they might use. Keep a record of your observations for each extract. Role-play some of the interesting/funny ones.

Fiction

Fiction writing comes from the imagination; it is made up. Stories are created by a writer who imagines people and events. However, real life can inspire a fiction writer, and they may base some of their characters and plots on real people and events.

Think about the old saying, 'Truth is stranger than fiction' and you wonder what is really real and what is really fiction!

The books you have enjoyed most from childhood to now have probably been fiction novels. Everyone loves a good story and an escape from the real world. Continue enjoying this escape, there are millions of books out there just waiting for you to pick them up.

Read these examples of fiction writing.

Wonder *by R.J. Palacio*

This is R.J. Palacio's first novel and it's a real page turner. August Pullman is the main character; he was born with a terrible facial abnormality, underwent many surgeries and was home-schooled up to the age of ten. Then at ten, he ventured into school to face the real world. The story is narrated by August himself, but also by his friends and family, so the reader gets a more complete picture of how August gets on and how others truly feel about him.

Ordinary

1. I know I'm not an ordinary ten-year-old kid. I mean, sure, I do ordinary things. I eat ice cream. I ride my bike. I play ball. I have an Xbox. Stuff like that makes me ordinary. I guess. And I feel ordinary. Inside. But I know ordinary kids don't make other ordinary kids run away screaming in playgrounds. I know ordinary kids don't get stared at everywhere they go.

2. If I found a magic lamp and I could have one wish, I would wish that I had a normal face that no one ever noticed at all. I would wish that I could walk down the street without people seeing me and then doing that look-away thing. Here's what I think: the only reason I'm not ordinary is that no one sees me that way.

3. But I'm kind of used to how I look by now. I know how to pretend I don't see the faces people make. We've all got pretty good at that sort of thing: me, Mom and Dad, Via. Actually, I take that back: Via's not so good at it. She can get really annoyed when people do something rude. Like, for instance, one time in the playground some older kids made some noises. I don't even know what the noises were exactly because I didn't hear them myself, but Via heard and she just started yelling at the kids. That's the way she is. I'm not that way.

4. Via doesn't see me as ordinary. She says she does, but if I were ordinary, she wouldn't feel like she needs to protect me as much. And Mom and Dad don't see me as ordinary, either. They see me as extraordinary. I think the only person in the world who realizes how ordinary I am is me.

5. My name is August, by the way. I won't describe what I look like. Whatever you're thinking, it's probably worse.

 ## A. Reading

Rate this text for 'readability'. Write the word/phrase of your choice into your copy.

VERY EASY ☐   **EASY** ☐   **OKAY** ☐   **HARD** ☐   **VERY HARD** ☐

 ## B. Literacy Questions

1. From paragraph 1, list three ordinary things or activities the writer does.
2. From paragraph 2, say what the writer would wish for if he found a magic lamp.
3. From paragraph 3, explain how the writer and his sister Via react differently to things.
4. Do you think that Via is a good sister to August (the writer)? Explain why you think this.
5. What do you think August looks like?
6. Would you like to read more of this book? Why or why not?

Proofread your answers and correct any mistakes.

The extract is told using 'I'. August is the narrator. He tells his story from his own point of view, from how he sees his world. This is called first person narration. You are already used to using first person narration – you tell stories yourself using 'I'.

 ## C. Oral Language

Talk to the person beside you. Tell them about yourself using ten 'I' statements.
For example:

- I like/don't like this school because…
- I love watching … on TV and also…
- I rarely listen to the radio. I prefer…
- I think that … are the best band around.
- Guess what happened to me recently? I was…

Back to Blackbrick *by Sarah Moore-Fitzgerald*

This is the debut (first) novel from Limerick author Sarah Moore-Fitzgerald. Take an exciting trip back in time with the narrator who, in trying to figure out how to solve problems in his present-tense world, unexpectedly finds himself back in the past, facing quite different issues and challenges.

People go through phases, and a lot of them come out the other side perfectly fine. I don't think you should write someone off just because they occasionally get a bit mixed up and have to be shown where the toilet is.

At dinner that night, Granddad frowned and chewed his food very slowly, not saying anything for ages. Then he looked up at my gran and he said, 'Where's Brian?'

'Oh dear now, don't distress yourself,' my gran said to him, which was kind of condescending as far as I was concerned.

'Brian fell out of a window,' I said helpfully.

'Did he?' said Granddad.

'Yes, my dear,' my gran said, moving closer to him and softly patting him on the hand, 'I'm afraid he did.'

'He's dead now, isn't that right?' he said.

'Yes, he is,' my gran replied.

'Oh,' my granddad replied. He clenched his jaw and he kept brushing something invisible off his jumper. 'Yes, that's what I thought. I mean of course. I knew that.' And he put his hand flat on his forehead and let out this shuddery sigh and we all stayed quiet for a while listening to the ticking of the clock on the wall.

There was nothing on the memory cure website that showed you what to do if talking about the past made the person you love start to cry, so me and my gran tried to move quickly on to cheering him up by talking about other people that Granddad loved, which was a bit difficult seeing as many of them had disappeared off to San Francisco or Australia.

ACTION NUMBER 2

- Label common household items and images clearly.
- As long as your loved one's reading capacity remains, this is a good way to help out with their day-to-day functioning.

I set up this quite good system by writing instructions on Post-its, and sticking them all over the place. They said things like: 'open the fridge and take out the CHEESE', or 'This is the TOILET, which is for PEEING into' and 'this is the DISHWASHER (for washing DISHES)'.

I also wrote out people's names and stuck them on all the photos:

'Brian (your grandson – DEAD)'

'Uncle Ted (your son – in San Francisco)'

'Sophie (your daughter – drumming up business in Sydney)'

On my gran's picture I wrote, 'Deedee, your wife'.

Those signs worked pretty well, except for Brian's, which didn't have that great an effect on any of us. I had to take it down quite quickly. It's one thing knowing that you've got a dead brother. It's another thing having to read it every single time you sit down to have a bowl of cereal.

So I wrote a new sign that said: 'Brian, your grandson. Gone away for a while.'

That seemed to comfort Granddad and in a funny kind of way it comforted me too. If you read something often enough, part of you can start to believe it. Even if it is a lie and even if you've written the lie yourself.

A. Reading

Rate this text for 'readability'. Write the word/phrase of your choice into your copy.

VERY EASY ☐   **EASY** ☐   **OKAY** ☐   **HARD** ☐   **VERY HARD** ☐

B. Literacy Questions

1. What happened to Brian?
2. What problem does Granddad have, in your opinion?
3. What did the narrator (the person telling the story) do to help his granddad?
4. Use a dictionary to find the meaning of *condescending* and *clenched* and use each one in a sentence.
5. Where did the narrator get his ideas from?
6. Did you find the extract humorous? Explain your answer.

Proofread your answers and correct any mistakes.

Poetry

Poems tell stories too, but they are usually much shorter than fiction novels or short stories. They are also written in a very different format, which you will learn more about later.

Poems are often personal; expressing the real emotions, fears, joys or concerns of the poet. Here are two short poems about family.

Holding His Hand *by Colm McGlynn*

Today we took a gentle stroll
From Rathfarnham Shopping Centre
To the post box in Templeogue village

And Dad, in his 83rd year,
Became so jaded
I had to hold his hand

Tears welled up in my heart
At this role reversal:

The man who held
my hand as a boy
now in need of mine.

A. Oral Language

Think about what has happened in the relationship between father and son in the poem. Talk to the person beside you about this. Think about your own grandparents. What kind of people are/were they? Do/did you get on well with them? What memories do you have of them? What important parties or events have you and your family celebrated with them?

B. Pairwork

Bring in some photos of yourself and your grandparents and discuss the events you have enjoyed with them. Use 'I' statements and tell anecdotes. **Anecdotes** are short stories about things that really happened to you. Some anecdotes are funny, some are sad, some are about coincidences, etc.

Night Singing *by David Cameron*

There comes a time in singing to a child,
As the small limbs go limp and the breaths deepen,
That you become aware of weight. It's then
You hear your voice, and in it something wild.
Why do fears come? Nothing on any shelf
Can tell you in this place of simple rhyme.
The child's asleep, and has been for some time.
You're only singing now to soothe yourself.

 ## A. Literacy Questions

1. Imagine the setting for this poem. Think about where the child and parent are. What is happening?

2. Make a list in your copy of (a) the nouns and (b) the adjectives in the poem.

3. In this poem, the parent singing to the child becomes aware that the child is already asleep. Have you ever thought that you were communicating with somebody and then realised that you weren't 'reaching' the other person? How did you feel? How do you think the parent feels in this situation?

 ## B. Drawing

Draw the scene or setting of the poem as you visualise it yourself. Use simple sketches and colours that you think would suit the scene.

Brahms's Lullaby

Lullaby and goodnight
In the sky stars are bright
May the moon, silvery beams, bring you sweet dreams
Close your eyes now and rest
May these hours be blessed
Till the sky's bright with dawn
When you wake with a yawn
Lullaby and goodnight, you are mother's delight
I'll protect you from harm and you'll wake in my arms

Sleepy head close your eyes for I'm right beside you
Guardian angels are near so sleep without fear
Lullaby and goodnight with roses be-deight
Lilies o'er head lay thee down in thy bed
Lullaby and goodnight you are mother's delight
I'll protect you from harm and you'll wake in my arms

A. Oral Language

Seamus Heaney, the famous Irish poet who died on 30 August 2013, wanted 'Brahms's Lullaby' to be played at the end of his funeral mass. It was played and was both moving and soothing. In pairs, discuss the lullabies that you remember from your early childhood.

B. Personal Writing – My Poem

In your **PORTFOLIO**, write a poem about relationships, for example mother/child, teenager/father or adult/grandparent.

ASSESSMENT

Complete this assessment in your **PORTFOLIO**.

Oral Assessment

Speak for 1-2 minutes on a topic of your choice. (Complete the Oral Assessment Checklist in your **PORTFOLIO**.)

Written Assessment

A. Personal Literacy

Write four 'I' sentences about yourself: your likes/dislikes, hobbies, etc.

I_____

I_____

I_____

I_____

(8 marks)

B. Sentences That Make Sense

Place a tick beside the sentences that make sense.

   1. Maud ran so fast that she didn't.

   2. Tom and Dan reached the forest at last and saw the new treehouse.

   3. He just wanted to get away from the fire because.

   4. They loved watching cartoons on TV.

   5. 'Isn't it great when you get a day off school?' said Anna.

(10 marks)

C. Capital Letters

Insert capital letters in the correct places in the following sentences.

   1. tom's favourite soccer team is manchester united, but bob loves liverpool.

   2. jenny flew to boston on monday, drove to new york on thursday and flew on to chicago on sunday.

   3. mum likes hyundai cars, but dad prefers ford or volkswagen.

   4. sheila read *matilda*, then the *harry potter* series, then the *twilight* series.

   5. on mondays sarah works in the bank of ireland in galway and on friday she works in mayo.

(10 marks)

D. Life Stories

Fill in the missing words in the sentences.

   1. An autobiography is written by someone who wants to tell the _____ of their own _____. It is written using 'I' _____. An example of an autobiography that I have heard about or read is: _____.   (4 marks)

   2. A biography is a _____ about a person's life written by _____ _____. An example of a biography that I have heard about or read is: _____. (3 marks)

   3. A diary is a p_____ record of events, experiences or thoughts. An example of a diary that I have heard about or read is: _____.   (2 marks)

   4. A biography tells about a person's whole life, but a memoir remembers a _____ of the writer's life.   (1 marks)

ASSESSMENT

E. Nouns and Adjectives

Highlight the nouns in one colour and the adjectives in another colour in the following passage:

Life of Pi by *Yann Martel*

With just one glance I discovered that the sea is a city. Just below me, all around, unsuspected by me, were highways, boulevards, streets and roundabouts bustling with submarine traffic. In water that was dense, glassy and flecked by millions of lit-up specks of plankton, fish like trucks and buses and cars and bicycles and pedestrians were madly racing about, no doubt honking and hollering at each other. The predominant colour was green. At multiple depths, as far as I could see, there were evanescent trails of phosphorescent green bubbles, the wake of speeding fish. As soon as one trail faded another appeared. These trails came from all directions and disappeared

in all directions. They were like those time-exposure photographs you see of cities at night, with the long red streaks made by the tail lights of cars. Except that here the cars were driving above and under each other as if they were on interchanges that were stacked ten storeys high. And here the cars were of the craziest colours. The dorados – there must have been over fifty patrolling beneath the raft – showed off their bright gold, blue and green as they whisked by.

Count the number of nouns you found: _____

Count the number of adjectives you found: _____

F. Self-Assessment

How well do you think you have done?

I did well in _____

The things that I found difficult were _____

The things that I don't fully understand are _____

I would like to improve _____

CHAPTER 2

Fiction: Tell Me It's Not True!

My Learning Expectations

In this chapter, I will:

- Learn about **narrative points of view** and **genres** of fiction

- **Give my opinion** on books and films

- Find out **what kind of reader** I am

- Read different **styles of writing**

- Figure out how writers create **descriptive language** using nouns, adjectives, verbs and adverbs

- **Listen to the opinions** of my classmates and teacher about books they have read

- Use and recognise **verbs, adverbs** and **apostrophes**

- Use the story ingredients (setting/plot/characters/atmosphere) to **write a short story**

- Write into my **PORTFOLIO** to keep a record of my **creative writing** (remember ACE from Chapter 1)

- **Continue to proofread and edit** my work

Fiction: Tell Me It's Not True!

Fiction

In Chapter 1, we learned that fiction writing involves an author creating a story in an **imaginary world**. We will look at different examples of fiction in this chapter. If you really enjoy one of these examples, you may have found a genre that you like!

Stories can be told from different points of view; this is called the narrative point of view.

Narrative Point of View

Every story is told by someone who gives their point of view. Stories are told using first person narration ('I') or third person narration ('he/she').

First Person Narration ('I')

If the story is told using 'I', this person is the narrator and is usually a character in the story. The narrator might be biased (unfairly for or against someone or something) or they might be fair and objective (basing their decisions on fact not emotion) in how they tell us the story.

For example:

*I wish Cam had long hair. I wish she looked glamorous. I wish she was something special like a film star. I wish she smiled more. She just slumps round all draggy and depressed. Over **me**.*

from *The Dare Game* by Jacqueline Wilson

Third Person Narration ('He/She')

If the narrator is not involved in the story, the story is told using 'he/she'.

For example:

*Artemis cleared **his** throat. 'Let us proceed under the assumption that the fairy folk do exist and that I am not a gibbering moron.' **Butler** nodded weakly. **Juliet** was unconvinced. 'Very well. Now, as I was saying, the People have to fulfil a specific ritual to renew their powers. According to my interpretation, they must pick a seed from an ancient oak tree by the bend in the river. And they must do this during the full moon.' The light began to dawn in **Butler's** eyes.*

from *Artemis Fowl* by Eoin Colfer

A. Pairwork

Working with a partner, say whether each of the following sentences is written in first person narration or third person narration.

1. 'I'm not going to help you ever again,' I screamed to Paul, furious at his deception.
2. Taking the dusty chest gingerly from the back of the wardrobe, I tiptoed downstairs.
3. 'She lost her 'phone again, Mum,' I said wearily as I limped into the kitchen.
4. They stopped at a clearing suddenly. Ned motioned to them to sit down.
5. I simply didn't know what to do next; it was all too complicated for me.

B. Research

Look at the books which you have read recently. List the titles and authors of each one. Find out if the narration is first or third person. Copy one or two sentences from each book to prove your point about how it is narrated.

Reading and You

What do you think about reading? Do you like it, dislike it or find it just OK? Do you prefer reading comics, magazines or newspapers to reading books? Do you prefer to read material on a screen using a tablet or PC rather than on a printed page? Would you like to read more often than you currently do? What's the best book you have ever read? This section will help you to see how you really feel about reading and what kind of reader you are.

Have you read any books by the following authors?

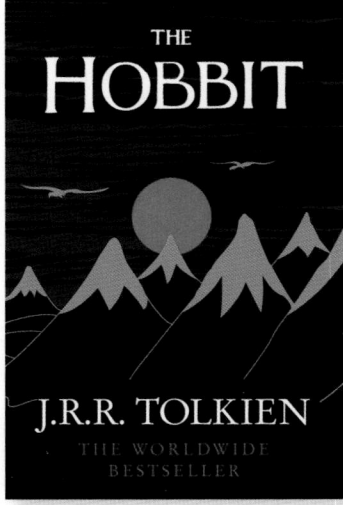

Anthony Horowitz	Jacqueline Wilson	Philip Pullman
Cathy Cassidy	Judi Curtin	Roddy Doyle
Darren Shan	Kate Thompson	Sarah Webb
Derek Landy	Meg Cabot	Siobhán Parkinson
Enid Blyton	Michael Morpurgo	Terry Pratchett
J.R.R. Tolkien	Patrick Ness	

Fiction Genres

There are many different types, or **genres**, of fiction. You should try different genres until you find the one that really interests you! You can choose from comedy, romance, detective, fantasy, thriller, adventure, mystery, horror, science fiction (sci-fi) and so on.
See Chapter 5 p.253 for more on genres.

Look at the book covers on this page and try to guess the genre of each book.

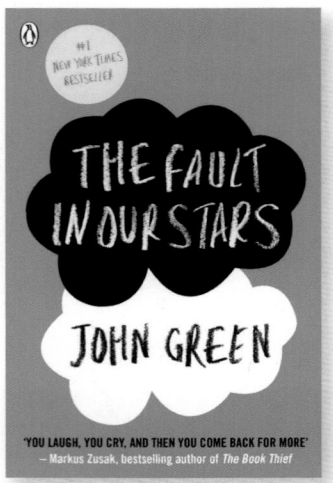  

Modern Fiction

Modern fiction has generally been written within the past few decades. It is difficult to give an exact date for when fiction became 'modern', and it is often a matter of opinion. Some might argue that fiction written within the past century is modern.

Look at the following list of modern fiction books and see if you have read any of them:

The Hunger Games trilogy by Suzanne Collins

Goodnight Mister Tom by Michelle Magorian (1981)

Holes by Louis Sachar (1998)

Rebecca Rocks by Anna Carey (2013)

Run With the Wind by Tom McCaughren (1983)

The *Artemis Fowl* series by Eoin Colfer

The *Boy in the Striped Pyjamas* by John Boyne (2006)

The *Cherub* series by Robert Muchamore

The *Harry Potter* series by J.K. Rowling

The *Twilight* series by Stephanie Meyers

Classic Fiction

Classic fiction 'stands the test of time'. It is considered to be very good and well worth reading. It can come from any time period. Many of the books that are considered 'classics' were written a long time ago. Ask your parents and grandparents what they liked to read when they were your age. Show them the list below to help jog their memories.

A Christmas Carol by Charles Dickens

Aesop's Fables translated by S.A. Handford

Alice's Adventures in Wonderland by Lewis Carroll

Anne of Green Gables by L.M. Montgomery

Black Beauty by Anna Sewell

Flambards by K.M. Peyton

Frankenstein by Mary Shelley

Heidi by Johanna Spyri

Just William by Richmal Crompton

Kidnapped by Robert Louis Stevenson

Little Women by Louisa May Alcott

Of Mice and Men by John Steinbeck

Oliver Twist by Charles Dickens

Peter Pan by J.M. Barrie

Silas Marner by George Eliot

Sherlock Holmes: The Hound of the Baskervilles by Arthur Conan Doyle

The Adventures of Huckleberry Finn by Mark Twain

The Adventures of Tom Sawyer by Mark Twain

The Borrowers by Mary Norton

The Call of the Wild by Jack London

The Catcher in the Rye by J.D. Salinger

The Chronicles of Narnia by C.S. Lewis

The Great Gatsby by F. Scott Fitzgerald

The Hobbit by J.R.R. Tolkien

The Lord of the Rings by J.R.R. Tolkien

The Railway Children by E. Nesbit

The Secret Garden by Frances Hodgson Burnett

The Swiss Family Robinson by Johann Wyss

The Wind in the Willows by Kenneth Grahame

The Wonderful Wizard of Oz by L. Frank Baum

Tom's Midnight Garden by Philippa Pearce

Treasure Island by Robert Louis Stevenson

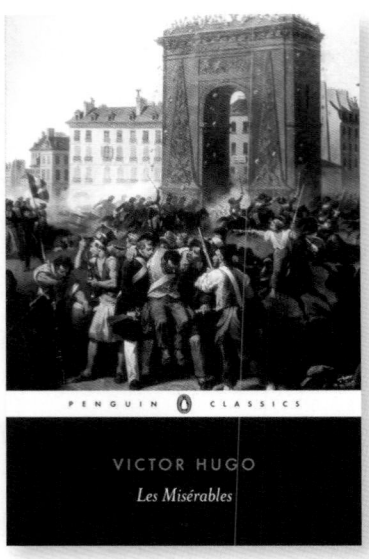

EMILY BRONTE
Wuthering Heights

CHARLES DICKENS
Great Expectations

VICTOR HUGO
Les Misérables

More Challenging Famous Classics

Anna Karenina by Leo Tolstoy

Great Expectations by Charles Dickens

Jane Eyre by Charlotte Brontë

Jean de Florette and Manon des Sources by Marcel Pagnol

Les Misérables by Victor Hugo

Pride and Prejudice by Jane Austen

The Grapes of Wrath by John Steinbeck

The Mayor of Casterbridge by Thomas Hardy

Wuthering Heights by Emily Brontë

Digital Reading

Nowadays you can choose to read almost anything on a **screen**, rather than on a printed page. You can read books, newspapers and magazines using a tablet, personal computer (PC), laptop or mobile phone. Look at the following list of ways that you might be reading digitally and see which ones relate to your life:

- Facebook
- Twitter
- Google searches
- eBooks
- Online magazines
- Blogs

A. Pairwork

1. Working with the person beside you, discuss which is better: the book or the film.

   - The *Harry Potter* series
   - The *Twilight* series
   - *The Hunger Games* trilogy
   - *The Flight of the Doves*
   - *Holes*
   - *Goodnight Mister Tom*
   - *The Boy in the Striped Pyjamas*
   - Any other example

2. In pairs, make a list in your copy of at least 10 writers that you have read in the last few years. Write the list in alphabetical order, starting with the author's surname, as in the sample below.

Author's Surname	First Name	Book Title
Collins	Suzanne	*The Hunger Games* trilogy
Colfer	Eoin	*Artemis Fowl* series

B. Writing

In your copy, try to put the books you named in task A Part 2 above in lists according to genre, as in the example below. This can be hard to do because some books fall into two or more genres. Just choose the genre you feel is most suitable.

Comedy	Romance	Detective	Fantasy	Thriller	Adventure	Sci-Fi
Just William	*Twilight*	*Sherlock Holmes*	*Harry Potter*	*The Hunger Games*	*The Chronicles of Narnia*	*The Host*

C. Oral Language

1. Choose your favourite book from your list. Tell the class **three** reasons why you like it so much.

2. Listen to Sinéad Gleeson interviewing *Artemis Fowl* author Eoin Colfer on The Book Show on RTÉ Radio 1. Eoin is talking about a short story he has written to be included in a series of eBooks for children. The series is to tie in with the 50th anniversary of the TV programme *Doctor Who*.

   i. What TV channels did Eoin have as a child?

   ii. How did Eoin know about Dr Who?

   iii. What is the name of the episode Eoin wrote?

   iv. In what way is the short story he wrote similar to the fairy-tale Peter Pan?

   v. What kind of writer did Eoin want to be when he was younger?

   vi. Why did Eoin stop writing Artemis Fowl books?

   vii. What genres of fiction does Eoin mention?

   viii. What kind of a person do you think Eoin Colfer is, having listened to the interview?

3. Imagine you are on Teen TV. Today's topic is 'Teens and Reading'. Work in pairs. **Person A** is the interviewer (the person asking the questions). **Person B** is the teenage respondent (the person replying to the questions). Take turns being Person A and Person B. Imagine that there is a live audience in the TV studio and imagine the cameras are filming you. (If you have your teacher's permission, why not try filming it?) Once you have rehearsed your interview, do it in front of the class.

Make a list of possible questions that the interviewer will ask. For example:

- How do you feel about reading?
- Do you think that teenagers today read regularly?
- What do you read?
- What do you think about the latest novel by...?
- Do you prefer magazines to books?
- Do you prefer films to books?
- What books or magazines do you think are really good reads?
- Some people say magazines are a waste of money. What do you think?

MY READING GOALS ☑

Choose some reading goals for the next six months and write them into your **PORTFOLIO**. Below are some examples of what these goals might be.

- Start reading books regularly again, perhaps by reading for 10 minutes at bedtime.

- Read one book a week/month.

- Finish my current book, entitled ....

....

......................................,
and start another, entitled

....

- Read magazines/newspapers because I like reading the sports pages, health and beauty, the celebrity gossip and the reviews of films/books/games, etc.

- Read the local newspapers, maybe starting with the sports pages, the pet corner, the entertainment section, etc.

- Read online using blogs, Twitter, Facebook, etc.

Creative Writing

Now that you've read some fiction, you might like to consider the following questions:

- What makes a book so good that you can't put it down?
- Why do you recommend a book to your friends and read it again and again?
- Have you got what it takes to write a good story?
- Can you write a good story working together as a group?

Writing an essay or a story requires ideas, imagination and patience, because usually you need to rewrite your work quite a lot to get it right. Most writers write lots of drafts until they are happy with their story. It's easy to write an ordinary, boring story or essay, but writing an original, interesting one takes time and hard work. Working in pairs or groups might make this task easier.

The **ingredients** in a story are:

- **Setting**
- **Plot** or storyline
- **Characters**
- **Atmosphere/tone**

Setting

The setting is *where* and *when* the action happens. It's the *time* and *place* in which the characters live. The story might be set in present day or a long time ago. It could be set in Ireland or America, or in a futuristic, apocalyptic time and place!

For example:

Harry Potter and the Philosopher's Stone is set in Surrey in England and then in fictional Hogwarts in Scotland.

Plot

The plot is what happens in a story or the **storyline**. The writer decides what happens and in what sequence. Stories can start at the beginning and move forward chronologically (in order of time) or they can mix past and present by using **flashback** or **flash forward**.

To make a plot interesting the writer usually includes the following:

- interesting beginning
- conflict/action
- resolution/ending

For example:

The plot of *Harry Potter and the Philosopher's Stone* begins when Harry, aged 11, discovers that he is a wizard. He then has to battle various enemies to get the Philosopher's stone. Conflict is created as Snape (the potions master) appears to hate Harry and seems to want the Philosopher's stone. Harry finds the Philosopher's stone in the end.

Characters

Characters are the people (or in some cases, the animals or aliens!) in the story. We are interested in what they are like, what they do and how things turn out for them in the end. There are main characters, who are very important to the story, and there are minor, less important characters.

For example:

The main characters in *Harry Potter* are Harry, Ron and Hermione.

Atmosphere/ Tone

Atmosphere or tone is the feeling or mood created by the writer's descriptions. There may be tension and suspense as excitement builds and the reader is unsure of what will happen next.

For example:

When you read the extract from *Great Expectations* on p.68-71 see if you can feel the tension.

Read the following fiction extracts to see how these ingredients work. If you like one a lot, you might read the whole book!

The Hunger Games *by Suzanne Collins*

Written in 2008, *The Hunger Games* is a novel by American writer Suzanne Collins. The story is told through the voice of 16-year-old Katniss Everdeen. She has a younger sister called Primrose and they are from a fictional nation called Panem, in North America. Years ago, the poor districts of Panem rebelled against the wealthy, ruling 'Capitol'. The Capitol beat the rebellion and decided to hold 'Hunger Games' each year to punish the districts. Every year, each district must choose one boy and one girl (ranging from age 12 to 18) to participate in a televised fight until only one is left alive.

Taking the kids from our districts, forcing them to kill one another while we watch – this is the Capitol's way of reminding us how totally we are at their mercy. How little chance we would stand of surviving another rebellion. Whatever words they use, the real message is clear. 'Look how we take your children and sacrifice them and there's nothing you can do. If you lift a finger, we will destroy every last one of you. Just as we did in District Thirteen.'

To make it humiliating as well as torturous, the Capitol requires us to treat the Hunger Games as a festivity, a sporting event pitting every district against the others. The last tribute alive receives a life of ease back home, and their district will be showered with prizes, largely consisting of food. All year, the Capitol will show the winning district gifts of grain and oil and even delicacies like sugar while the rest of us battle starvation.

'It is both a time for repentance and a time for thanks,' intones the mayor. Then he reads the list of past District 12 victors. In seventy-four years, we have had exactly two. Only one is still alive. Haymitch Abernathy, a paunchy, middle-aged man, who at this moment appears hollering something unintelligible, staggers on to the stage, and falls into the third chair. He's drunk. Very. The crowd responds with its token applause, but he's confused and tries to give Effie Trinket a big hug, which she barely manages to fend off.

The mayor looks distressed. Since all of this is being televised, right now District 12 is the laughing stock of Panem, and he knows it. He quickly tries to pull the attention back to the reaping by introducing Effie Trinket.

Bright and bubbly as ever, Effie Trinket trots to the podium and gives her signature, 'Happy Hunger Games! And may the odds be ever in your favour!' Her pink hair must be a wig because her curls have shifted slightly off-centre since her encounter with Haymitch. She goes on a bit about what an honour it is to be here, although everyone knows she's just aching to get bumped up to a better district where they have proper victors, not drunks who molest you in front of the entire nation.

Through the crowd, I spot Gale looking back at me with a ghost of a smile. As reapings go, this one at least has a slight entertainment factor. But suddenly I am thinking of Gale and his forty-two names in that big glass ball and how the odds are not in his favour. Not compared to a lot of the boys. And maybe he's thinking the same thing about me because his face darkens and he turns away. 'But there are still thousands of slips,' I wish I could whisper to him.

It's time for the drawing. Effie Trinket says as she always does, 'Ladies first!' and crosses to the glass ball with the girls' names. She reaches in, digs her hand deep into the ball, and pulls out a slip of paper. The crowd draws in a collective breath and then you can hear a pin drop, and I'm feeling nauseous and so desperately hoping that it's not me, that it's not me, that it's not me.

Effie Trinket crosses back to the podium, smoothes the slip of paper, and reads out the name in a clear voice. And it's not me.

It's Primrose Everdeen.

GLOSSARY

Paunchy: Has a large belly.

Unintelligible: Can't be understood.

Fend off: Try to stop something from happening.

Reaping: The selection process for the Hunger Games contestants.

Nauseous: Feel like getting sick.

A. Reading

Rate this text for 'readability'. Write the word/phrase of your choice into your copy.

VERY EASY ☐   **EASY** ☐   **OKAY** ☐   **HARD** ☐   **VERY HARD** ☐

B. Literacy Questions

1. What kind of a setting is described in this extract?

2. What is the benefit of winning the Hunger Games?

3. Do you like the character Effie Trinket? Scan the text for information on her. To back up your answer include sentences from the text (quotes).

4. How is suspense created before the name of the next contestant is read out at the end?

Proofread your answers and correct any mistakes.

C. Numeracy Questions

1. For how many years have the *Hunger Games* been taking place?
2. How many times has *District 12* won?
3. If Gale's name is in the draw 42 times and there are 1,000 names in total in the draw, what are the chances (or odds) of his name being drawn?

Writing Style: Fiction

Did you notice that the style of writing in the above fiction extract is different to the style that you might use in your everyday conversations and in your own writing? Fiction writers use **descriptive language** to make that world come alive for the reader. They use interesting words and they put effort into describing places, characters, events and atmosphere. They help the reader to imagine and visualise the characters, the setting or location, the dialogue and the action. They do this by making good use of nouns, adjectives, verbs and adverbs.

Verbs and Adverbs

Verbs

Verbs are action words. They are used to describe an action taking place; it could be the wind *howling*, a dog *barking* or a child *skipping*. Verbs have different **tenses**, which show when the action took place. You use verbs in lots of tenses all the time without thinking about them.

I **walked** to school yesterday. (**Past** tense)
I **walk** to school every day. (**Present** tense)
I **am walking** to school now. (**Present continuous** tense)
I **will walk** to school tomorrow. (**Future** tense)

The plain form of the verb is known as the **infinitive.** This is when the verb is not in a tense and when it usually has the word 'to' in front of it. For example, to sneeze, to laugh, to run, to dance, to gloat, to mock, to cook, to sing, to stand.

What tenses are used in these sentences?

- Jane *danced* while Mark *swam* and later they *ate* pizza for dinner.
- Hannah *texted* Tom about *going* to the cinema.
- They *giggled* as the clown deliberately *tripped* and *fell*.
- 'I'm *driving* home first,' *said* Mum, 'then I'll *ring* you and *meet* you later.'
- The audience *sighed* and *cried* at the end of the show.

A. Reading

Pick out the verbs in the following sentences. The first one has been done for you.

1. She ran away laughing wildly.
2. Robin snapped the branch and tossed it into the bonfire.
3. They swam across the bay and sighed with relief when they reached the pier.
4. It was burnt so he simply dumped it and started again.
5. George tugged at the roots until they loosened; then he pulled them up easily.
6. Sonia teased three-year-old Margery so much that the poor child began to cry.
7. Philip and Tony raced to the woods.
8. Aunt Joan sighed, dropped the book and slowly went indoors.
9. 'Run for your lives,' shouted the fireman as the forest caught fire.
10. They giggled, and then danced merrily around the fairy fort.

B. Writing

1. Fill in the rest of this table in your copy. The first few have been done for you.

Infinitive	Present tense	Past tense	Future tense
to swallow	I swallow it I'm swallowing it	I swallowed it	I will swallow it
to shout	I shout I'm shouting	I shouted	I will shout
to swim			
to dance			
to eat			
to buy			
to clean			
to look			
to go			
to give			

2. Write 12 sentences in any tense using the following verbs:

to scribble	to haggle	to smile
to laugh	to complain	to surrender
to holler	to drink	to chatter
to freeze	to click	to fix

3. Write a paragraph about the activities or hobbies that you are involved in. Once the paragraph is written, read over it and underline or highlight the verbs in it. How many verbs did you use?

4. Swap copies with the person next to you. Read the other person's work. What verbs did he/she use?

5. Rewrite the sentences below. Use the verbs from the list to fill in the blanks?

i. The chef _____ the potatoes with milk, butter and salt.

ii. The wolf _____ as he searched hungrily for food.

iii. Mary _____ all alone in the quiet church.

iv. The starving children barely _____ the food and they greedily _____ the milk.

v. Tom _____ the seeds to the hungry chickens.

vi. The thief _____ as he happily escaped with the loot.

vii. The confident children _____ on stage and performed beautifully.

viii. John's horse _____ easily to victory in the race.

ix. Karen didn't notice the wet floor and she _____ .

x. Joe _____ onions, garlic and carrots for the dinner.

xi. The cross teacher _____ loudly at the unruly children.

xii. The starving lion _____ hungrily for food.

xiii. Milo _____ all the milk but was still thirsty, so he _____ for more.

xiv. The weary travellers _____ the last 2 km home.

xv. The happy children _____ at the antics of the clown and the magician.

chewed	guzzled	prayed	sniggered
chopped	howled	prowled	trudged
cried	laughed	roared	
drank	mashed	scattered	
galloped	pranced	slipped	

 C. **Oral Language**

Working in pairs, decide who is **Person A** and who is **Person B**.

Person A: Ask person B the following questions. Listen to the verbs that they will use in the **past tense**.

1. How did you travel home from school yesterday?
2. What was the first thing you did when you got home?
3. When did you have dinner?
4. Did you do any homework?
5. Did you watch TV?
6. What time did you go to bed?
7. Did you read in bed? If you answered 'yes', what did you read? Tell me a little about it.

Person B: Ask person A the following questions. Listen to the verbs that they will use in the **future tense**.

1. Where will you go on holidays next summer?
2. What will you put on your birthday wish list?
3. What will you do when you go home this evening?
4. What will you do this weekend?

Adverbs

Adverbs describe verbs (action words: sing, smile, dance, run). They usually end in –ly.

For example:

- They sang sweetly / loudly / quietly / horribly / atrociously / poorly / badly / marvellously.
- She danced beautifully / gracefully / softly / elegantly / merrily / silently.
- He ran swiftly / quickly / lightly / sprightly / heavily / frantically / hurriedly / happily / nervously.

 ## A. Writing

1. In your copy add adverbs to these sentences.

i. The monkeys scrambled _____ up the tree.

ii. Jacob and Tom ran _____ to the sweet shop.

iii. The raft drifted _____ down the river.

iv. Susie looked _____ at the crying child.

v. The witch cackled _____ as she stirred the cauldron.

vi. Larry swam _____ to the shore.

vii. The teacher shouted _____ at the noisy class.

viii. The snake slithered _____ towards the boy.

ix. Having won the Lotto, Maura danced _____.

x. He sighed _____ at the amount of work he had to do.

xi. The sun shone _____ on the wedding party.

xii. Amy tiptoed _____ up the stairs.

xiii. The baby slept _____ all night.

xiv. Wasps and bees buzz _____.

2. Put the following adverbs into sentences.

hastily	suddenly	lovingly
poorly	repeatedly	lazily
happily	rarely	cheerily
frighteningly	narrowly	madly

3. Write the opposite of these adverbs.

sadly	nicely	tenderly
quickly	patiently	neatly
nervously	perfectly	loudly
angrily	widely	sweetly

 ## B. Pairwork

Write the headings below into your copy. Working in pairs, fill in the columns under each heading by finding the relevant words from the extract from *The Hunger Games* on p. 59-60. Some examples have been filled in for you.

Type of narration (first/third)	Style of writing	Nouns	Adjectives	Verbs	Adverbs
	witty	delicacies	paunchy	staggers	desperately
	humorous	sugar	drunk	falls	slightly

The Chronicles of Narnia: The Magician's Nephew *by C.S. Lewis*

The Chronicles of Narnia is a series of seven fantasy novels by C.S. Lewis, published between 1950 and 1954. In these books, children from the real world are magically transported to a fantasy world called Narnia. In *The Magician's Nephew,* the sixth book in the series, two children, Digory Kirke and Polly Plummer, decide to explore the attic connecting their houses.

The Wrong Door

Their adventures began chiefly because it was one of the wettest and coldest summers there had been for years. That drove them to do indoor things: you might say, indoor exploration. It is wonderful how much exploring you can do with a stump of candle in a big house, or in a row of houses. Polly had discovered long ago that if you opened a certain little door in the box-room attic of her house you would find the cistern and a dark place behind it which you could get into by a little careful climbing. The dark place was like a long tunnel with brick wall on one side and sloping roof on the other. In the roof there were little chunks of light between the slates. There was no floor in this tunnel: you had to step from rafter to rafter, and between them there was only plaster. If you stepped on this you would find yourself

falling through the ceiling of the room below. Polly had used the bit of the tunnel just beside the cistern as a smugglers' cave. She had brought up bits of old packing cases and the seats of broken kitchen chairs, and things of that sort, and spread them across from rafter to rafter so as to make a bit of floor. Here she kept a cash-box containing various treasures, and a story she was writing and usually a few apples. She had often drunk a quiet bottle of ginger-beer in there: the old bottles made it look more like a smugglers' cave.

Digory quite liked the cave (she wouldn't let him see the story) but he was more interested in exploring.

'Look here,' he said. 'How long does this tunnel go on for? I mean, does it stop where your house ends?'

'No,' said Polly. 'The walls don't go out to the roof. It goes on. I don't know how far.'

'Then we could get the length of the whole row of houses.'

'So we could,' said Polly. 'And oh, I say!'

'What?'

'We could get *into* the other houses.'

'Yes, and get taken up for burglars! No thanks.'

'Don't be so jolly clever. I was thinking of the house beyond yours.'

'What about it?'

'Why, it's the empty one. Daddy says it's always been empty ever since we came here.'

'I suppose we ought to have a look at it then,' said Digory. He was a good deal more excited than you'd have thought from the way he spoke. For of course he was thinking, just as you would have been, of all the reasons why the house might have been empty so long. So was Polly. Neither of them said the word 'haunted'. And both felt that once the thing had been suggested, it would be feeble not to do it.

'Shall we go and try it now?' said Digory.

'All right,' said Polly.

'Don't if you'd rather not,' said Digory.

'I'm game if you are,' said she.

'How are we to know when we're in the next house but one?' They decided they would have to go out into the box-room and walk across it taking steps as long as the steps from one rafter to the next. That would give them an idea of how many rafters went to a room. Then they would allow about four more for the passage between the two attics in Polly's house, and then the same number for the maid's bedroom as for the box-room. That would give them the length of the house. When they had done that distance twice they would be at the end of Digory's house; any door they came to after that would let into an attic of the empty house.

'But I don't expect it's really empty at all,' said Digory.

'What do you expect?'

'I expect someone lives there in secret, only coming in and out at night, with a dark lantern. We shall probably discover a gang of desperate criminals and get a reward. It's all rot to say a house would be empty all those years unless there was some mystery.'

GLOSSARY

Cistern: The tank for storing the water to flush the toilet.

Rafter: A wooden beam or thick plank used in roofs and attics.

A. Reading

Rate this text for 'readability'. Write the word/phrase of your choice into your copy.

VERY EASY ☐   **EASY** ☐   **OKAY** ☐   **HARD** ☐   **VERY HARD** ☐

B. Literacy Questions

1. What is the setting for this story?
2. Why did the children play indoors during this particular summer?
3. What kind of wonderful place did Polly discover in the box-room attic?
4. List the things Polly used to make a floor across the rafters.
5. What kind of house do you think Polly lived in? Was it a detached house, a semi-detached house or a terraced house? Explain your answer.
6. Describe the characters Digory and Polly.

Proofread your answers and correct any mistakes.

C. Numeracy Questions

1. How were the children going to figure out how many rafters were in the box room?
2. How many rafters did they allow for the passage between the two attics in Polly's house?
3. How many rafters do you think were in the maid's room?
4. How were they going to figure out the length of the house?

 ## D. Pairwork

Write the headings below into your copy. Working in pairs, fill in the columns under each heading by finding the relevant words from the extract from *The Magician's Nephew* on p. 65-66. Some examples have been filled in for you.

Type of narration (first/third)	Style of writing	Nouns	Adjectives	Verbs	Adverbs
	conversational	adventures	wonderful	was	chiefly
	intriguing	summers	wettest	discovered	

 ## E. Drawing

This task may be done in your copy or using IT.

- Imagine you are an architect. Think about the house in the extract. Sketch the plan of the upstairs of the house.
- Draw the first attic/box-room, the passage to the second attic, the second attic itself and the maid's room.
- Draw the attic/box-room and the items that Polly has brought up to it. Imagine it as a 'smuggler's cave'.
- Colour in the drawing.

Great Expectations *by Charles Dickens*

Great Expectations was first published in 1861 and is set among the marshes of Kent and in London in the early to mid-1800s. Some of the English language in it is much different to the English that is used today. These are the opening paragraphs from this classic novel and they describe the sudden and terrifying encounter between the narrator, Pip, as he visits his parents' grave, and a dangerous, escaped convict. It is narrated in the first person.

Chapter 1

1. My father's family name being Pirrip, and my christian name Philip, my infant tongue could make of both names nothing longer or more explicit than Pip. So, I called myself Pip, and came to be called Pip.

2.   I give Pirrip as my father's family name, on the authority of his tombstone and my sister – Mrs Joe Gargery, who married the blacksmith. As I never saw my father or my mother, and never saw any likeness of either of them (for their days were long before the days of photographs), my first fancies regarding what they were like, were unreasonably derived from their tombstones. The shape of the letters on my father's, gave me an odd idea that he was a square, stout, dark man, with curly black hair. From the character and turn of the inscription, *'Also Georgiana Wife of the Above,'* I drew a childish conclusion that my mother was freckled and sickly. To five little stone lozenges, each about a foot and a half long, which were arranged in a neat row beside their grave, and were sacred to the memory of five little brothers of mine – who gave up trying to get a living, exceedingly early in that universal struggle – I am indebted for a belief I religiously entertained that they had all been born on their backs with their hands in their trouser-pockets, and had never taken them out in this state of existence.

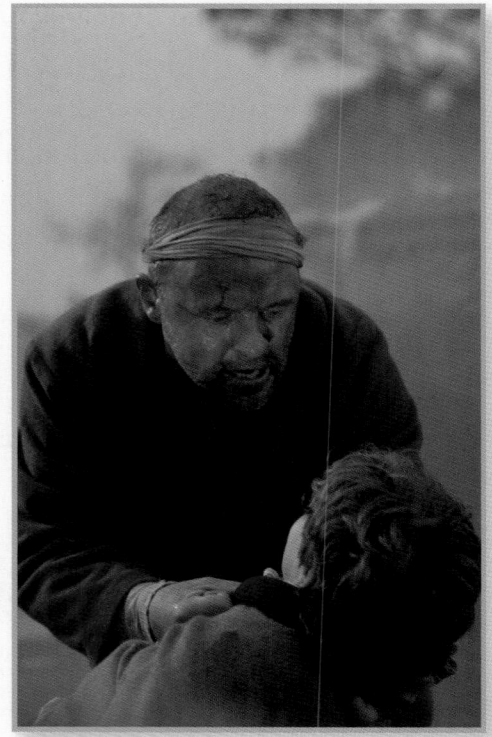

3.   Ours was the marsh country, down by the river, within, as the river wound, twenty miles of the sea. My first most vivid and broad impression of the identity of things, seems to me to have been gained on a memorable raw afternoon towards evening. At such a time I found out for certain, that this bleak place overgrown with nettles was the churchyard; and that Philip Pirrip, late of this parish, and also Georgiana wife of the above, were dead and buried; and that Alexander, Bartholomew, Abraham, Tobias, and Roger, infant children of the aforesaid, were also dead and buried; and that the dark flat wilderness beyond the churchyard, intersected with dykes and mounds and gates, with scattered cattle feeding on it, was the marshes; and that the low leaden line beyond, was the river, and that the distant savage lair from which the wind was rushing, was the sea; and that the small bundle of shivers growing afraid of it all and beginning to cry, was Pip.

4.   'Hold your noise!' cried a terrible voice, as a man started up from among the graves at the side of the church porch. 'Keep still, you little devil, or I'll cut your throat!'

A fearful man, all in coarse grey, with a great iron on his leg. A man with no hat, and with broken shoes, and with an old rag tied round his head. A man who had been soaked in water, and smothered in mud, and lamed by stones, and cut by flints, and stung by nettles, and torn by briars; who limped, and shivered, and glared and growled; and whose teeth chattered in his head as he seized me by the chin.

'O! Don't cut my throat, sir,' I pleaded in terror. 'Pray don't do it, sir.'

'Tell us your name!' said the man. 'Quick!'

'Pip, sir.'

'Once more,' said the man, staring at me. 'Give it mouth!'

'Pip. Pip, sir!'

'Show us where you live,' said the man. 'Pint out the place!'

I pointed to where our village lay, on the flat in-shore among the alder trees and pollards, a mile or more from the church.

The man, after looking at me for a moment, turned me upside down and emptied my pockets. There was nothing in them but a piece of bread. When the church came to itself – for he was so sudden and strong that he made it go head over heels before me, and I saw the steeple under my feet – when the church came to itself, I say, I was seated on a high tombstone, trembling, while he ate the bread ravenously.

'You young dog,' said the man, licking his lips, 'what fat cheeks you ha' got.'

I believe they were fat, though I was at that time undersized for my years, and not strong.

'Darn me if I couldn't eat 'em,' said the man, with a threatening shake of his head, 'and if I han't half a mind to't!'

I earnestly expressed my hope that he wouldn't, and held tighter to the tombstone on which he had put me; partly to keep myself upon it; partly to keep myself from crying.

'Now then, lookee here!' said the man. 'Where's your mother?'

'There, sir!' said I.

He started, made a short run, and stopped and looked over his shoulder.

'There, sir!' I timidly explained. 'Also Georgiana. That's my mother.'

'Oh!' said he, coming back. 'And is that your father alonger your mother?'

'Yes, sir,' said I, 'him too; late of this parish.'

'Ha!' he muttered then, considering. 'Who d'ye live with – supposin' you're kindly let to live, which I han't made up my mind about?'

'My sister, sir – Mrs Joe Gargery – wife of Joe Gargery, the blacksmith, sir.'

'Blacksmith, eh?' said he. And he looked down at his leg.

After darkly looking at his leg and at me several times, he came closer to my tombstone, took me by both arms, and tilted me back as far as he could hold me; so that his eyes looked most powerfully down into mine, and mine looked most helplessly up into his.

'Now lookee here,' he said, 'the question being whether you're to be let to live. You know what a file is.'

'Yes, sir.'

'And you know what wittles is.'

'Yes, sir.'

After each question he tilted me over a little more, so as to give me a greater sense of helplessness and danger.

'You get me a file.' He tilted me again. 'And you get me wittles.' He tilted me again. 'You bring 'em both to me.' He tilted me again. 'Or I'll have your heart and liver out.' He tilted me again.

5.   I was dreadfully frightened, and so giddy that I clung to him with both hands, and said, 'If you would kindly please to let me keep upright, sir, perhaps I shouldn't be sick, and perhaps I could attend more.'

He gave me a most tremendous dip and roll, so that the church jumped over its own weather-cock. Then, he held me by the arms, in an upright position on the top of the stone, and went on in these fearful terms:

'You bring me, to-morrow morning early, that file and them wittles. You bring the lot to me, at that old Battery over yonder. You do it, and you never dare to say a word or dare to make a sign concerning your having seen such a person as me, or any person sumever, and you shall be let to live. You fail, or you go from my words in any partickler, no matter how small it is, and your heart and your liver shall be tore out, roasted and ate. Now, I ain't alone, as you may think I am. There's a young man hid with me, in comparison with which young man I am an Angel. That young man hears the words I speak. That young man has a secret way pecooliar to himself, of getting at a boy, and at his heart, and at his liver. It is in wain for a boy to attempt to hide himself from that young man. A boy may lock his door, may be warm in bed, may tuck himself up, may draw the clothes over his head, may think himself comfortable and safe, but that young man will softly creep and creep his way to him and tear him open. I am a keeping that young man from harming of you at the present moment, with great difficulty. I find it wery hard to hold that young man off of your inside. Now, what do you say?'

6.   I said that I would get him the file, and I would get him what broken bits of food I could, and I would come to him at the Battery early in the morning.

'Say Lord strike you dead if you don't!' said the man.

I said so and he took me down.

'Now,' he pursued, 'you remember what you've undertook, and you remember that young man, and you get home!'

'Goo-good night, sir,' I faltered.

'Much of that!' said he, glancing about him over the cold wet flat. 'I wish I was a frog. Or a eel!'

At the same time, he hugged his shuddering body in both his arms – clasping himself, as if to hold himself together – and limped towards the low church wall. As I saw him go, picking his way among the nettles, and among the brambles that bound the green mounds, he looked in my young eyes as if he were eluding the hands of the dead people, stretching up cautiously out of their graves, to get a twist upon his ankle and pull him in.

When he came to the low church wall, he got over it, like a man whose legs were numbed and stiff, and then turned round to look for me. When I saw him turning, I set my face towards home, and made the best use of my legs. But presently I looked over my shoulder, and saw him going on again towards the river, still hugging himself in both arms, and picking his way with his sore feet among the great stones dropped into the marshes here and there, for stepping-places when the rains were heavy, or the tide was in...

... I looked all around for the horrible young man, and could see no signs of him. But, now I was frightened again, and ran home without stopping.

GLOSSARY

Fancies: Thoughts, imaginings, images.

Character: Handwriting (in the context of paragraph 2).

Stone lozenges: Small headstones.

Aforesaid: Previously mentioned or referred to.

A great iron on his leg: A piece of iron like handcuffs, which are on his leg because he's an escaped convict.

Alonger: Along with.

File: An instrument used to cut through iron.

Wittles: Food.

Over yonder: Over there.

Sumever: Whatsoever.

Partickler: Particular.

Pecooliar: Peculiar.

In wain: In vain – no use trying.

A. Reading

Rate this text for 'readability'. Write the word/phrase of your choice into your copy.

VERY EASY ☐   **EASY** ☐   **OKAY** ☐   **HARD** ☐   **VERY HARD** ☐

B. Literacy Questions

1. What is the narrator's Christian name, surname and nickname?
2. What age do you think he is? Search for clues to this question and explain your answer.
3. What has happened to the boy's parents?
4. Why do you think five of his infant siblings died?
5. What does the man threaten to do to the boy?
6. Describe the characters of the boy and of the man as revealed in the extract.
7. Is the boy afraid? Give examples from the text to support your answer.

Proofread your answers and correct any mistakes.

C. Pairwork

Write the headings below into your copy. By putting nouns with adjectives and verbs with adverbs, the author creates **descriptive writing**. Working in pairs, write examples of descriptive writing from the extract from *Great Expectations* above. Some examples have been filled in for you.

Adjectives and nouns	Verbs and adverbs
raw afternoon	he ate the bread ravenously
dark, flat wilderness	I timidly explained
savage lair	his eyes looked most powerfully down into mine

D. Writing

Imagine you are the man, an escaped convict in the 1860s. Write a short paragraph from the man's point of view, continuing the story from where it ends above.

E. Drawing

Imagine the setting or scene (the place/location) of the above extract. Draw the setting and draw the boy and the man as you imagine them to be. Here are some hints to get you started:

- **Setting/scene:** Churchyard, tombstones, church steeple, graveyard, river, fields, cattle, nettles, marsh, evening/night-time.
- **Man:** Coarse grey, iron on his leg, wet, fearful, broken shoes, rag around his head.
- **Boy:** Small bundle of shivers, afraid, small for his years, crying, helpless.

F. Oral Language

Act out the fearful scene above, taking turns to play the role of Pip and the convict. Read the dialogue from your book as you role-play the action.

Apostrophes

Apostrophes have two uses in written English.

1. They are used to show **ownership or possession** of something. As well as showing ownership and possession of actual things, like cars, bikes, toys and books, apostrophes are also used to show 'ownership' of feelings, qualities, attributes, skills, talents and emotions. Notice that all the 'owned' things listed below are nouns.

   For example:

   Jane**'s** hair is very wavy.

   Adam**'s** feelings were hurt.

   Lucy**'s** bike was stolen.

   Brian**'s** skin broke out in a rash.

   The nurse**'s** car was brand new.

The games get pretty crazy at the English teachers' parties.

2. Apostrophes are used to show where a letter has been left out in a word. This happens when a word is shortened, or contracted.

   For example:

It's a gorgeous day.	**It is** a gorgeous day.
We've plenty of time.	**We have** plenty of time.
He **could've** cooked a nice meal.	He **could have** cooked a nice meal.
She **shouldn't** have slammed the door.	She **should not** have slammed the door.
They'll be home soon.	**They will** be home soon.

 # Writing

1. Write these sentences in your copy and add apostrophes where needed:

   i. The girls shoelaces opened and she almost tripped and fell.

   ii. Tinas headcold got worse and she felt miserable.

   iii. Barrys new pup was gorgeous.

   iv. The managers workload was too heavy.

   v. The captains ship sailed swiftly into the ocean.

   vi. Hughs eyes are a deep green.

   vii. Japans trains run on time.

   viii. Lindas cat is scary.

   ix. The dragons fangs were fierce.

   x. The postmans whistle was annoying.

2. Rewrite the following sentences in your copy, using apostrophes to show ownership. The first one has been done for you.

   i. The scissors of the hairdresser were sharp. The **hairdresser's scissors** were sharp.

   ii. The fangs of the wolf were long and white.

   iii. The temper of the boy raged furiously.

   iv. The warmth of the sun thawed the frozen earth.

   v. The delight of the little child was heart-warming.

   vi. The dry skin of the woodcutter was cracked and raw.

   vii. The laughter of the boy was heard by all.

   viii. The feelings of the girl were hurt by the sharp comment.

   ix. The strength of the tiny mouse shocked the lion.

   x. The greed of the witch was astounding.

3. Write these sentences in your copy and add apostrophes where needed.

   i. Naomis eyes are blue and her hands are short and cute.

   ii. The boats hull was damaged in the storm.

   iii. The nurses watch fell and broke.

   iv. The childs tooth fell out.

   v. My sisters cat drank all the milk.

   vi. Her mothers hair was dark and smooth as silk.

   vii. The mechanics car was blue and sleek.

   viii. The farmers tractor trundled slowly through the floods.

   ix. We knew that Marks homework would be the best.

   x. The babys rattle fell and the babys dad picked it up.

4. Write these sentences in your copy and add apostrophes where needed.

   i. Its a miserable day for a walk by the river.

   ii. Its a fabulous time of year, Christmas.

   iii. Isnt it great to get a day off school when it snows?

   iv. Havent you finished that essay yet?

   v. She shouldve been home an hour ago.

   vi. Its great fun going ice-skating.

   vii. The owl blinked its eyes as the moon gleamed brightly.

   viii. Her voice lost its sharpness as she listened to the recitations.

   ix. Its your own fault if youre late.

   x. Weve no room at the inn today.

Just William *by Richmal Crompton*

Just William is a book of short stories about a young boy, William Brown, who is adventurous and mischievous. It was published in 1922 and was so successful that a series of books followed. The stories were adapted for film, television and radio.

Chapter VII: William Joins The Band of Hope

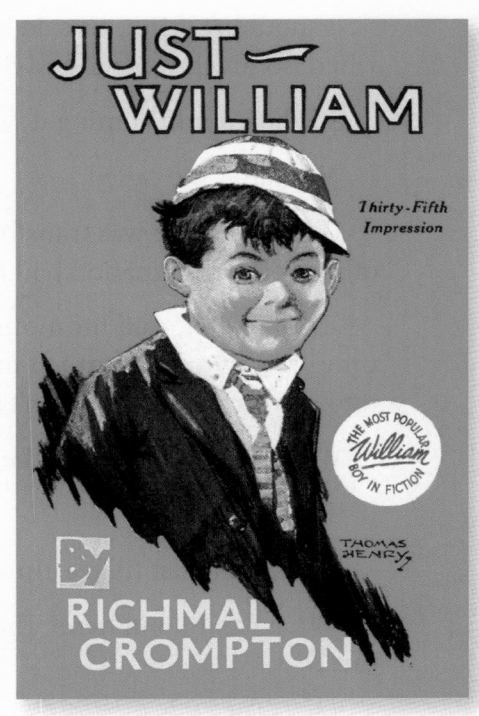

'WILLIAM! You've been playing that dreadful game again!' said Mrs Brown despairingly.

William, his suit covered with dust, his tie under one ear, his face begrimed and his knees cut, looked at her in righteous indignation.

'I haven't. I haven't done anything what you said I'd not to. It was "Lions an' Tamers" what you said I'd not to play. Well, I've not played "Lions an' Tamers", not since you said I'd not to. I wouldn't *do* it— not if thousands of people asked me to, not when you said I'd not to. I—'

Mrs Brown interrupted him.

'Well, what *have* you been playing at?' she said wearily.

'It was "Tigers an' Tamers"', said William. 'It's a different game altogether. In "Lions an' Tamers" half of you is lions an' the other half tamers, an' the tamers try to tame the lions an' the lions try not to be tamed. That's "Lions an' Tamers". It's all there is to it. It's quite a little game.'

'What do you do in "Tigers and Tamers"?' said Mrs Brown suspiciously.

'Well—'

William considered deeply.

'Well,' he repeated lamely, 'in "Tigers an' Tamers" half of you is tigers – you see – and the other half—'

'It's exactly the same thing, William,' said Mrs Brown with sudden spirit.

'I don't see how you can call it the same thing,' said William doggedly. 'You can't call a *lion* a tiger, can you? It jus' isn't one. They're in quite different cages in the Zoo. "*Tigers* an' Tamers" can't be 'zactly the same as "*Lions* an' Tamers".'

'Well, then,' said Mrs Brown firmly, 'you're never to play "Tigers and Tamers" either. And now go and wash your face.'

William's righteous indignation increased.

'My *face*?' he repeated as if he could hardly believe his ears. 'My *face*? I've washed it twice today. I washed it when I got up an' I washed it for dinner. You told me to.'

'Well, just go and look at it.'

William walked over to the looking glass and surveyed his reflection with interest. Then he passed his hands lightly over the discoloured surface of his face, stroked his hair back and straightened his tie. This done, he turned hopefully to his mother.

'It's no good,' she said. 'You must wash your face and brush your hair and you'd better change your suit— and stockings. They're simply covered with dust!'

William turned slowly to go from the room.

'I shouldn't think,' he said bitterly, as he went, 'I shouldn't think, there's many houses where so much washin' and brushin' goes on as in this, an' I'm glad for their sakes.'

She heard him coming downstairs ten minutes later.

'William!' she called.

He entered. He was transformed. His face and hair shone, he had changed his suit. His air of righteous indignation had not diminished.

'That's better,' said his mother approvingly. 'Now, William, do just sit down here till tea-time. There's only about ten minutes, and it's no good your going out. You'll only get yourself into a mess again if you don't sit still.'

William glanced round the drawing-room with the air of one goaded beyond bearing.

'Here?'

'Well, dear, just till tea-time.'

'What can I do in here? There's nothing to do, is there? I can't sit still and not do anything, can I?'

'Oh, read a book. There are ever so many books over there you haven't read, and I'm sure you'd like some of them. Try one of Scott's,' she ended rather doubtfully.

William walked across the room with an expression of intense suffering, took out a book at random, and sat down in an attitude of aloof dignity, holding the book upside down.

It was thus that Mrs de Vere Carter found him when she was announced a moment later.

Mrs de Vere Carter was a recent addition to the neighbourhood. Before her marriage she had been one of *the* Randalls of Hertfordshire. Everyone on whom Mrs de Vere Carter smiled felt intensely flattered. She was tall, and handsome, and gushing, and exquisitely dressed. Her arrival had caused quite a sensation. Everyone agreed that she was 'charming'.

On entering Mrs Brown's drawing room, she saw a little boy, dressed very neatly, with a clean face and well-brushed hair, sitting quietly on a low chair in a corner reading a book.

'The little dear!' she murmured as she shook hands with Mrs Brown.

William's face darkened.

GLOSSARY

Righteous indignation: Annoyance at what is seen as unfair treatment.

Doggedly: With persistence and determination.

Goaded: Provoke to get a reaction.

Aloof: Not friendly, cool, distant.

A. Reading

Rate this text for 'readability'. Write the word/phrase of your choice into your copy.

VERY EASY ☐   EASY ☐   OKAY ☐   HARD ☐   VERY HARD ☐

B. Literacy Questions

1. Why does Mrs Brown forbid William from playing his game 'Lions and Tamers'?

2. Do you think that William is an obedient or a disobedient boy? Explain your answer. Find evidence in the text to support your view.

3. Find five examples of words with 'apostrophes' in the above text. If applicable, write out the full version of the words.

4. Did you find moments in the story humorous (funny)? Explain your answer using examples from the text.

Proofread your answers and correct any mistakes.

C. Pairwork

Find examples of descriptive writing in the extract above. List some phrases/sentences in your copy. Then try to sort the words into nouns, adjectives, verbs and adverbs. Read right through the extract and make your list as long as possible.

D. Creative Writing – Continue a Story

Use the story ingredients on p. 57 to write a brief story in your **PORTFOLIO** continuing from these first sentences:

The door slammed behind him. This was it. It was now or never. He took a deep breath and…

Remember Analyse, Create and Edit (ACE) from Chapter 1.

- **Analyse/think** about the setting, characters, problems and a way of solving problems in the end.
- **Create** the text.
- Then keep creating by rereading it and **cutting out any clichés** (overused phrases and/or predictable material).
- **Improve the verbs** (action words), **adverbs** (words that describe verbs) and **adjectives** (words that describe nouns).
- **Insert short sentences** to create a dramatic effect, e.g. He fled. / She howled. / It happened again. / They paused in horror.
- **Edit** your text by **proofreading** it and correct any spelling, grammar or punctuation mistakes.

Dictionary and Thesaurus

Dictionary

Dictionaries are delightful! You'll be amazed at what you can learn from them.

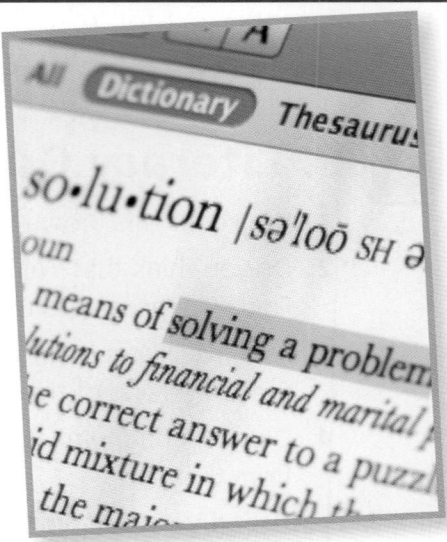

- You can check the **meaning** or the **spelling** of a word.
- Beside the word, it will indicate if the word is a **noun** (*n.*), **adjective** (*adj.*), **verb** (*v.*) or **adverb** (*adv.*).
- It will **explain** the word. There may be a few different meanings.
- It will give the **origin** of the word – whether it was originally a Latin or a French word, etc.

 ## Reading

Look up the following words in a dictionary and record your results in your copy, using the headings in the sample below.

bow, arm, chart, defend, eternal, floret, horrible, inlet and *jar*.

The first one has been done for you.

Word	Part of speech	Meaning 1	Meaning 2	Origin
bow	Noun	A knot tied with two loops and two loose ends	A weapon for shooting arrows	None given

Thesaurus

A thesaurus is a book that groups words with the same or similar meanings (synonyms). For example, if you look up the word *boat* you will be shown other words such as *craft, ship, ferry, dinghy, yacht* and *kayak*.

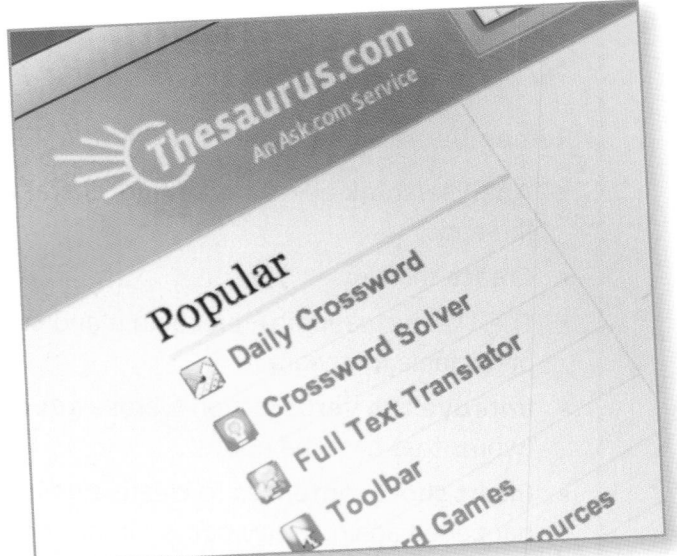

 ## Reading

Look up the following words in a thesaurus and record your results in your copy:

keg, lovely, mist, none, orb, plane, quarry, repair, sever, term, unclean, veil, wake, X-ray and *zero*.

The first two have been done for you.

Word	Synonyms (words with similar meanings)
keg	barrel, bask, drum, firkin, hogshead, tun, vat
lovely	admirable, adorable, amiable, attractive, beautiful, charming, comely, exquisite, nice

Revision: Grammar

In the extracts in Chapters 1 and 2 we have seen writers use nouns, adjectives, verbs and adverbs to great effect. Are you getting better at using them too?

Writing

1. **Nouns** are objects/things, people and places, e.g. window, car, pen, Joan, Frank, Cork, Africa. In your copy, write down some examples of nouns that you see in the following pictures.

2. **Adjectives** describe nouns, e.g. broken windows, new cars, green pens, beautiful Joan, witty Frank, historic Cork, amazing Africa.
In your copy, list adjectives that describe nouns in the pictures opposite.

3. **Verbs** are action words, e.g. dance, sing, laugh, surf, jump, scream, cry. Write ten sentences using ten different verbs in your copy.

4. **Adverbs** describe verbs, e.g. happily, noisily, faintly, painstakingly.
In your copy, list adverbs that describe the dancers in the picture opposite.

ASSESSMENT

Complete this assessment in your PORTFOLIO.

Oral Assessment

Describe your favourite novel to the class. Tell them why you like it. (Complete the Oral Assessment Checklist in your **PORTFOLIO.**)

Written Assessment

A. Nouns

Underline the nouns in the following sentences.

1. Mark bought new runners, socks and shin guards in Elvery's summer sale.
2. They raced happily along the pier until they reached the ice-cream van.
3. Doctors and nurses work unsociable hours.
4. The sun shone brightly on the shoreline.
5. 'There are only strawberries left; all the melons and grapes are sold,' she said.

Now count up the number of nouns you found. _____ **(5 marks)**

B. Adjectives

Underline the adjectives in the following sentences.

1. The dreary rain poured incessantly against the window-pane.
2. She loved dark chocolate but detested white.
3. The girl had frizzled hair, sharp elbows and spotless nails.
4. He dipped the stale biscuit into the warm tea.
5. The pungent smoke stung his cold, narrow eyes.

Now count up the number of adjectives you found. _____ **(5 marks)**

C. Verbs

Underline the verbs in the following sentences.

1. They played cards, read books, watched TV and went to bed.
2. 'Will you bring it to the sink and wash it?' she asked.
3. One Direction played three concerts in Dublin last year.
4. The flames rapidly spread to the roof of the cottage.
5. In a flash of fury, she flung the pearls from her neck.

Now count up the number of verbs you found. _____ **(10 marks)**

D. Adverbs

Fill in adverbs in the following sentences.

1. The choir sang _____ and were applauded _____.
2. She shook the tree _____ and tons of apples flew off it.

ASSESSMENT

3. He stirred the soup _____.

4. The starving men ate their dinner _____.

5. The wolf growled _____.

6. Farmers work _____ in all weathers and in all conditions.

7. She stumbled _____ in her new high heels.

8. They danced _____ at the disco.

9. Brian _____ won the race.

10. Sonia jumped _____ on the bouncy castle.

(10 marks)

E. Contractions

Rewrite the following sentences and contract the words that you can, using apostrophes to replace missing letters. The first one has been done for you.

1. He **should have** brought an umbrella since rain was forecast.
   He **should've** brought an umbrella since rain was forecast.

2. They did not see their favourite programme because they were late getting home.

3. If my sister had any patience she would have finished the task.

4. We will walk the first mile; then we will jog the rest.

5. If they do not hurry they will miss the plane.

6. She did not stir the mixture enough so the cake did not rise properly.

7. I am tired so I am going home early.

8. I do not have enough money so I cannot buy the new tablet.

9. They could not see in the fog so they were not able to travel far.

10. Can you not find the treasure?

(10 marks)

F. Personal Writing

Write five sentences about your love of reading OR sport OR music.

ACE this question!

Peer assessment: Swap your draft 1 with a classmate and correct each other's personal writing. Underline any errors that you find. Learning from each other is very important.

Share your results with your classmates to see how you all responded to the assessment. Compare how many nouns, adjectives and verbs you all found. See who found the most correct ones.

(10 marks)

G. Self-Assessment

I did well in _____

The things that I found difficult were _____

The things that I don't fully understand are _____

I would like to improve _____

CHAPTER 3

Songs and Poems: Storytelling

My Learning Expectations

In this chapter, I will:

- See the **storytelling** that is in songs and poems

- Recognise the **styles of writing** used in songs and poetry

- Read some **poetry** – classic, modern, acrostics, haiku and limericks

- Understand the **themes** in poems and songs

- Recognise and learn how to use **features of language**: alliteration, assonance, onomatopoeia, repetition, rhythm, rhyme, sibilance, similes, metaphors and personification

- Write into my **PORTFOLIO** to keep a record of my **creative writing** (remember ACE from Chapter 1)

- Use and recognise **pronouns** and **plurals**

- **Revise** capital letters, full stops, commas, nouns, adjectives, apostrophes, verbs and adverbs

- Assess **my progress** to see how I am getting on with English

Songs and Poems: Storytelling

Songs

In Chapter 2, you became familiar with the style of writing used in novels. Fiction is narrated in the first or third person and is descriptive. It is often written using full sentences that make up paragraphs. The story is then usually divided into chapters.

Songs are descriptive too and they often tell stories. The style of a song is very different to a novel. **Songs** are written in **verses** rather than in paragraphs and there is usually a **chorus** that is repeated.

The type of music that most people listen to is called pop music. Most often, these songs are between 2 and 5 minutes in length.

Can you name the artists in the pictures below? Can you name any of their hits?

A. Writing

1. Think about songs you like. They could be:
   - Childhood songs
   - Christmas songs
   - Songs from musicals, concerts or variety shows
   - Songs that are special to you personally for whatever reason

   Pick out one song in particular. In your copy explain what this song is about.
   Is there a story in it? Is it happy or sad?

2. Make a list of ten songs that you like and which tell stories.

B. Pairwork

1. With a partner, discuss your favourite songs.
2. Compare each other's lists from task A above. What kinds of music do each of you like?
3. Now vote for your class group's top ten favourite songs!
   Write the top ten on a chart and display it in the classroom.

C. Numeracy Question

Below are the birthdays of the band members of One Direction. How old, to the day, are they?

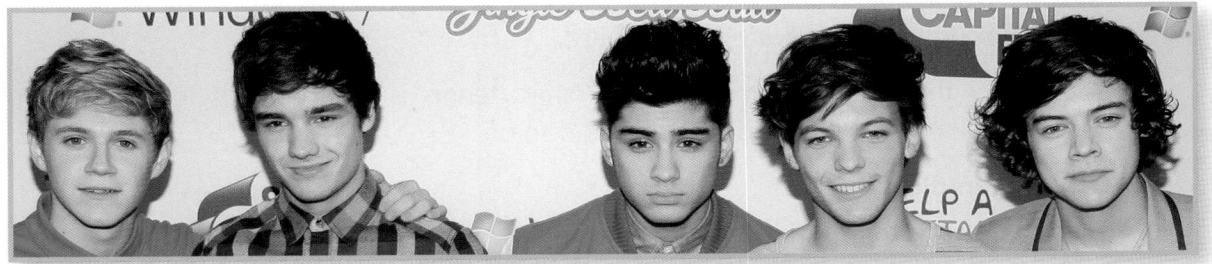

Niall Horan	13 September 1993	Harry Styles	1 February 1994
Zayn Malik	12 January 1993	Louis Tomlinson	24 December 1991
Liam Payne	29 August 1993		

D. Listening

Listen to Ryan Tubridy from RTÉ 2FM interviewing Aidan Davitt and answer the questions below.

1. What is Aidan Davitt's title?
2. Name five famous singers or bands from Mullingar.
3. What is the plan for the town council building?
4. What are the advantages of having a music museum in Mullingar?
5. Why was Ryan in Mullingar? Where did he visit when he was there?
6. What other job does Aidan have?

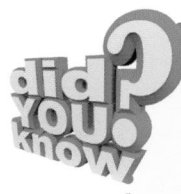

If they weren't in a successful band, these are the careers the One Direction members said they'd choose:

Niall	Football player	Harry	Astronaut
Zayn	SWAT team member	Louis	Power Ranger
Liam	Fireman		

Pronouns

A pronoun is used instead of a noun or a noun phrase. Pronouns give nouns a rest from over-use so they act as substitutes for them.

Personal pronouns	Object pronouns	Possessive pronouns
I	me	my/mine
you	you	your/yours
he/she	him/her/it	his/her/its
we	us	our/ours
you (plural)	you	yours
they	them	their/theirs

For example:

Here is a piece of text with no pronouns:

Amelia loves to play tennis. Amelia plays tennis every day. Amelia's brother, James, plays tennis too. James has a new tennis racket. James's tennis racket is very expensive. Amelia and James hope to win some competitions. Amelia and James practice hard.

Here is the same piece using pronouns:

Amelia loves to play tennis. *She* plays *it* every day. Her brother, James, plays tennis too. *He* has a new tennis racket. *His* tennis racket is very expensive. Amelia and James hope to win some competitions. *They* practice hard.

You can see that 'Amelia' is replaced with 'she', 'tennis' is replaced with 'it', James is replaced with 'he', 'James's' is replaced with 'his' and so on.

Other examples:

This hat belongs to *me*. This hat is *mine*.
Give the book to Barry. Give *it* to *him*.
It is Barry's book. It is *his* book.
Take your sweets. *They* are *yours*.
A relative pronoun 'relates' to the subject in the earlier part of the sentence:

Relative pronouns	
That	Who
Where	Whom
Which	Whose

For example:

The girl *who* went to the shop is my friend.
'Who' refers to the girl, she is the subject in the sentence.

The shop, *which* is on the corner, is well stocked.
'Which' refers to the shop.

The boy, *whose* father owns the shop, came out to talk to her.
'Whose' refers to the boy.

The chocolate *that* she bought was delicious.
'That' refers to the chocolate.

A. Writing

1. Identify (pick out) and list the relative pronouns in the following sentences.

    i. The bike which belonged to Marco was then passed on to Emmet.
    ii. The children, whose toys were damaged in the flood, received new ones.
    iii. Henry and Allie, who had been swimming in the morning, then read books in the afternoon.
    iv. Sherlock Holmes, whose assistant is Watson, is truly a genius.
    v. Our house, which is 100 years old, is cold and draughty.

2. Replace the nouns with personal pronouns.
    Susie ran home after school. Susie was in a hurry because she had arranged to meet Mandy and Antonia at the cinema at 4.30pm and Susie didn't want to be late. Susie quickly changed out of the school uniform into comfy jeans and a t-shirt. Realising that she had managed the time well, Susie relaxed and Susie strolled the short distance to the Apollo to meet her friends.

3. Rewrite the sentences using pronouns.
    i. The nurse cleaned the wound, then the nurse bandaged it and the nurse gave Peter a painkiller.
    ii. The children raced to the water slide and the children yelled in delight as the children whooshed and splashed down the slide.
    iii. Maud put the lead on the dog and Maud walked the dog for 40 minutes. Maud and the dog took a short cut home and Maud and the dog were thirsty after Maud and the dog's trek.
    iv. The band rocked the stadium for two hours and the band were excellent. The band received great applause and the band had to do two encores.
    v. Paulina left her locker key at home so Paulina had to suffer all day without her books for class and Paulina had to share with her friends in every class.

**Peer Assessment** – *Swap copies to correct each other's work*

B. Pairwork

In pairs create five sentences *without* pronouns, and then write them *with* pronouns. Use the examples above as a guide.

Themes

Think about your list of favourite songs. These songs tell stories about love, joy, heartache, loss, beauty, loneliness, defeat, success, emigration, isolation, hope, fear, death, etc. These are **themes** in the songs. Read (or listen to) the following song and try to work out the theme of the song.

Let Her Go *by Passenger*

Mike Rosenberg is a successful British singer-songwriter. He played with a band called Passenger from 2003 to 2009. When the band broke up, Mike kept their name, using it for his solo career. 'Let Her Go' is one of his most successful songs to date.

Well you only need the light when it's burning low
Only miss the sun when it starts to snow
Only know you love her when you let her go
Only know you've been high when you're feeling low
Only hate the road when you're missing home
Only know you love her when you let her go
And you let her go

Staring at the bottom of your glass
Hoping one day you'll make a dream last
But dreams come slow and they go so fast

You see her when you close your eyes
Maybe one day you'll understand why
Everything you touch surely dies

But you only need the light when it's burning low
Only miss the sun when it starts to snow
Only know you love her when you let her go
Only know you've been high when you're feeling low
Only hate the road when you're missing home
Only know you love her when you let her go

Staring at the ceiling in the dark
Same old empty feeling in your heart
'Cos love comes slow and it goes so fast

Well you see her when you fall asleep
But never to touch and never to keep
'Cos you loved her too much and you dived too deep

Passenger

Well you only need the light when it's burning low
Only miss the sun when it starts to snow
Only know you love her when you let her go
Only know you've been high when you're feeling low
Only hate the road when you're missing home
Only know you love her when you let her go
And you let her go
And you let her go
And you let her go
Well you let her go

'Cos you only need the light when it's burning low
Only miss the sun when it starts to snow
Only know you love her when you let her go

Only know you've been high when you're feeling low
Only hate the road when you're missing home
Only know you love her when you let her go
'Cos you only need the light when it's burning low
Only miss the sun when it starts to snow
Only know you love her when you let her go
Only know you've been high when you're feeling low
Only hate the road when you're missing home
Only know you love her when you let her go
And you let her go

 ## A. Literacy Questions

1. What is the theme of this song? Use quotes from the song to support your answer.
2. Is the song written in verses or paragraphs?
3. How many times is the **chorus** repeated?
4. List the opposites mentioned in the song, e.g. *light / dark*.
5. List the words which rhyme in each verse, e.g. *glass / last / fast*.

 ## B. Writing

1. Match three songs from your favourite list with some of the themes listed on p. 88.
2. Songs use descriptive words (adjectives and adverbs). Can you list descriptive words from a song that you like or know well?

C. Research

Think of songs that are about places in Ireland.

For example:

'The Rose of Tralee'

'The Mountains of Mourne'

'It's a Long Way to Tipperary'

'The Banks of My Own Lovely Lee'

'Limerick You're a Lady'

'Galway Girl'

'My Lovely Rose of Clare'

There are songs for almost every county. See how many you can name using the list of counties below.

Antrim	Galway	Monaghan
Armagh	Kerry	Offaly
Carlow	Kildare	Roscommon
Cavan	Kilkenny	Sligo
Clare	Laois	Tipperary
Cork	Leitrim	Tyrone
Derry	Limerick	Waterford
Donegal	Longford	Westmeath
Down	Louth	Wexford
Dublin	Mayo	Wicklow
Fermanagh	Meath	

Poetry

Poems are written in **stanzas** rather than paragraphs. They can come in many different styles and formats, from sonnets (14 lines) to Japanese Haiku (3 lines). Poems are generally written in **verse**, which means with a rhythm or rhyme.

Poems are often like puzzles or jigsaws. You have to think about the hints and clues in them and work out the overall picture in your head.

Poetic Techniques

Poems tell stories in a descriptive way, using some of the following features of language.

Alliteration is the repetition of initial consonants in a series of words. For example:

- I **w**aited and **w**himpered and **w**hinged – the 'w' is repeated
- **L**ake water **l**apping with **l**ow sounds – the 'l' is repeated
- The **b**usy **b**ee **b**umbled **b**ravely **b**eyond the **b**ough – the 'b' is repeated
- The **gl**ow-worm **gl**immered in the **gl**oomy **gl**ade – the 'gl' is repeated

Assonance is the repetition of vowel sounds in a series of words.

Soft broad vowels (a, o, u) are repeated in:
Peace comes dropping slow, dropping from the veils of the morning to where the cricket sings

Harsh slender vowels (i, e) are repeated in:
icy rivulets of rain dripping into his eyes

Metaphors are comparisons which do not use 'like' or 'as'. Metaphors compare one thing to another more directly. They say something *is* something else. For example:

- Her smile is a summer's day
- The moon is a golf ball
- Homework is an itch which will not go away
- The sea is a hungry dog
- The night is coal-black
- 'Roses were young girls hanging from the sky' (from 'Spraying the Potatoes' by Patrick Kavanagh)

Onomatopoeia is when you can almost hear the sound of the word itself: *clash, whizz, bang, clang, clatter, rattle, hum, crack, crash.*

Repetition occurs when words or sentences are repeated. For example:

> *I will arise and go now, and go to Innisfree*
> *… I will arise and go now, for always night and day*

(from 'The Lake Isle of Innisfree' by W.B. Yeats, see p.102)

> *I get up every day torn in two*
> *I trudge to the minimart torn in two*
> *I buy my sliced pan torn in two*

(from 'Torn in Two' by Paul Durcan, see p.122)

Rhyme: Words with the same or similar endings sound the same, and when used together form a rhyme. For example: *street/feet, light/night, lose/shoes, while/smile, shake/snake, tame/same.*

Rhythm is a regular, repeated sound pattern. It is created in a poem by using rhyme and/or a particular pattern of syllables. A **syllable** is a unit of sound. Words are made up of syllables; for example *wa-ter* has two syllables, *char-ac-ter* has three and *a-ccomm-o-da-tion* has five. The word 'syllable' has three syllables: *syll-a-ble*.

Here are two lines from 'Let Her Go':
Star-ing at the cei-ling in the dark   (9 syllables)
Same old emp-ty fee-ling in your heart   (9 syllables)

The combination of the same number of syllables and the similar sounding words at the end makes these two sentences have rhythm. Say them out loud to hear the rhythm and the rhyme.

Sibilance is the repetition of 's' sounds. For example:
- **S**wift a**s** an antelope run**s** from the hou**s**e**s** toward**s** **S**uir Road
- **S**he **s**ell**s** **s**ea**s**hell**s** by the **s**ea **s**hore
- **S**oft **s**alted **s**heet**s** of **s**ea water **s**pla**s**hed the **s**andy **s**horeline

Similes are comparisons using the words 'like' or 'as'. For example:
- Cars crawl and stop **like** carapaces
- He gleams **like** the skin on these tracks
- I feel **like** a foreigner in my native land
- Fangs that snap **like** a murder trap
- I wandered lonely **as** a cloud
- The Grand Canal is as silvery **as** a new coin
- A man, swift **as** an antelope
- Legs, long **as** spears

A. Writing

Invent five examples of each of the following poetic techniques: alliteration, rhyme, sibilance and similes. Work in pairs if you need to.

B. Oral Language

Do you think there are similarities between poems and songs? Have you ever written a poem or song? Discuss this with the person beside you.

Dancing on the Table *by Margot Bosonnet*

We've got a table
big and square;
we dance on the table
when Mammy's not there.

We've got a table
sturdy and stout;
we dance on the table
when Mammy is out.

We've got a table
and it's able
to be a stage or a mountain top
and underneath is a cave or a shop
or the vilest hold of a sailing sloop
where prisoners are chained to the legs by loops.
It's a nomad's tent in the Gobi desert,
it's a snow dugout on the slopes of Everest
in the wildest storm that tries to sweep
us to our deaths,
it's a pothole deep.
It's a caravan trading merchandise,
it's a pond for skating, thick with ice.

We've got a table chipped in patches,
we've got a table with lots of scratches
but it feels so silky when our feet are bare
that we dance on the table and *we* don't care!

We dance on the table
and we clamour and shout;
we dance on the table
till we're all danced out…

A. Literacy Questions

1. What do the children love to do on the table when 'Mammy is out'?
2. The children use the table to play games. List three games that the children play.
3. Make a list of the words that rhyme in the poem. List them in pairs, e.g. *square/there.*
4. List the words or sentences that are repeated in the poem. What effect does this repetition have?

Proofread your answers and correct any mistakes.

B. Writing

Think about the games you played when you were younger. What was the most exciting or fun one? Write a short paragraph (four to six sentences) about it.

Literature and Translation

Imaginative or creative writing in the form of novels, poems, short stories, dramas and film scripts belong to what is called **literature**. You'll see more on short stories, dramas and film in the following chapters.

Translation means changing text from one language to another. Literature is translated so that people all over the world can enjoy the writings of good authors, no matter which language they write in.

Street Dancer *by Gabriel Rosenstock*

Gabriel Rosenstock was born in 1949 in Limerick. He is an author, translator and poet and he writes in English, Irish and German. He has written or translated over 100 books.

There once was a boy who danced on the street,
danced with his arms, danced with his feet.
He danced all day from the sun's first light –
danced with stars in the purple night.
'Nothing to lose!' he cried, 'Nothing to lose!
nothing at all but the soles on my shoes!'
And people would stop and stare a while
shaking their heads with a little smile…
Sometimes he'd wriggle and sometimes he'd shake
sometimes he'd wriggle just like a snake.
At times he was wild, at times he was tame –
no two dances were ever the same.
He had names for his dances: *Falling Snow*
was the name of a dance that was terribly slow.
He made up others as he went along:
Polish Goose and *Tibetan Gong*.
A lovely little dance was *Broken Lip*
With a hop and a leap and a hop and a skip
Sometimes he'd chant, sometimes he'd hum –
mostly he just preferred to be *shtumm*.
He loved to go dancing up in the zoo
With a stripy old zebra and a white cockatoo.
And the hippos would watch him with tears in their eyes
For they couldn't dance with their fat heavy thighs!
Was he born to dance? Nobody knows…
but when he was born he wriggled his toes.
He was dancing as soon as he learned to walk
dancing before he was able to talk.
'Hello, I see you're dancing too!'
he whispered once to a shy bamboo.

One day he met a holy man
who said, 'Things dance as best they can!
Everything – look! Even that table!
No, nothing is solid, nothing is stable!'
And the boy understood that dancing was good,
everything dances as everything should.
'Well, I'll dance the blue sky!' the little boy said,
'I'll dance the green sea and the flat ocean bed,

I'll dance for the young, dance for the old,
dance in the heat, dance in the cold.
I'll dance every colour, dance every sound,
dance in the air, dance on the ground.
I'll dance you a river! Dance you a lake,
the falling leaves and the crooked rake.
Dance you the whales that roam the sea,
dance you Time and Eternity.
The sickle moon, the planet Mars,
the thousands and thousands and millions of stars!

Yes, I will become the dance,' said he.
'I am the dance, the dance is me!'

 ## A. Literacy Questions

1. Read some of the poem aloud. What makes it easy to read?
2. What gives the poem its rhythm or beat?
3. Read the poem again. Pick out an example of one wild and one tame dance that the boy did.
4. What do you think the boy meant in the last two lines?

 ## B. Drawing

The boy loves dancing and believes that 'everything dances': people, nature, animals. Draw some of the things mentioned in the poem that dance.

 ## C. Oral Language

1. Do you like to dance? What kind of dancing do you like? Discuss in pairs.
2. Discuss and try to identify songs that are very lively and which make you want to dance! For example:
   - Lively pop/rap songs
   - Lively jigs and reels
   - Lively songs in films

The following two poems are not in English, but have words which look and sound like some words in English. See what you can figure out.

Sa Bhaile *by Una Leavy*

Una Leavy has written many books for children. She works as a primary school teacher in County Mayo.

Níl aon tinteán
Mar do thinteán féin.

Croch suas do chóta,
Bain díot do bhróga,
faigh cupán tae agus
suigh cois na tine.

Cuirtíní dúnta,
seanchlog ag bualadh,
gaoth ins an simléar
ag cogar sa chiúnas.

An cat is an madra
'na gcodladh araon.
Níl aon tinteán
mar do thinteán féin.

 Literacy Questions

1. How many words in this Irish poem sound or look like English words? List them in your copy.
2. Try to write a translation of this poem.

Mon Cartable *by Pierre Gamarra*

Pierre Gamarra was born in Toulouse in 1919. He was a poet, novelist and literary critic. He died in 2009.

Mon cartable a mille odeurs.
Mon cartable sent la pomme,

Le livre, l'encre, la gomme,
Et les crayons de couleurs.
Mon cartable sent l'orange,
Le buisson et le nougat.
Il sent tout ce que l'on mange
Et ce qu'on ne mange pas.
La figue et la mandarine,
Le papier d'argent et d'or,
Et la coquille marine,
Les bateaux sortant du port.
Les cow-boys et les noisettes,
La craie et le caramel,
Les confettis de la fête
Les billes remplies de ciel
Les longs cheveux de ma mère
Et les joues de mon papa,
Les matins dans la lumière
La rose et le chocolat.

 ## A. Literacy Questions

1. How many words in this French poem sound or look like English words? List them in your copy. Translate as much of the poem as you can.

2. Think about the languages that you speak and which you are studying. Are you able to translate from one to the other?

3. Think of a simple sentence, e.g. 'I like sweets.' Translate it into a few languages.

4. What happens to words and their order and meaning when you translate?

 ## B. Writing

Write a paragraph about your schoolbag (how it looks, smells, what it means to you, what you've been through together, etc).

ACE this question!

Creative Day in Class

Everyone has a special talent or gift. Find out what yours is and develop it. Think about things you produced in primary school.

- Are you musical, artistic, poetic, scientific, mathematical or logical?
- Do you have a flair for languages?
- Are you a good listener or talker?

Everyone in the class should decide what they will contribute to a 'Creative Day in Class'. You can work alone on something, in pairs or in groups, whatever you prefer. Keep the activities short, simple and fun.

Here are some suggestions:

- Have your own short variety show.
- Create simple visual displays. (In groups, each individual shapes themselves to form a letter so that the group displays words like LOVE, FUN, HAPPY, etc.)
- Do a mime.
- Act in a mini-drama.
- Make a short film clip.
- Write a poem and read it aloud.
- Choose a poem written by someone else and read it aloud.
- Write a short story and read it aloud. (A story can be as short as six words, here is one attributed to the famous American writer Ernest Hemingway: *For sale: baby shoes, never worn*.)
- Create a crossword, a Sudoku puzzle or a wordsearch.
- Draw a picture.
- Exhibit some interesting photos.
- Exhibit your own creations. What can you make or craft?
  Can you make something out of sticks? Can you sew, knit or crochet?
- Sing a song: a solo or duet or sing in a group.
- Bring in a musical instrument and play it.

It's your fun day in English class, so enjoy it.

Classic Poetry

As we saw in Chapter 2, if something is called 'classic' it is valued, well-liked and worth having. For example, there are classic cars, films, novels and there is also classic fashion. Classic poems are great poems worth learning about, so read on.

William Wordsworth

I wander'd lonely as a cloud

by William Wordsworth

William Wordsworth was born in 1770 in the Lake District, a very scenic area in north-west England. He had four siblings, but was closest to his sister Dorothy. His father encouraged him to read poetry and he loved walking on the moors (an open area of hills) where his grandparents lived. Wordsworth was the Poet Laureate from 1843 to 1850. (A Poet Laureate is a poet specially chosen by the government to write poems for special occasions.) He died in 1850.

> I wander'd lonely as a cloud
>   That floats on high o'er vales and hills,
> When all at once I saw a crowd,
>   A host, of golden daffodils;
> Beside the lake, beneath the trees,
> Fluttering and dancing in the breeze.
>
> Continuous as the stars that shine
>   And twinkle on the Milky Way,
> They stretch'd in never-ending line
>   Along the margin of a bay;
> Ten thousand saw I at a glance
> Tossing their heads in sprightly dance.
>
> The waves beside them danced, but they
>   Outdid the sparkling waves in glee:
> A poet could not but be gay,
>   In such a jocund company:
> I gazed – and gazed – but little thought
> What wealth the show to me had brought:
>
> For oft, when on my couch I lie
>   In vacant or in pensive mood,
> They flash upon that inward eye
>   Which is the bliss of solitude;
> And then my heart with pleasure fills,
> And dances with the daffodils.

GLOSSARY

Vales: Valleys.
Sprightly: Lively, full of energy.
Jocund: Cheerful and light-hearted.
Oft: Often.
Vacant: Empty.
Pensive: Thinking deeply, reflecting.
Inward eye: Imagination, mind's eye.
Solitude: Being alone.

 A. Literacy Questions

1. List the rhyming words in this poem in pairs, e.g. *cloud/crowd*.

2. What is the location, or setting, of the poem?

3. Is the speaker (poet) happy, in your opinion? Why or why not?

4. Wordsworth wrote in the late 18th century, so some of the words he used at that time are different to the words you use today. Read the poem aloud yourself. What words were hard to *pronounce* or say? Why? List them in your copy.

5. Put each of the words in the glossary into a sentence that makes sense.

Proofread your answers and correct any mistakes.

 B. Writing

Write out the poem using words that you would use instead of the poet's words.

Imagery

You've probably noticed that songs and poems often have some of the same features:

- Rhyme
- Repetition
- Descriptive words

Vivid imagery is another important feature of all good writing, especially in songs and poems. When reading, images are pictures that you see in your mind's eye. You visualise what is being described using your imagination. Think about what you can see in your imagination when you read the following poems.

Stopping by Woods on a Snowy Evening

by Robert Frost

Robert Frost was born in 1874 in San Francisco in the United States. When his father died in 1885, the family moved east to New England. Even though he grew up in the city, in later years, when he was married, he lived on a farm. Many of his poems are about nature and rural life. He died in 1963.

Robert Frost

Whose woods these are I think I know.
His house is in the village though;
He will not see me stopping here
To watch his woods fill up with snow.

My little horse must think it queer
To stop without a farmhouse near
Between the woods and frozen lake
The darkest evening of the year.

He gives his harness bells a shake
To ask if there is some mistake.
The only other sound's the sweep
Of easy wind and downy flake.

The woods are lovely, dark and deep.
But I have promises to keep,
And miles to go before I sleep,
And miles to go before I sleep.

 Literacy Questions

1. What images do you like in the poem? Explain why you like them.
2. List four examples of rhyme in the poem.
3. List the positive and negative words in the poem.
4. What effect does repeating the line at the end have?

Proofread your answers and correct any mistakes.

The Lake Isle of Innisfree *by W.B. Yeats*

William Butler Yeats was born in 1865 in Dublin. He was educated in Dublin and in London. He spent much of his childhood in Sligo where his mother was from. He loved listening to the servants' stories about fairies and this sparked his interest in Irish legends and mythology. He also fell in love with the landscape of County Sligo and it inspired much of his work. In 1889, he fell in love with a woman called Maud Gonne but she didn't return his love and she married someone else. This had a great influence on Yeats's life and poetry. In 1923, he was awarded the Nobel Prize for Literature. He died in 1939.

William Butler Yeats

I will arise and go now, and go to Innisfree,
And a small cabin build there, of clay and wattles made;
Nine bean-rows will I have there, a hive for the honey-bee,
And live alone in the bee-loud glade.

And I shall have some peace there, for peace comes dropping slow,
Dropping from the veils of the morning to where the cricket sings;
There midnight's all a-glimmer, and noon a purple glow,
And evening full of the linnet's wings.

I will arise and go now, for always night and day
I hear lake water lapping with low sounds by the shore;
While I stand on the roadway, or on the pavements grey,
I hear it in the deep heart's core.

GLOSSARY

Innisfree: A small island in Lough Gill near Sligo.

Wattles: Small twigs/branches used to make houses. You may have come across the word in history, studying the homes of the Neolithic farmers who used wattle and daub making their homes.

Glade: A meadow or open space in a wood/forest.

A. Literacy Questions

1. Write down any words or phrases that strike you. Explain your choices.
2. Make a list of the words in the poem that are old-fashioned and not used nowadays.
3. Where is the poem set or located?
4. What sounds can you imagine you hear?
5. Why does the poet want to move to the island?
6. Do you think that he likes nature? Why or why not?

Proofread your answers and correct any mistakes.

B. Writing

Imagine you are the poet and you have gone to the island for a holiday. Write a **postcard** home telling everyone how you are getting on. Describe two nice things about the island as mentioned in the poem.

He Wishes for the Cloths of Heaven *by W.B. Yeats*

Had I the heavens' embroidered cloths,
Enwrought with golden and silver light,
The blue and the dim and the dark cloths
Of night and light and the half-light;
I would spread the cloths under your feet:
But I, being poor, have only my dreams;
I have spread my dreams under your feet;
Tread softly because you tread on my dreams.

GLOSSARY

Enwrought: Finely decorated.

 ## A. Literacy Questions

1. List the words which are repeated in the poem.
2. What imagery does the poet use?
3. Do you like the images he uses? Explain your answer.
4. What do you think the poem is about?
5. What do you think the poet means in the last line?

Proofread your answers and correct any mistakes.

 ## B. Pairwork

In pairs or groups discuss your dreams, not the ones you have when you sleep, but the things you'd like to do/achieve in your life.

The Fiddler of Dooney *by W.B. Yeats*

When I play on my fiddle in Dooney,
Folk dance like a wave of the sea;
My cousin is priest in Kilvarnet,
My brother in Mocharabuiee.

I passed my brother and cousin:
They read in their books of prayer;
I read in my book of songs
I bought at the Sligo fair.

When we come at the end of time
To Peter sitting in state,
He will smile on the three old spirits,
But call me first through the gate;

For the good are always the merry,
Save by an evil chance,
And the merry love the fiddle,
And the merry love to dance:

And when the folk there spy me,
They will all come up to me,
With "Here is the fiddler of Dooney!"
And dance like a wave of the sea.

GLOSSARY

Peter sitting in state: This is a reference to St Peter, who greets souls at the gates of heaven and has a book with the names of those who are to be saved. He is regarded as the keeper of the keys of the kingdom of heaven. (*Matthew 16:19*)

 ## A. Literacy Questions

1. What kind of a person is 'The Fiddler of Dooney?
2. List all the pairs of rhyming words in the poem.
3. What effect has the rhyme on the poem?
4. Identify and explain any similes (comparisons using the words 'like' or 'as') in the poem.

Proofread your answers and correct any mistakes.

 ## B. Research

Do some research on the place-names in the poem. Are they real?

The Song of Wandering Aengus *by W.B. Yeats*

I went out to the hazel wood,
Because a fire was in my head,
And cut and peeled a hazel wand,
And hooked a berry to a thread;
And when white moths were on the wing,
And moth-like stars were flickering out,
I dropped the berry in a stream
And caught a little silver trout.

When I had laid it on the floor
I went to blow the fire aflame,
But some thing rustled on the floor,
And someone called me by my name:
It had become a glimmering girl
With apple blossom in her hair
Who called me by my name and ran
And faded through the brightening air.

Though I am old with wandering
Through hollow lands and hilly lands,
I will find out where she has gone,
And kiss her lips and take her hands;
And walk among long dappled grass,
And pluck till time and times are done
The silver apples of the moon,
The golden apples of the sun.

A. Literacy Questions

1. Identify the magical or fantastical elements in each stanza of the poem.
2. Explain why Aengus is wandering.
3. List six examples of rhyme in the poem.
4. List three examples of alliteration (repetition of initial consonants in a series of words).
5. Find two examples of assonance (repetition of vowel sounds in a series of words).
6. Choose one image from the poem which you really liked. Explain what you liked about it.

Proofread your answers and correct any mistakes.

B. Drawing

Visualise and draw the scenes described in each stanza. Begin with Stanza 1, then do Stanzas 2 and 3.

Leisure *by William H. Davies*

William Henry Davies was born in 1871 in Wales. His father died when he was three and his mother sent William and his two siblings to live with their grandparents. William became involved in petty crime. He travelled to America and Canada, but was a tramp (travelling from place to place looking for work or begging) until he self-published his first book of poems and gradually became successful. He died in 1940.

What is this life if, full of care,
We have no time to stand and stare.

No time to stand beneath the boughs
And stare as long as sheep or cows.

No time to see, when woods we pass,
Where squirrels hide their nuts in grass.

No time to see, in broad daylight,
Streams full of stars, like skies at night.

No time to turn at Beauty's glance,
And watch her feet, how they can dance.

No time to wait till her mouth can
Enrich that smile her eyes began.

A poor life this if, full of care,
We have no time to stand and stare.

 ## A. Literacy Questions

1. List the things that the poet feels people should take time to look at and care about.
2. List examples of alliteration in the poem.
3. Why do you think the words 'no time' are repeated in the poem?
4. Why do you think the title of the poem is 'Leisure'?
5. Do you think people today take the time to 'stand and stare'? Explain your answer.

Proofread your answers and correct any mistakes.

 ## B. Writing

Write a modern copy or imitation of the poem. Use words and images that apply to our lives today in the 21st century.

ACE this question!

 ## C. Research

William H. Davies had a very interesting and varied life, spending time in jail and on the road. Do some research into his life and present your findings to the class.

Plurals

Plural means more than one.

Easy Plurals simply get an 's'	cliff → cliffs
	egg → eggs
	horse → horses
	room → rooms
	biro → biros
Add es	gas → gases
	box → boxes
	glass → glasses
	tomato → tomatoes
	potato → potatoes
	dish → dishes
	watch → watches
	brush → brushes
	bench → benches
f/fe → ves	life → lives
	knife → knives
	dwarf → dwarves
	scarf → scarves
	wife → wives
	thief → thieves
y → ies	Baby → babies
	lady → ladies
	family → families
Tricky Plurals	woman → women
	man → men
	child → children
No change	sheep
	deer
	salmon

Writing

Write the plurals of the following words:

baby	cow	prize
banana	foot	ship
box	goose	solo
buffalo	knife	thief
chief	library	tomato
piano	lily	torpedo
child	loaf	volcano
church	potato	wolf

Peer Assessment – *Swap copies to correct each other's work*

Golden Stockings *by Oliver St John Gogarty*

Oliver St John Gogarty was born in 1878 in Dublin. Oliver was sent to boarding school in Mungret College, Limerick and to Clongowes Wood College in Kildare. He studied medicine, wrote poetry and was friends with James Joyce. He was also a senator from 1922 to 1936 and was a close friend of Michael Collins and Arthur Griffith. He was deeply affected by their deaths and performed the autopsies on both men. Oliver died in 1957.

Golden stockings you had on
In the meadow where you ran;
And your little knees together
Bobbed like pippins in the weather,
When the breezes rush and fight
For those dimples of delight,
And they dance from the pursuit,
And the leaf looks like the fruit.

I have many a sight in mind
That would last if I were blind,
Many verses I could write
That would bring me many a sight.
Now I only see but one,
See you running in the sun
And the gold-dust coming up
From the trampled buttercup.

GLOSSARY

Pippins: Yellow and red apples; pippin comes from the French word for pip, *pépin*.

 ## A. Literacy Questions

1. In your opinion, what is the most striking element/feature about this poem? Explain your answer.
2. What image strikes you the most? Explain your answer.
3. Find two similes in the poem; explain the comparisons which each simile is making.
4. Circle the words which best describe the mood or tone of the poet:

   sad   happy   nostalgic   sentimental   wistful

Proofread your answers and correct any mistakes.

 ## B. Oral Language

1. In pairs, recite the poem carefully. Try to count the number of syllables (units of sound in a word) in each line. For example:

   Line 1   7 syllables   Gold-en stock-ings you had on
   Line 2   7 syllables   In the mead-ow where you ran;

2. What effect does the regular pattern of syllables have on how you read/learn the poem?

 ## C. Research

Oliver St John Gogarty was a very witty and interesting person. Do some research on him and present your findings to the class.

Personification

Images are easier to visualise or see if some of the following techniques are used to create them:

- Metaphors [see p. 91]
- Similes [see p. 92]
- Personification

Personification is when we use human qualities/ characteristics to describe things.

For example:

- The wind howled bitterly, the storm raged furiously and the trees sighed softly.
- The waves beside them danced but they outdid the waves in sparkling glee.
- Jet aeroplanes circling moaning overhead.
- Silence shuffled forward with its hands up in the air.

A. Writing

1. Invent five examples of personification and put them into sentences.
2. Personify the following nouns: *book, phone, grass, rain and car*.

B. Drawing

Draw pictures to illustrate two of your examples of personification.

C. Oral Language

Read out your examples of personification giving them meaning with your tone and gestures.

Silver *by Walter de la Mare*

Walter de la Mare was born in 1873 in Kent, England. He didn't like the name Walter, so instead was called Jack. He worked as a statistician (analysing statistics) but wrote poetry and children's books in his free time. He died in 1956 and his ashes are buried in the crypt in St Paul's Cathedral in London.

Slowly, silently, now the moon
Walks the night in her silver shoon:
This way, and that she peers, and sees
Silver fruit upon silver trees;
One by one the casements catch
Her beams beneath the silvery thatch;
Couched in his kennel like a log,
With paws of silver sleeps the dog;
From their shadowy cote the white breasts peep
Of doves in a silver-feathered sleep;
The harvest mouse goes scampering by,
With silver claws, and silver eye:
And moveless fish in the water gleam,
By silver reeds in a silver stream.

GLOSSARY

Shoon: Possibly a word created by the poet to mean 'the shine' of the moonlight. Writers often create their own words; this is called 'poetic licence'.
Casement: A window, usually one which opens on a vertical hinge, like a door.
Thatch: A roof of straw.
Cote: A shelter with nest holes for birds; the doves shelter in their dovecote.

 # A. Literacy Questions

1. The poet uses personification (giving something human qualities) in this poem, such as 'the moon walks...' Read the entire poem and explain fully what the moon/person does.

2. The poem is written in rhyming couplets (every two lines rhyme). What effect does this rhyme have on the poem?

3. List examples of sibilance (the repetition of 's' sounds) in the poem.

4. Count the number of times the word 'silver' is repeated in the poem. Why is it repeated, what is the poet trying to emphasise?

5. Do you like the poem? Explain your answer.

Proofread your answers and correct any mistakes.

 # B. Writing

Adapt this poem by writing about the sun instead of the moon.

Dover Beach *by Matthew Arnold*

Matthew Arnold was born in 1822 in England. His father was a headmaster. In 1834, his family holidayed in the Lake District, close to William Wordsworth's home. In 1842, his father died and Matthew went to live in the Lake District. He got a job as a school inspector and married in 1851. He travelled widely on the railways inspecting schools across England. In 1849, he published his first book of poetry. He died suddenly of heart failure in 1888.

This is an excerpt from the poem.

> The sea is calm tonight.
> The tide is full, the moon lies fair
> Upon the straits; on the French coast the light
> Gleams and is gone: the cliffs of England stand,
> Glimmering and vast, out in the tranquil bay.
> Come to the window, sweet is the night-air!
> Only, from the long line of spray
> Where the sea meets the moon-blanch'd land,
> Listen! you hear the grating roar
> Of pebbles which the waves draw back, and fling,
> At their return, up the high strand,
> Begin, and cease, and then again begin,
> With tremulous cadence slow, and bring
> The eternal note of sadness in.

GLOSSARY

Straits: A narrow passage of water connecting two seas, probably referring to the English Channel separating England and France.
Blanch'd: Whitened by moonlight.
Tremulous: Shaking or quivering.
Cadence: The rhythm of sounds.

 ## A. Literacy Questions

1. What is the poet describing, what is the scene or the setting?
2. List the words which rhyme in the poem.
3. List the words which you don't understand. Use a dictionary to find out what they mean.

Proofread your answers and correct any mistakes.

 ## B. Drawing

Draw the scene as described in the poem. (Hints: A beach in the moonlight, cliffs, someone at the window looking out to sea, waves flinging pebbles on the shore.)

The Express *by Stephen Spender*

Stephen Spender was born in 1909 in London. His father was a journalist, his mother an artist. He attended Oxford University but never completed his degree. He said of himself that he had never passed an exam in his life. He spent many years in Germany and worked as a poet and novelist. He died in 1995.

After the first powerful, plain manifesto
The black statement of pistons, without more fuss
But gliding like a queen, she leaves the station.
Without bowing and with restrained unconcern
She passes the houses which humbly crowd outside,
The gasworks and at last the heavy page
Of death, printed by gravestones in the cemetery.
Beyond the town there lies the open country
Where, gathering speed, she acquires mystery,
The luminous self-possession of ships on ocean.
It is now she begins to sing—at first quite low
Then loud, and at last with a jazzy madness—
The song of her whistle screaming at curves,
Of deafening tunnels, brakes, innumerable bolts.
And always light, aerial, underneath,
Retreats the elate metre of her wheels.
Steaming through metal landscape on her lines,
She plunges new eras of white happiness,
Where speed throws up strange shapes, broad curves
And parallels clean like trajectories from guns.
At last, further than Edinburgh or Rome,
Beyond the crest of the world, she reaches night
Where only a low stream-line brightness
Of phosphorous on the tossing hills is light.
Ah, like a comet through flame, she moves entranced,
Wrapt in her music no bird song, no, nor bough
Breaking with honey buds, shall ever equal.

GLOSSARY

Manifesto: A public declaration of aims. It comes from Latin, *manifestare*, 'to make public'. The train's noise made its intent clear.

Pistons: Tubes or valves used in engines.

Elate metre: Ecstatic rhythm, joyous movement.

Trajectory: The path followed by a moving object, in this case, the train.

Comet: An object of gas and ice created in space, usually known for moving very fast.

A. Literacy Questions

1. The train is personified. Explain what the train is personified as.
2. Is it an old train or a modern one? Use quotes from the poem to support your answer.
3. Find words, phrases and comparisons which suggest that the train is very powerful.
4. In what way does the train 'begin to sing'?
5. Is the train happy? Find quotes to support your view.
6. Track the journey of the train; list the things and places which it passes.

Proofread your answers and correct any mistakes.

B. Oral Language

In pairs discuss your experiences of trains:

- Did you play with trains when you were younger?
- What train journeys have you been on?
- What are the advantages/disadvantages of travelling by train?
- Have you seen any films about trains that you particularly liked (such as Polar Express, Murder on the Orient Express, Strangers on a Train, Von Ryan's Express)? Explain why you liked the movie you choose.

Challenge yourself to speak to the class for one minute on one of the topics you discussed.

O my luve's like a red, red rose *by Robert Burns*

Robert Burns was born in 1759 in Scotland, where he is known as Robbie Burns and is regarded as the national poet. His birthday, 25 January, is known as Burns Day in Scotland. His poem and song 'Auld Lang Syne' is often sung at celebrations on New Year's Eve, or Hogmanay as it is known in Scotland. He died in 1796.

O my luve's like a red, red rose,
That's newly sprung in June:
O my Luve's like the melodie
That's sweetly play'd in tune.

As fair art thou, my bonie lass,
So deep in luve am I:
And I will luve thee still, my dear,
Till a' the seas gang dry:

Till a' the seas gang dry, my dear,
And the rocks melt wi' the sun;
I will luve thee still, my dear,
While the sands o' life shall run.

And fare thee weel, my only Luve,
And fare thee weel awhile!
And I will come again, my Luve,
Tho' it were ten thousand mile.

 ## A. Literacy Questions

1. List the Scottish words in the poem and explain what each one means.
2. List the old-fashioned words in the poem. What do you think they mean?
3. Identify the similes in the poem and explain what is being compared.
4. The poet says he is deeply in love. How does he prove this point?
5. Re write the poem, replacing the old words with modern ones.

Proofread your answers and correct any mistakes.

 ## B. Research

Find out what the traditions are for Burns Day in Scotland and report back to the class (Hint: Haggis).

The Chess-Board *by Edward Bulwer-Lytton*

Edward Bulwer-Lytton was born in 1803 in Hertfordshire, England. His father died when he was four and his mother moved the family to London. He wrote verse/poetry in his teenage years and obtained a BA (Bachelor of Arts) degree in Cambridge University. He was a novelist, poet, playwright, and politician. He died in 1873. His most famous quotation, 'the pen is mightier than the sword', is from his play *Richelieu*:

'... beneath the rule of men entirely great, the pen is mightier than the sword.'

My little love, do you yet remember
Ere we were grown so sadly wise,
Those evenings in the bleak December,
Curtained warm from the snowy weather,
When you and I played chess together,
Checkmated by each other's eyes?
Ah, still I see your soft white hand
Hovering warm o'er Queen and Knight,
Brave Pawns in valiant battle stand:
The double Castles guard the wings:
The Bishop, bent on distant things,
Moves, sidling, through the fight,
Our fingers touch; our glances meet,
And falter; falls your golden hair
Against my cheek; your bosom sweet
Is heaving. Down the field, your Queen
Rides slow her soldiery all between,
And checks me unaware.
Ah me! The little battle's done:
Dispers't is all its chivalry;
Full many a move, since then, have we
'Mid life's perplexing chequers made,
And many a game with Fortune play'd; –
What is it we have won?
This, this at least – if this alone; –
That never, never, never, more,
As in those old still nights of yore,
(Ere we were grown so sadly wise)
Can you and I shut out the skies,
Shut out the world, and wintry weather,
And, eyes exchanging warmth with eyes,
Play chess, as then we played, together!

GLOSSARY

Valiant: Brave.

Sidling: To walk in a furtive/secretive manner.

Soldiery: A group of soldiers.

Dispers't: Dispersed or scattered.

Chivalry: Knightly qualities of courage, manners, etc.

Perplexing: Confusing.

 # A. Literacy Questions

1. What memories does the poet describe in the poem?
2. Identify two warm, cosy images from the poem and two cold ones.
3. List six examples of words which rhyme in the poem.
4. The chess game is a metaphor. The poem compares the game of chess to the game of life. Find two examples of this comparison and explain them.
5. How do you think that the poet feels in the poem?

Proofread your answers and correct any mistakes.

 # B. Pairwork

Discuss your experiences of games which you like to play in:

Those evenings in the bleak December,

Curtained warm from the snowy weather,

Modern Poetry

Modern poetry is simply poetry that isn't very old. It's difficult to give it an exact date but poems written from the 1900s onwards would probably be considered modern. To you, that may seem like ages ago and so not modern. But in terms of the poets writing centuries ago, it is modern!

 # Frogs *by Norman Mac Caig*

Norman Mac Caig was born in Edinburgh in 1910. He obtained a degree in Classics in 1932 from the University of Edinburgh. He worked as a primary school teacher in his early career and later worked in the universities in Edinburgh and in Stirling. His first collection of poetry, *Far Cry*, was published in 1943. He died in 1996.

Frogs sit more solid
Than anything sits. In mid-leap they are
Parachutists falling
In a free fall. They die on roads
With arms across their chests and
Heads high.

I love frogs that sit
Like Buddha, that fall without
Parachutes, that die
Like Italian tenors.

Above all, I love them because,
Pursued in water, they never
Panic so much that they fail
To make stylish triangles
With their ballet dancer's
Legs.

 ## A. Literacy Questions

1. List three things to which frogs are compared.
2. List one example of a simile in the poem.
3. List one example of a metaphor in the poem.
4. What does the poet love most about frogs?

Proofread your answers and correct any mistakes.

 ## B. Writing

Do you like frogs? Write a short paragraph about your childhood memories of tadpoles, frogspawn, frogs, river banks, lakeshores, nature, etc.

ACE this task!

Prayer to Laughter *by John Agard*

John Agard was born in 1949 in British Guiana (now Guyana) and now lives in East Sussex, having moved to England in 1977. He studied English, French and Latin for his A-Levels and always loved words and writing. He has published numerous collections of poetry and received many awards. In 2012 he was awarded the Queen's Gold Medal for Poetry.

O Laughter
giver of relaxed mouths

you who rule our belly with tickles
you who come when not called
you who can embarrass us at times

send us stitches in our sides
shake us till the water reaches our eyes
buckle our knees till we cannot stand

we whose faces are grim and shattered
we whose hearts are no longer hearty
O Laughter we beg you

crack us up
crack us up

A. Literacy Questions

1. What is the poem about, explain the theme?
2. Does laughter hurt; find evidence in the poem to support your view?
3. List an example of sibilance ('s' being repeated in a series of words) in the poem.
4. Why do people sometimes cry when they laugh? Find a line in the poem which refers to this.
5. What do you think the last two lines mean?

Proofread your answers and correct any mistakes.

B. Oral Language

In pairs swap stories/anecdotes about hilarious, side-splitting moments in your lives. Can you remember being in a place where you had to stifle (stop) or control your laughter? In a church or a classroom for example? Be brave, speak out and share your funny story with the class.

The Worm *by Ralph Bergengren*

Ralph Bergengren was born in 1871 in Gloucester, Massachusetts. He loved writing children's poetry using rhyme and light-hearted topics. He married a writer in 1900 and they lived in Boston. He died in 1947.

When the earth is turned in spring
The worms are fat as anything.

And birds come flying all around
To eat the worms right off the ground.

They like worms just as much as I
Like bread and milk and apple pie.

And once, when I was very young,
I put a worm right on my tongue.

I didn't like the taste a bit,
And so I didn't swallow it.

But oh, it makes my Mother squirm
Because she *thinks* I ate that worm!

A. Literacy Questions

1. The poem is written using rhyming couplets (two lines together with a rhyme at the end of each line). List all the words which rhyme in the poem, for example 'Spring/anything'.

2. Would you agree that this poem is about a personal experience? Explain your answer.

Proofread your answers and correct any mistakes.

B. Writing

Write 3-4 sentences about a personal experience which you had with the world of nature when you were younger, for example finding a dead bird, feeling caterpillars or ladybirds crawl on your skin, feeling a butterfly flapping between your closed hands, the sting of a wasp, catching a fish, etc.

ACE this task!

C. Pairwork

In pairs, try to write a similar poem, copy the format above of 6 rhyming couplets. Write your poem about any season or experience or event.

Blackberry-Picking *by Seamus Heaney*

Seamus Heaney was born in 1939 on a small farm called Mossbawn in County Derry, Northern Ireland. He was the eldest of nine children. At 12 years of age, he won a scholarship to St Columb's College, a Catholic boarding school in Derry City. In 1961, he graduated from Queen's University, Belfast with a first class honours degree in English Language and Literature. He published his first major collection of poetry in 1966 and was appointed lecturer in Modern English literature in Queen's University. He won the Nobel Prize for Literature in 1995. He died in August 2013, aged 74 following a short illness. Heaney was much loved and respected. Two days after his death, the 81,000 spectators at the All-Ireland football semi-final in Croke Park, acknowledged Heaney with a round of applause lasting over three minutes.

Seamus Heaney

Late August, given heavy rain and sun
For a full week, the blackberries would ripen.
At first, just one, a glossy purple clot
Among others, red, green, hard as a knot.
You ate that first one and its flesh was sweet
Like thickened wine: summer's blood was in it
Leaving stains upon the tongue and lust for
Picking. Then red ones inked up and that hunger
Sent us out with milk-cans, pea-tins, jam-pots
Where briars scratched and wet grass bleached our boots.
Round hayfields, cornfields and potato-drills
We trekked and picked until the cans were full,
Until the tinkling bottom had been covered
With green ones, and on top big dark blobs burned
Like a plate of eyes. Our hands were peppered
With thorn pricks, our palms sticky as Bluebeard's.

We hoarded the fresh berries in the byre,
And when the bath was filled we found a fur,
A rat-grey fungus, glutting on our cache.
The juice was stinking too. Once off the bush
The fruit fermented, the sweet flesh would turn sour.
I always felt like crying. It wasn't fair
That all the lovely canfuls smelt of rot.
Each year I hoped they'd keep, knew they would not.

GLOSSARY

Potato-drills: Rows of potatoes sown in soil.
Hoarded: Stored carefully for future use.
Byre: Cowshed.
Glutting: Having too much.
Cache: A hidden collection of things.
Fermented: Juices changed to alcohol.

 ## A. Literacy Questions

1. List the examples of alliteration in the poem.
2. List five examples of rhyme in the poem.
3. List the similes in the poem.
4. This poem appeals to our senses of sight and smell; what words/images help us to see and smell the blackberries?

Proofread your answers and correct any mistakes.

 ## B. Oral Language

Have you ever gone blackberry picking? Tell the class about your experience.

 ## C. Research

Seamus Heaney has been described as the greatest Irish poet since W.B. Yeats. Find out more about this extraordinary poet and present your findings to the class.

Torn in Two *by Paul Durcan*

Paul Durcan was born in 1944 in Dublin. He grew up in Dublin and also spent happy times in Turlough, County Mayo where his mother was from. He studied law and economics at UCD and had his first collection of poems published in 1967. His work is witty and quirky yet deep and thought-provoking.

Paul Durcan

That twenty-two page love letter in which
I slopped out my heart to you,
Comparing you, my mountain woman,
With a hoard secreted in loughwater
Under a thorn tree in Rear Cross –
How I waited day after day for a reply,
Week after week, month after month.
When after seven months a reply came
I did not recognise your hand on the envelope
But inside there it was, my letter,
My twenty-two page love letter, all of it,
Which you had torn in two.

I get up every day torn in two.
I trudge to the minimart torn in two.
I buy my sliced pan torn in two.
I buy my low-fat milk torn in two.
I traipse back home torn in two.
I crouch in front of the TV torn in two.
I gobble my microwave dinner torn in two.
I kneel down at my bed torn in two.
I whisper my bedtime prayers torn in two.
I clamber into bed torn in two.
But I cannot go to sleep torn in two.
I read about the Taliban torn in two.
I spend the night on my back torn in two.
I get up every day torn in two.
Have I no hope of being one with you?
I am a bright man torn in two.

 Literacy Questions

1. What kind of letter did the poet write and post in Stanza 1?
2. Pick out a metaphor from Stanza 1.
3. How is the atmosphere/tone different in Stanza 2? Why is that?
4. Give examples of repetition in the poem. How does it make you feel?

Proofread your answers and correct any mistakes.

Checkout Girl *by Paul Durcan*

A week back in Ireland from Japan,
But I cannot stop bowing.
Only ten minutes ago in the supermarket
I bowed to the checkout girl
With the red cheeks and the limp.

I bowed from the waist to her
And she blushed and I think
When she limps home this afternoon,
Collecting her toddler from the crèche,
It may be with an extra spring in her limp.

A. Literacy Questions

1. What is the poem about?
2. Why did the girl blush?
3. Why does he think the incident will put a 'spring in her limp'?

Proofread your answers and correct any mistakes.

B. Creative Modelling – A Poem

The poem tells us about an interesting, yet ordinary, experience which the poet had. In your **PORTFOLIO**, write a similar poem yourself about an experience you've had. Try copying the format of this poem, two stanzas with five lines in each.

ACE this task!

Did you know that bowing in gratitude is a custom in Japan?

Mud Between the Toes *by Evelyn Cosgrave*

Evelyn Cosgrave is a poet, novelist and a teacher living and
working in Limerick.

Evelyn Cosgrave

What can I do but smile at myself?
Four years old, rooted in the rain scourged mud
in the upper yard of my grandfather's farm –
only the elegant red rubber of my brand new wellies
between me and the backends of cows.

What I did was cry
while my Dad looked on laughing
telling me it was only my boots were stuck, not me
and all I had to do was leave them behind,
pick my way between rocks and cakes of dung,
let the good earth come oozing
between my little curled toes.
And when I got used to the feel of it
I could go anywhere, no field would be too wet
to keep me out, no slope too slippery
under the roughening soles
of my city white feet.

But I wouldn't budge.
I waited and whimpered and whinged
until he came to lift me out, first me
out of my boots then my boots out of the land
and brought me back to the parlour
where my uncles laughed and made faces
and gave me sweet cake and asked me
what I learned in school.

What can I do now that the upper yard is concrete
and all the upper and lower fields a golf course
and I'm still rooted to the spot,
still afraid of a little mud between the toes.

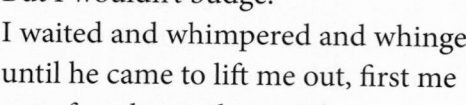

A. Literacy Questions

1. Give one example of alliteration in the poem.
2. List at least 10 adjectives and adverbs from the poem. Use them to write new sentences.
3. What do you think the poet means in the last four lines?
4. What colour wellies did you have as a child? What kind of fun did you have when you
   wore them?

Proofread your answers and correct any mistakes.

B. Writing

The poem tells a story about the child getting stuck in muck. What kinds of scrapes or moments of yuckiness did you experience as a child? Write three to six sentences narrating this anecdote.

ACE this task!

C. Drawing

Imagine the locations or settings in the poem – field, farmhouse, golf course – and draw them as best you can.

Saving Time *by Evelyn Cosgrave*

When my sister was small
she kept a box of treasures.
In it were ribbons and scented rubbers
paper clips, plastic earrings,
all the chocolate she didn't eat for Lent –
and the hour she saved
each winter when the clocks
went back.

She kept the hours
as she kept the chocolate –
for those odd vacuums in her day
that needed filling.

She angered my father
and worried my mother.
But she was defiant.
Thrusting her wrist in their faces,
She let her Telstar watch face
tell the story.

Afterwards,
with an earring,
she'd prick the hour
backwards, acknowledge
its absence from the box,
close it,
return it to beneath her bed.
Not entirely unaware
of what she had done.

A. Literacy Questions

1. List the treasures that the poet's sister kept.
2. When the clocks go back in winter, how does this affect you, how do you feel about it?

Proofread your answers and correct any mistakes.

B. Oral Language

What treasures did you store away as a child? Share your treasured memories of secret stashes or hoards with the person beside you.

Boy at the Window *by Richard Wilbur*

Richard Wilbur was born in 1921 in New York. He was eight when his first poem was published in a magazine. He published his first poetry collection in 1947. Wilbur is also a writer of children's books and a literary translator. Like Robert Frost, Wilbur finds wonder in everyday experiences. He was named Poet Laureate in 1987.

Seeing the snowman standing all alone
In dusk and cold is more than he can bear.
The small boy weeps to hear the wind prepare
A night of gnashings and enormous moan.
His tearful sight can hardly reach to where
The pale-faced figure with bitumen eyes
Returns him such a god-forsaken stare
As outcast Adam gave to Paradise.

The man of snow is, nonetheless, content,
Having no wish to go inside and die.
Still, he is moved to see the youngster cry.
Though frozen water is his element,
He melts enough to drop from one soft eye
A trickle of the purest rain, a tear
For the child at the bright pane surrounded by
Such warmth, such light, such love, and so much fear.

GLOSSARY

Bitumen: Tar or asphalt used to surface roads.

Adam: A reference to the Bible story of Adam, who sinned in the Garden of Eden and was expelled from God's Paradise.

 ## A. Literacy Questions

1. In which season is the poem set? Use quotes to support your answer.
2. Why is the small boy weeping in Stanza 1?
3. Why is the snowman 'content' or happy in Stanza 2?
4. List four examples of rhyme in the poem.
5. List one example of sibilance and one example of onomatopoeia (you can almost hear the sound of the word) in the poem.
6. What do you think the poet means in the last line of the poem?

Proofread your answers and correct any mistakes.

 ## B. Drawing

Draw the scene as you can imagine it from Stanzas 1 and 2 in the poem.

 ## C. Research

1. Ask your teacher to show you the John Lewis Christmas advertisements from 2011 and 2012. Can you see connections between them and this poem?
2. Do you know the story (and the film) by Raymond Briggs, The Snowman? Watch it (or your teacher may show it to you) and write a brief personal response to the story.

The door *by Miroslav Holub*

Miroslav Holub was born on in 1923 in Plzen, in what is now the Czech Republic. He wrote poetry, as well as essays and articles. His poems generally lack rhyme and have been translated into over 30 languages. His work was first published in English in the *Observer* newspaper in 1962. He died in 1998.

Go and open the door.
   Maybe outside there's
   a tree, or a wood,
   a garden,
   or a magic city.

Go and open the door.
   Maybe a dog's rummaging.
   Maybe you'll see a face,
or an eye,
or the picture
       of a picture.

Go and open the door.
   If there's a fog
   it will clear.

Go and open the door.
   Even if there's only
   the darkness ticking,
   even if there's only
   the hollow wind,
   even if
      nothing
         is there,
go and open the door.

At least
there'll be
a draught.

A. Literacy Questions

1. What command is repeated in the poem? Why is it repeated, do you think?
2. List the positive and negative things the poet suggests may be outside.
3. Look at the shape of the poem, what do you think it symbolises?
4. What do you think is the message of the poem?

Proofread your answers and correct any mistakes.

B. Drawing

Using a storyboard format (boxes in a sequence),
draw the images described in each stanza of the poem.

Encounter *by Czeslaw Milosz*

Czeslaw Milosz was born in 1911 in what is now known as Lithuania. He was fluent in Russian, Lithuanian, Polish, French and English. He considered himself a Polish, rather than Lithuanian poet, because his family had spoken Polish since the 16th century. He had a varied career in Paris, Poland and America and in 1980 won the Nobel Prize for Literature. He died in 2004.

> We were riding through frozen fields in a wagon at dawn.
> A red wing rose in the darkness.
>
> And suddenly a hare ran across the road.
> One of us pointed to it with his hand.
>
> That was long ago. Today neither of them is alive,
> Not the hare, nor the man who made the gesture.
>
> O my love, where are they, where are they going
> The flash of a hand, streak of movement, rustle of pebbles.
> I ask not out of sorrow, but in wonder.

A. Literacy Questions

1. What do you think the poem is about? Think about the title.
2. What season is it in Stanza 1 of the poem and what time of the day is it?
3. What is the significance or importance of the incident with the hare?

Proofread your answers and correct any mistakes.

B. Writing

Think about a random, unexpected incident which you have experienced in your life. Write four sentences about it.

ACE this task!

In Memory of My Mother *by Patrick Kavanagh*

Patrick Kavanagh was born in 1904 in Inniskeen, County Monaghan. He was the fourth of ten children. His father was a shoemaker and a farmer and always bought the newspaper, which encouraged Patrick's love of reading, writing and journalism. Patrick worked on the farm and as a shoemaker by day, and wrote poetry and prose by night. In 1954, he was diagnosed with lung cancer and had a lung removed. While recovering from his illness, he spent time on the banks of the Grand Canal in Dublin and rediscovered the beauty of nature. This inspired some of his most famous poems. He died in 1967.

I do not think of you lying in the wet clay
Of a Monaghan graveyard; I see
You walking down a lane among the poplars
On your way to the station, or happily

Going to second Mass on a summer Sunday –
You meet me and you say:
"Don't forget to see about the cattle –"
Among your earthiest words the angels stray.

And I think of you walking along a headland
Of green oats in June,
So full of repose, so rich with life –
And I see us meeting at the end of a town

On a fair day by accident, after
The bargains are all made and we can walk
Together through the shops and stalls and markets
Free in the oriental streets of thought.

O you are not lying in the wet clay,
For it is a harvest evening now and we
Are piling up the ricks against the moonlight
And you smile up at us – eternally.

A. Literacy Questions

1. Explain two examples of the ordinary things which the poet sees his mother doing.
2. What images help you to visualise this farming and rural scene?
3. What impression do you get of the relationship between the mother and son?
4. Identify one example of alliteration and one example of assonance in the poem.

Proofread your answers and correct any mistakes.

B. Research

Patrick Kavanagh is one of Ireland's best-loved poets. Do some research on his life and write down five interesting things that you find out.

Woman Work *by Maya Angelou*

Maya Angelou was born in 1928 in America. She was called Marguerite, but her older brother nicknamed her Maya because he always referred to her as 'mya sister'. She has published autobiographies, books of poetry and essays and has won numerous awards. She is a highly-respected spokesperson for the black community and for women, and her work is on the curriculum in schools and universities in America and elsewhere.

I've got the children to tend
The clothes to mend
The floor to mop
The food to shop
Then the chicken to fry
The baby to dry
I got company to feed
The garden to weed
I've got the shirts to press
The tots to dress
The cane to be cut
I gotta clean up this hut
Then see about the sick
And the cotton to pick.

Shine on me, sunshine
Rain on me, rain
Fall softly, dewdrops
And cool my brow again.

Storm, blow me from here
With your fiercest wind
Let me float across the sky
'till I can rest again.

Fall gently, snowflakes
Cover me with white
Cold icy kisses and
Let me rest tonight.

Sun, rain, curving sky
Mountains, ocean, leaf and stone
Star shine, moon glow
You're all that I can call my own.

A. Literacy Questions

1. Where do you think this woman lives and in what era? Use quotes to support your answer.
2. The first stanza outlines all the chores she has to do. What do the other stanzas focus on?
3. What relationship does she have with nature?
4. What do you think she means in the last stanza?

Proofread your answers and correct any mistakes.

B. Research

1. Do some research on the poet Maya Angelou. She is a famous African-American writer who has had a very interesting life. Do a brief PowerPoint Presentation using around six slides.
2. The slaves who worked on the cotton, sugar cane and tobacco plantations in America up to the 1860s sang beautiful songs about their experiences. Are you familiar with any of them? Do some research in pairs and play some of the songs for the class.

Introduction to Night and Day: Twenty four hours in the life of Dublin City *by Dermot Bolger*

Dermot Bolger was born in 1959 in Dublin. He is one of Ireland's best-known writers. He has won numerous awards for his novels, plays and poetry. When he was growing up, he thought that writers were distant, highly-intelligent people and that ordinary people like him couldn't enter into that world or have a career as a writer. However, his natural talent came through and he has enjoyed great success as a writer over the past decades.

Dermot Bolger

In 2008, he published a book of poems and photographs that had initially been displayed as posters and murals all about South Dublin. He then invited poets in the locality to send him poems about day-to-day life that connected with the themes in his poems. This meant that, in the finished book, which is entitled *Night & Day: Twenty four hours in the life of Dublin City*, Bolger's poems about life in the area are interwoven with poems by writers from the area who capture aspects of their own lives. It was a project that South Dublin County Council funded over a two-year period. In the following extract from the introduction to the book, Dermot explains the background to the project.

Part 1

1. As a poet you can witness the start of a poem's journey. This generally begins as a stray thought which sparks with such sudden electricity that you feel you must find a pen and paper and write it down before whatever unexpected magic exists there disappears. This is the stage of a poem's journey that the writer can control. In each <u>successive</u> draft the poem remains a secretive thing, an <u>embryo</u> that you nurture in your mind, working towards the final draft when you risk bringing it out into the light, but always aware that if you <u>procrastinate</u> for too long you risk worrying to death whatever slim magic once existed in the words.

2. The poems you send out may be pebbles that make a splash somewhere, but the ocean seems so vast that ripples rarely stretch back to you. Sometimes you may also have a sense that the audience that the poem has reached (while welcome, because one feels a sense of <u>privilege</u> if a poem reaches any audience) is not necessarily the intended audience for which it was written.

3. That is because when you post off your poem to whatever <u>periodical</u> may publish it, you lose control of the process by which it finds its audience. The poem is no longer your secret: it has slipped beyond you into an environment where you have little influence on how or where it may be read.

4. Once anyone begins to write – be it poetry or fiction or song lyrics or simply keeping a diary – this seems to me to be a declaration of independence. In a world which increasingly wants you to exist purely as a consumer, it shows that you may be refusing to be seduced by the great lies. Instead you are using words to form your own judgements that may challenge readers and far more importantly, challenge yourself, as you probe down to the bedrock of the hopes, fears and <u>contradictions</u> that <u>constitute</u> us all.

A. Literacy Questions

1. In your own words, explain the journey of a poem according to how it happens for Dermot Bolger.
2. Dermot Bolger uses interesting comparisons (metaphors) to describe the journey of a poem. Find these comparisons/metaphors and explain what he compares them to.
3. Look up the underlined words in the dictionary.
4. What do you think the writer means in the first sentence in paragraph 4?

Proofread your answers and correct any mistakes.

B. Pairwork

Discuss some of the 'hopes, fears and contradictions' that you have had that are a natural part of growing up.

Part 2

1. The poems in *Night and Day* are deliberately rooted in one time and place, South Dublin County. My poems were first published as posters or as murals on walls in places as diverse as the Belgard Luas stop in Tallaght or the gable of the Cúnas and Cairdeas Centre in Neilstown – which houses the local Drugs Task Force.

2. I grew up in an environment where I felt that my experiences weren't reflected in literature. Therefore as a writer I've always tried to write in a way that touches upon hidden lives. I began as a teenager by selling photocopied broadsheets of work by local poets in Finglas pubs, hoping to reach a readership who rarely encountered poetry. Now – though Ireland has greatly changed – I have found that in this present project I have echoed that process in some ways by trying to initially display my poems in unexpected locations across South Dublin County where people may rarely encounter poetry.

3. I am not naïve enough to imagine that poems by me or by anyone are likely to ever affect a broad <u>constituency</u> when displayed in any public space. But always I was seeking the one person in five hundred who turns a familiar corner and is surprised to see some hint of their own experience reflected back at them from a wall.

4. These posters and murals became my way of leaving the sort of sign which I had longed for as a <u>disaffected</u> youth, a glimpse into another method of seeing things, an <u>affirmation</u> of the <u>validity</u> of thinking in a different way, or – perhaps even better – a sense that the writer has got it wrong and you could find better words to describe what he wanted to capture.

5. In *Night and Day*, I wanted to strip away the 'I' from my poetry and use instead the 'eye' through which we <u>perpetually</u> observe fellow commuters, strangers we pass on streets, people with whom we share busy lifts or supermarket check-out queues, the others whose lives we find ourselves unconsciously speculating about. This project allowed me this time to be an observer, to journey through Clondalkin and Rathfarnham and Tallaght and other places and to imaginatively reinvent the thoughts of a woman I saw waiting for a tram, a foreign worker alighting from one, a teenage girl on a street, a man walking alone at night, a woman trapped in the glacier of a bottle-necked motorway, the people we generally pass and forget, people whose lives I suddenly had time to <u>speculate</u> upon or people I met who took time to talk to me about their lives.

6. Therefore real and reinvented lives jostle throughout these pages. A writer's work is essentially solitary, as they try to breathe life into the phantoms of their imaginations and engage in <u>tentative</u> projects that they do not know anyone else will ever read.

 # A. Literacy Questions

1. When he was a teenager, how did Dermot Bolger promote poetry amongst people who rarely read it?

2. What did he hope to achieve with the *Night and Day* collection?

3. Look up the underlined words in the dictionary.

4. Name two difficulties he says are experienced by writers?

Proofread your answers and correct any mistakes.

 # B. Drawing

In writing his poems, Dermot Bolger said that he used the 'eye' through which we constantly watch or see other people in our daily lives. Think about your daily journey to and from school. What do you see from early morning through to evening and night-time? Draw these images in your copy. You can use a storyboard format like the example below if you like.

 # C. Writing

Write a diary entry describing the events in your drawing above.

ACE this task!

The following three poems – 'Warriors', 'Reflections' and 'Spy in the Sky' – all come from the *Night and Day* collection.

Warriors *by Eileen Casey*

The Grand Canal is silvery as a new coin.
I'm on the Luas thinking of nothing in particular
when a man, swift as an antelope,
runs from the houses towards Suir Road.

Legs, long as spears, gather speed
This Luas is a wild one
broken free from the herd.

On the grass, thawing frost steams a mirage,
dust rises.
His winter coat, shirt and navy trousers
dissolve to gorgeous Maasai colours.
He gleams like the skin on these tracks,
each muscle and sinew
zig zagging a perfect quarter arc

bearing down on the metal beast
and I'm back on the Midland streets
sidestepping pools of greenish-
hued cow dung. Straw
straggles from trailers, haggling
wasps swarm around my ears.

A cow breaks from a loose bunch,
is chased by a farmer in breeches
held up with braces, his face berry red,
legs akimbo: the stick in his hand
orchestrating a fair day.
Later, there'll be whiskey in the pubs
chocolate for children of the tribe
creeping in to sit on the long benches.

My warrior comes on board
scarcely out of breath. Beyond
Rialto
Fatima
St. James
Heuston Station
we journey towards the city.

GLOSSARY

Mirage: Something that seems real but is not there.

Maasai: An African tribe known for their colourful clothing.

Gleams: Shines.

Sinew: Tissue that connects muscle to bone.

Bearing down: Approaching.

Midland streets: Streets in the midlands of Ireland.

Hued: Of a certain colour.

Straggles: Falls behind.

Haggling: Bargaining.

Breeches: Trousers.

Akimbo: Turned outwards.

 ## A. Literacy Questions

1. Identify the metaphors in the poem.

2. What action takes place in the poem? Write out the events that take place in the poem. (Hints: Man running to catch a Luas, passenger watches him, he reminds her of a childhood memory when a cow broke loose on a market/fair day, the man hops on the Luas, the journey continues.)

3. Do you know the places-names in the poem (Rialto, Fatima, St. James, Heuston Station)? Find them on a transport map of Dublin.

Proofread your answers and correct any mistakes.

 ## B. Pairwork

Working in pairs or groups, rewrite the action of the poem as a short story (go from stanzas to paragraphs).

- Use the ACE (Analyse, Create, Edit) tips in Chapter 1.
- Write it in the third person (he/she).
- Use short, simple sentences for draft 1.
- Use paragraphs.
- In draft 2, use descriptive **adjectives**, e.g. 'tall, fit, lean man'.
- Use descriptive **adverbs**, e.g. 'ran lithely / quickly / speedily / gracefully / purposefully', etc.
- Proofread draft 2 and correct any mistakes.
- Ask someone else to proofread draft 2 and create draft 3.

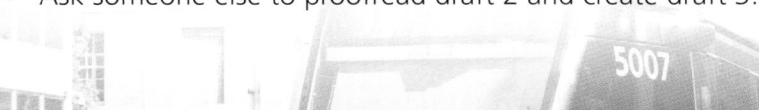

Reflections *by Betty Keogh*

Through the window
Their features look familiar,
Yet I don't understand their tongue.

Luas stop after stop
People board and alight,
Dusk turns into dark.

We whizz past streetlights:
Factories, houses, the Square,
Apartments climbing skyward.

I feel like a foreigner
In my native land.

 ## A. Literacy Questions

1. What is the poet reflecting on or thinking about?
2. If you have ever felt like the poet feels in the final two lines of the poem, then you can connect with her and relate to her experience. Has there been a time when you too have felt like a foreigner in your native land? Explain your answer, giving details of your experience.

Proofread your answers and correct any mistakes.

 ## B. Writing

Imagine you are on a train. Describe the people sitting around you and what you imagine about their lives.

ACE this task!

Spy in the Sky *by Mae Newman*

As I sit unseen, I silently watch
Cars crawl and stop like carapaces.
Inside these shells people drink

Coffee, eat breakfast, shave,
Scratch, pluck eyebrows, use mobiles.
Ask the mirror – is this life?

They're too busy going somewhere,
Getting nowhere, to wonder
Am I lost, cast aside or rejected.

Some say I'm cute, I'm lovely.
Others that I'm cruel, I'm vermin.

A lonely grey squirrel, sitting
On a signpost over the bypass

GLOSSARY

Vermin: **Harmful wild animals.**

A. Literacy Questions

1. What is the squirrel doing?
2. How does the squirrel feel?
3. Use a dictionary to find the meaning of *carapaces*.
4. List the activities that the squirrel sees people doing in their cars.
5. Can you think of a different title for the poem? Explain your choice.

Proofread your answers and correct any mistakes.

B. Oral Language

In pairs explain to each other your reasons for the title you chose in question 5 above.
Perhaps stand up and explain to the class.

The Nomad *by Dermot Bolger*

This poem is from a volume of poetry called *External Affairs*, published in 2008.

Always in my mind the landscape of Waterford
Awaits beyond the boundaries of foreign towns.
On childhood nights I swore one day to explore
High into the wilds of the Knockmealdowns,
To see Dungarvan, Passage East and Tramore:
Places sounding distant and impossibly strange.

No encounter has quenched the sense of wonder
That fuelled this life of hostels and train stations,
A life spent seeking a home, yet needing to wander,
Never able to settle on one job, one lover, one abode,
Imagining that beyond the next set of mountains,
The next city block, I'll discover a narrow road

Beckoning in the dark between hawthorn bushes,
To a bend where I will stare up at an attic window,
To see a child's face looking out into the darkness,
Listening to his mother sing in the kitchen below,
His hands at the glass pane, his gaze rapturous,
Already in his mind a nomad, a wandering hobo.

 Literacy Questions

1. What kind of person is the poet do you think?
2. Can you find and explain an example of personification in the poem?
3. List in pairs the words which rhyme in the poem.
4. Do you like travelling to, exploring and discovering new places? Explain your answer.

Proofread your answers and correct any mistakes.

Acrostics, Limericks and Haiku

Poems can be written in lots of ways and styles. They can be long or short. They can rhyme or not rhyme. You have already seen some poems written in stanzas. In the following pages, you will see examples of acrostic, haiku and limerick poems.

Acrostic Poems

Acrostic poems are written using the letters in a word to start each line of the poem. For example, here we see the letters of a girl's name (Sinéad) and a boy's name (Thomas) used to start each line of the poem.

Sinéad

She loves writing, doodling, scribbling

Inking her fingers with reds, pinks and greens

Never minding where her doodles take her

Every scrawl an escape from the humdrum

A celebration of the imagination

Delightful, daring and deliciously time-wasting!

Thomas

Truth be told he's very bold

Heaps clothes on the floor, refuses to fold

Only showers once a week

Makes faces and gives cheek

Asks nosy questions and spills the beans

Sighs with remorse, then eats his greens.

 ## Writing

1. Using your first name, write an acrostic poem all about yourself.
2. Listen to funny poems on www.gigglepoetry.com. Try writing your own funny poem. Then swap poems with each other for fun.

Limericks

Limericks are short, funny, witty poems that are only five sentences long. The rhyme is organised so that lines 1, 2 and 5 rhyme and lines 3 and 4 rhyme using a different sound.

For example:

There was a young lady from **Leeds**	Line 1
Who swallowed a package of **seeds**.	Line 2
Now this sorry young **lass**	Line 3
Is quite covered in **grass**,	Line 4
But has all the tomatoes she **needs**.	Line 5

Writing

Try writing your own limericks.

Haiku

A haiku is a traditional Japanese poem. It is a short poem, organised around syllables. A syllable is a part of a pronounced word. The word 'haiku' has two syllables: *hai-ku*. Haiku consist of three lines. The first and last lines of a haiku have five syllables and the middle line has seven syllables, so a 5-7-5 pattern. The lines rarely rhyme.

did you know?

Haiku comes from the Japanese, *hai* (amusement) and *ku* (verse).

Haiku are short poems, like tweets. They are usually written about things that are recognisable to the reader.

Here's a haiku to help you remember:

Haiku

I am first with five

Then seven in the middle –

Five again to end.

What am I?

Green and speckled legs,

Hop on logs and lily pads

Splash in cool water.

A. Writing

Try writing your own haiku. Find examples online.

B. Creative Writing – A Poem

Choose a type of poem that you like from any you have seen in this chapter.
Using the poem you have chosen as a template, write a poem about any topic into
your **PORTFOLIO**.

ACE this task!

ASSESSMENT

Complete this assessment in your **PORTFOLIO**.

Oral Assessment

Describe your favourite poem to the class. Tell them why you like it. (Complete the Oral Assessment Checklist in your **PORTFOLIO**.)

Written Assessment

A. Writing Style

List **two** features of the writing style used for **each** of the following.

Songs _____ (2 marks)

Poems _____ (2 marks)

B. Features of Poetry and Song

Alliteration is _____

Example: _____ (4 marks)

Assonance is _____

Example: _____ (4 marks)

A metaphor is _____

Example: _____ (4 marks)

Onomatopoeia is _____

Example: _____ (4 marks)

Personification means _____

Example: _____ (4 marks)

Repetition means _____

Example: _____ (4 marks)

Rhythm means _____

Example: _____ (4 marks)

Rhyme means _____

Example: _____ (4 marks)

Sibilance is _____

Example: _____ (4 marks)

A simile is _____

Example: _____ (4 marks)

ASSESSMENT

C. Grammar Revision

- A **capital letter** is used at the _____ of a sentence. (2 marks)

- A **full stop** goes at the _____ of a sentence.   (2 marks)

- **Commas** go after words in a _____. No comma is needed before the word

  _____.   (2 marks)

- Insert full **stops** and **commas** in the following text.   (14 marks)

  The rain and wind lashed the shore It was a very sudden storm No one had expected
  it The morning had been so glorious The sun shone since dawn and they had all
  scurried off happily to the beach Now however they scurried to gather buckets
  spades picnic baskets wind breakers towels sandals books and other bits and bobs
  Then they dashed to the car soaked and disappointed

- **Nouns** are words for p_____, p_____ and t_____.   (3 marks)

- **Adjectives** describe _____, for example, the _____ teacher, the

  _____ boy, the _____ day, the _____ sun, the _____

  ice-cream.   (6 marks)

- **Apostrophes** show that someone _____ something. For example, _____

  _____   (2 marks)

- **Verbs** are _____ words that describe when an _____ is being done.

                                                                            (2 marks)

- **Adverbs** describe _____, for example, he drove _____, she cried

  _____, they sang _____ and we fought _____.   (5 marks)

D. Self-Assessment

I did well in _____

The things that I found difficult were _____

The things that I don't fully understand are _____

I would like to improve _____

CHAPTER 4

Non-literary Texts: What's Your Point?

My Learning Expectations

In this chapter, I will:

- Listen and read carefully to distinguish between **formal** and **informal language**

- Learn how to use **formal writing** in interviews, questionnaires, surveys, instructions, press releases, petitions, memos, reviews, letters, application forms, brochures, invitations and broadsheet newspaper articles

- Learn how to use **informal writing** in interviews, letters, newsletters, blogs and tabloid newspaper articles

- Recognise informal **persuasive writing** in advertising, travel writing and reviews

- Write into my **PORTFOLIO** to keep a record of my formal and informal writing (remember RAFT from Chapter 1)

- Use and recognise **prepositions** and regular, comparative and superlative **adjectives**

- Recognise **multimodal texts** with icons, signs and symbols

- Research for a **radio documentary**, then write it, record it, present it!

Non-literary Texts: What's Your Point?

Non-literary Texts

There are many kinds of texts you can write that are not telling a story like the biographies, novels and poems that you have seen so far. These are **non-literary texts** and they have many purposes. It is important to understand the purpose of these texts so that you can use the correct style of writing/speaking.

The literary texts which you have seen so far use **figurative language** (similes, metaphors, personification, etc.) whereas non-literary texts are less descriptive. They fall into two broad categories: informal and formal. These categories often overlap depending on the audience and the purpose of the text.

Informal texts use relaxed language and don't follow rigid, specific rules. In this chapter, we will see the following kinds of informal writing:

- Questions for informal interviews
- Letters and blogs
- Tabloid newspaper articles
- Travel writing

Formal texts use structured writing and are for a specific purpose.
They are shaped depending on the purpose. We will look at the following formal texts:

- Questions for formal interviews
- Surveys and questionnaires
- Instructions and rules
- Press releases
- Petitions

- Memos
- Reviews
- Debates
- Letters and e-mails
- Newsletters
- Application forms

- Brochures, pamphlets and leaflets
- Invitations
- Advertisements
- Documentaries
- Articles

Interviews

An interview is a conversation between two or more people where one person is asking questions, and the other is answering them. Interviews are generally held to learn more about a person or topic.

Who Conducts Interviews?

- The **media** (TV, radio, newspapers, magazines, websites, etc.) regularly conduct interviews with famous people, politicians, artists, etc.
- **Employers** interview people who are looking for work.
- **Researchers** interview people to find out information for their research projects.

Informal Interviews

Informal interviews are relaxed and easy-going. The interviewer lets the interview travel along its own natural path rather than directing it along a specific route with the questions. A lot of media interviews are in this category as the interviewers are usually asking famous people about their talents.

Everyone has a unique talent or gift. Students in your class and in your school are talented and successful in music, sport, English, science, maths, languages, etc. and may also show their skills through community involvement. If you were interviewing someone about their talent, you would ask both personal and specific questions.

Personal information

- Name
- Age
- Where they live
- Where they go to school, college, work
- Details on parents and siblings
- Hobbies and interests
- Early influences

Specific questions

- When did they start dancing/singing/writing/playing their particular sport, etc.?
- What was their first real success?
- How often do they train or practise?
- How did their family and friends react to their success?
- What impact does the time spent on this activity have on their leisure time?
- What are their future goals, both in the short term and long term?
- How do they fit study and exams into their busy schedule?
- What was their worst defeat or failure or a low point they experienced?
- What was their best moment, a high point in their life so far?

A. Pairwork

With a partner, make a list of possible interview questions that could be asked of someone who is on a chat show for *one* of the reasons listed below. Include **personal** and **specific** questions. Match the questions to the reason for the interview, because different interviews require different questions. For example, if you interview a poet, you may ask about poetry readings and writing workshops; if you interview an artist you may ask about exhibitions and oils or pastels, etc.

Reasons:

- Their special talents, gifts or skills: They are an excellent singer/dancer/actor/writer/ sportsperson.
- Their connection to an organisation, e.g. Red Cross, Scouts, Girl Guides, Rotary International, community/disability/voluntary group.
- They won a competition, e.g. Young Scientist, Young Social Innovator, short story competition, poetry competition, Press Pass journalism competition, talent show, X Factor.
- They have a serious illness that they struggle to live with.
- Their innovation and entrepreneurship: they have started something new and important.

B. Listening

Listen to Eliza Doolittle being interviewed on Weekenders on 2FM. Listen to how this informal interview flows and answer the following questions.

1. How long was Eliza touring?
2. List two things that Eliza likes about Los Angeles.
3. Where is 'home' for Eliza?
4. Who is Eliza's best friend in LA?
5. How many siblings does Eliza have?
6. Name her new single.

C. Oral Language

In pairs, interview each other using the list of questions you created in task A. One person is the interviewer and the other is the respondent/interviewee. Give the respondent time to answer.

Interviewers prefer respondents who talk and develop their points, rather than those who say little and give 'yes' or 'no' answers, so develop your answers, explain and expand on the topic or issue. Enjoy the chat.

Formal Interviews

Formal interviews are more serious and more specific than informal ones. The interviewer has a set of specific questions to ask in order to find out particular information. Serious topics on TV or radio or in newspapers require formal interviews.

A job interview is one of the most common types of formal interview. The employer wants to find out whether or not the applicant is suitable for the job and suited to the company or organisation.

 ## A. Oral Language

Imagine that you have applied for a summer job in the music shop in the ad below.

MEGA MUSIC SHOP

Birdhill Shopping Centre, Wicklow

REQUIRES PART-TIME SALES ASSISTANT FOR THE SUMMER

Must be efficient, friendly and reliable.

Apply in writing to the manager at the above address.

Role-play the job interview in groups of three. Use two interviewers and one interviewee. Take turns being the interviewers and the interviewee. These are the kinds of questions you would ask:

1. You are living in the local area. Tell us a little bit about the locality.
2. Are there many facilities for teenagers in this area?
3. Suggest one improvement you would like to see made in this area.
4. Describe your school for us.
5. Tell us about your hobbies and interests.
6. Why do you want to work for Mega Music?
7. Tell us about your favourite singers or bands.
8. Are you available to work half days on Saturdays and Sundays?
9. How would you deal with a cross or angry customer?
10. Would you be confident using a cash register?
11. Are you available for work all summer?
12. Have you any previous work experience?
13. Have you any experience doing voluntary work?
14. Do you think uniforms in schools and in workplaces are a good or a bad idea?
15. How would you describe yourself?
16. Have you any idea what you would like to do when you leave school?
17. What are your favourite subjects in school?

B. Reading

Examine the list of job interview questions above. In your copy, fill in the table below by putting each question into a category. Some have been done for you.

Questions to relax the interviewee	Interviewee's skills/ ability to do the job	Personality type and interests of the interviewee	General abilities and potential of the interviewee
Q1	Q9	Q5	Q3

C. Writing Task – Interview Questions

In your **PORTFOLIO**, compile six to eight interview questions for *one* of the following summer jobs. Use the above list as a guide and include questions from the four categories shown in the above table.

- Sales assistant in a gardening centre
- Waiter/waitress in a café
- Sales assistant in a sports shop

ACE this task! Remember RAFT.

D. Pairwork

1. Role-play the interview for the position you chose in task C above.
2. There is a difference in language and tone between informal chat show interviews and more serious, formal job interviews. Discuss this with your partner and tell the class about five differences that you agree on.

Surveys

A **survey** is the gathering of information for a certain purpose. Surveys can be conducted in many ways, for example by telephone, interview or using a **questionnaire**. Questionnaires can be online or in printed form.

Who Conducts Surveys?

- **Companies** (market research or customer service): What do customers think about the service from the TV company/bin company/clothing shop/supermarket/phone company, etc.?
- **Education providers**: How can the school or college improve its service?
- **Employers**: How can the workplace be improved?
- **Healthcare industry**: How healthy are people? How can services and products be improved?
- **Entertainment industry**: How did the concert/TV programme/radio show/play, etc. go? How can it be improved?
- **Bloggers**: Who are my readers and what do they like/think/want?

Market Research Survey

If you are setting up a new business, it is important to understand what people (the customers or potential target market) think about the products or services they are already using that will compete with yours. One way of finding this out is to conduct a **market research survey**. Part of that survey could involve giving people questionnaires to answer. (Transition year students often do surveys before they set up a new mini-company. Ask the TY mini-companies in your school for examples of their surveys!)

Questionnaires

A questionnaire is a list of questions that are answered by the **respondent**. Questions are compiled based on what it is that the person or organisation wants to find out. Questions can be either open-ended or closed-ended.

With **open-ended** questions, the respondent puts in their own answer, for example:

What is your favourite toothpaste? _____

With **closed-ended** questions, the respondent is given options from which they must choose (**multiple-choice**), for example:

Which toothpaste do you prefer?   Colgate ☐   Aquafresh ☐   Other ☐

How to Create a Questionnaire

Step 1	Choose your **topic**.
Step 2	Decide **who** you will survey.
Step 3	Create the **questions**, tease them out until they are correct; answer them yourself to see if they work and to see what response options match them best. [Tip] Choose **closed-ended questions** for your survey because they are easier to create and to analyse.
Step 4	**Proofread** your questions and correct any mistakes. It will give a very negative impression of you and your survey if there are any grammar or punctuation errors.
Step 5	**Distribute** the questionnaire and give a time limit to fill it in. You can print it and hand it out, e-mail it, or create it online with Google Docs or Survey Monkey (*www.surveymonkey.com*)
Step 6	**Collect** the responses.
Step 7	**Analyse** the responses.
Step 8	Graph the results.
Step 9	Draw **conclusions**.
Step 10	**Present** your findings.

How to Analyse and Graph the Results

 Example: Basic Survey using Closed Questions

SPORT

1) **Do you like sport?**
   Yes ☑   No ☐

2) **Which of the following sports do you most like?**
   Soccer ☐   Swimming ☐   Hurling ☐   Rugby ☐
   Basketball ☑   Camogie ☐   Hockey ☐

3) **How often do you play sport?**
   Regularly ☑   Occasionally ☐   Rarely ☐

1. **Count** up the number of **surveys** returned.
2. List the questions in a copy and set up **tables/grids**. Complete each table by ticking the right box depending on the answer/response given.
   [Tip] You can do this in an excel spreadsheet.

   For this example, ten surveys were returned. Here is the analysis table for Q2:

Q 2	Football	Swimming	Hurling	Rugby	Basketball	Camogie	Hockey
Survey 1	✓						
Survey 2					✓		
Survey 3					✓		
Survey 4			✓				
Survey 5				✓			
Survey 6			✓				
Survey 7					✓		
Survey 8				✓			
Survey 9		✓					
Survey 10	✓						

3. **Count** up the **responses** for **each question**.

Sport Survey Response Count

Q 1	Yes	No					
No. of responses	8	2					
Q 2	Football	Swimming	Hurling	Rugby	Basketball	Camogie	Hockey
No. of responses	2	1	2	2	3	0	0
Q 3	Regularly	Occasionally	Rarely				
No. of responses	5	3	2				

4. Calculate the **percentages**.
   Calculations:

8 out of 10 like sport	= (8/10) x 100 = 80%
2 out of 10 don't like sport	= (2/100) x 100 = 20%

5. You can use bar or pie charts to visually **present your findings** to your audience/class.

Sport Survey Response Count and Percentages

Q 1	Yes	No					
No. of responses	8	2					
Percentage	80%	20%					
Q 2	Football	Swimming	Hurling	Rugby	Basketball	Camogie	Hockey
No. of responses	2	1	2	2	3	0	0
Percentage	20%	10%	20%	20%	30%	0%	0%
Q 3	Regularly	Occasionally	Rarely				
No. of responses	5	3	2				
Percentage	50%	30%	20%				

Question 2

Camogie 0%
Hockey 0%
Football 20%
Swimming 10%
Hurling 20%
Rugby 20%
Basketball 30%

Conclusions

- A large majority (80%) of students like sport. This is a very positive finding, which leads us to conclude that these students are in favour of sport and exercise.
- 80% play sport, this again is very positive, leading us to conclude that they enjoy being active and that they are benefitting from exercise.
- Since none of the respondents chose camogie or hockey, we might conclude that this is a boy's school. (Surveys are usually confidential and anonymous. You do not write your name on the survey and you may not be given names of schools/companies/people involved in it.)
- Half of the respondents play sport regularly, which is positive. 30% play occasionally, so we can assume that almost 80% play sport at least occasionally. Again this is positive.
- 20% do not like sport, and 20% rarely do sport. We would recommend targeting this group in terms of promoting the benefits of sport, the fun associated with it, the team bonding, the social aspect of it as well as the obvious physical benefits.

Sample Questionnaires

Here are some examples of questions that might be asked in questionnaires for different topics. In a real questionnaire, there would be spaces to write in the answers.

Sample A: Health

These questions might appear in a questionnaire from a health authority.

HEALTH AUTHORITY QUESTIONNAIRE

1. How physically healthy are you?
   Very healthy ☐   Fairly healthy ☐   Unhealthy ☐

2. Do you take nutritional supplements?
   Yes ☐   No ☐

3. How important is exercise to you?
   Very important ☐ A bit important ☐ Not important ☐

4. In a typical week, how many times do you exercise?
   6–8 times ☐   4–5 times ☐   0–3 times ☐

5. How much exercise do you feel you get?
   Too little ☐   The right amount ☐

6. In a typical day, how many of your meals or snacks include vegetables?
   0 <3 ☐   <5 ☐

Sample B: Films

These questions might appear in a questionnaire for a celebrity magazine:

QUESTIONNAIRE

1. How often do you watch movies?
2. What is your favourite movie?
3. What is your least favourite movie?
4. Who is your favourite movie celebrity living today?
5. Who is your least favourite movie celebrity living today?
6. Who do you think is the most badly behaved movie celebrity living today?

Sample C: TV

These questions might appear in a questionnaire for a TV company:

QUESTIONNAIRE

1. How often do you watch television?
2. What is your favourite TV show?
3. What is your least favourite TV show?
4. Who is your favourite television celebrity living today?
5. Who is your least favourite television celebrity living today?
6. What makes a good TV programme for you?

Did you notice that Sample A has closed-ended questions, but Samples B and C have open-ended ones? Read Samples B and C again and think about what response options each question might have if they were multiple choice.

A. Writing

In your copy, match each question below with the most likely set of answer choices from the list given. This first one has been done for you.

Topic: Sense of Community

Questions

1. How many of your neighbours do you know? All ☐ Most ☐ Some ☐ A few ☐ None ☐
2. How strong is the sense of community in your neighbourhood?
3. How often do you attend events in your neighbourhood?
4. How often do you visit the park in your neighbourhood?
5. Are you satisfied with the facilities in your neighbourhood?
6. Do you feel safe in your neighbourhood?
7. In general is your neighbourhood clean?
8. This is a nice neighbourhood.

Answer Choices

Always	Regularly	Often	Rarely	Never
Daily	Weekly	Monthly	Annually	Rarely
7–10 times	5–7 times	3–5 times	Rarely	Never
Yes	Sometimes	No	Occasionally	Rarely
Very strong	Strong	Fair	Weak	Very weak
Strongly agree	Agree	Somewhat agree	Disagree	Strongly disagree
All	Most	Some	A few	None

B. Pairwork

Working in pairs or groups, create a questionnaire of 5–10 questions. You want to survey your class on *one* of the following topics:

- Sports and sports facilities in my school or area
- Takeaway foods – your likes and dislikes
- Attitudes towards fundraising and charities
- The school shop or canteen/lunch facilities

The questions you ask depend on what you want to find out. Think about the following:

- Gender (male/female)
- Age
- Occupation, e.g. student, teacher, parent, nurse, etc.
- Likes, dislikes or preferences
- Amount of time people spend on a service, activity or product
- Benefits of a service, activity or product
- Cost/price/value for money of a service, activity or product
- Satisfaction or dissatisfaction with a service, activity or product
- Suggestions to improve a service, activity or product

Follow the 'How to Create a Questionnaire' instructions on p. 152.

Prepositions

A **preposition** is a word that **shows the relationship** between a noun or a pronoun and another word in the sentence. Prepositions do this in many ways.

They can **indicate location**.

For example:

The dog is *in* the kennel. (Shows the relationship between the dog and the kennel)
The wine comes *from* France. (Shows the relationship between the wine and France)
She hid *under* the table. (Shows the relationship between 'she' and the table)

If we change the preposition, we change where the dog is, in relation to the kennel.

For example:

The dog is *under* the kennel.
The dog is *behind* the kennel.

They can show **when something happens**.

For example:

She arrived *after* dinner.
It rained *throughout* the morning.
He had perfect eyesight *until* recently.
He *always* drinks tea.

Other examples:

She wanted to work *for* the school.
He acted *as* leader *for* the day.
Where do you come *from*?
Maud ran *towards* the sea.
Jason sat *up* then ran *off* quickly.
I strolled home *with* my friends.

Due to his grammar mistake, Wilbur found a job. It just wasn't the one he expected.

What should Wilbur's sign say?

Writing

Put each of the prepositions in the box below into a sentence. See if you can write a sentence with more than one preposition.

in	off	up	after	from	behind	beneath
under	on	around	near	out	above	over
with	at	against	through	for	down	
towards	between	among	below	into	about	

Peer Assessment – *Swap copies to correct each other's work*

Instructions and Rules

When you buy a new product, it usually includes a set of **instructions**. Do you read the instructions? What is the purpose of the instructions? Are they usually written using formal or informal language? Can you think of products you received that came with a set of instructions?

Instructions describe and explain how to do something. This is usually in a step-by-step sequence. Look at the difference below between the personal writing on the board game Monopoly, and the way that instructions can be written for the game.

Personal Writing about Monopoly

Even though I love my iPad, my phone and my DS, I still really enjoy playing Monopoly on holidays or on miserable, boring, 'stuck inside' rainy days. I enjoy deciding how to spend my money, and taking rent from my family when they land on my properties. It's great to collect money when you pass GO when you are running low on funds! I rarely go bankrupt as I'm very good at playing the game.

Instructions for Monopoly

- Select one player to be banker.
- Choose a token.
- Start with €1500.
- Each player rolls the dice to move around the board.
- You can purchase a property if you land on it and have enough money.
- Collect rent when a player lands on one of your properties.
- Collect €200 each time you pass GO.
- Players can trade money or property, if both players agree to the trade.
- Mortgage a property if you need to.
- When you have no more money you are bankrupt and lose the game.

When playing any game there needs to be **rules**. Instructions tell you *how* to play, but rules tell you what you *can and cannot* do in the game. To understand a game, you need to know the instructions and rules.

Rules and Instructions for the Game of Soccer

- There are two opposing teams with 11 players on each team.
- The aim is to score goals in the opponent's net.
- The team with the most goals scored at the end of the game wins.
- Players kick the ball into the net of the opposing team.
- Only the goalkeeper can handle the ball.
- Teams are allowed six substitute players but can only bring on three during a match.
- A referee monitors the game for fair play.
- Fouls outside the box can lead to free kicks.
- Fouls inside the box can lead to penalties.
- Fouls are penalised. Warnings are given with a yellow card. After two yellow cards, a red card means a player is sent off and will not be replaced.
- The game is 90 minutes long (plus any injury time).
- After 45 minutes, it's half-time and there is a 15-minute break.
- If there's an equal score at the end it's called a draw.
- The game can be replayed at a later date if there's a draw or the winning team can be determined by a penalty shoot-out.

Writing Task – Instructions

Choose any game or sport, such as Connect 4, chess, hurling, camogie. In your **PORTFOLIO**, write brief instructions and rules on how to play.

- Use bullet points for this task.
- Keep your sentences short and concise.
- Use formal language.
- Full sentences are not always required.

Proofread your instructions and correct any mistakes.

Press Releases

Press releases are statements and/or documents given to the media informing them of an event.

'The press' is another term for 'the media'. There are two types of media:

- **Broadcast media**: TV stations, radio stations, internet.
- **Print media**: Newspapers and magazines.

Who Issues Press Releases?

Anyone can issue a press release if they think they have something newsworthy to say!

- **Companies:** To inform the public about their latest product or service, e.g. new technology from Apple or Microsoft.
- **Organisations:** To inform the public about events, e.g. a new fundraising event from Barnardos.
- **Government agencies**: To inform the public of new initiatives, e.g. the official opening of a new skate park.
- **Celebrities:** To inform their fans about their latest news, e.g. U2 to release a new album.

How to Write a Press Release

Structure your information as follows and make sure you cover the 5 Ws (who, what, when, where, why):

- **Who:** Name of company/organisation/person
- Date of press release
- **What:** Title of the event
- **When:** Date of event
- **Where:** Location
- **Why:** Introduction
- Additional information/background details
- Contact details

Example 1: Skate Park Opening

PRESS RELEASE

Athlone Town Council
Joan Ryan, Manager
Athlone Town Council
Castle Street
Athlone

20 July 2015

Skate Park Opening 31 July

The council is pleased to announce the official opening of the new skate park on 31 July in Shannon Lane at 10 am.

This is an important day for the local children and teenagers, who will benefit hugely from this new recreational facility.

The town manager will officially cut the ribbon at 10.30 am following a speech informing the public about work that the local community and the council did in order to build the facility.

Members of the local council, local businesses and the public are welcome to attend. Refreshments will be served afterwards.

Further details available from Joan Ryan at 0904-333444 or e-mail jryan@atc.ie.

Example 2: Replacing Water Mains

PRESS RELEASE

Dublin City Council

Tracey Lyons,
Executive Manager (Engineering)
with Dublin City Council

Friday, 6 June 2016

Dublin City Council progresses with replacing another 19 km of old and leaking water mains in Dublin City

Following approval by the Minister for Environment, Community and Local Government, the Dublin Region Water Mains Rehabilitation Project will commence another major improvement contract in Dublin City to replace old leaking Victorian water mains next Monday, 9 June 2016. This next phase of water mains improvements will take place in Gardiner Street, Camden Street Upper and Clanwilliam Place.

'The project, managed by Dublin City Council, has already replaced 140 km of water mains as part of an overall integrated investment programme across Dublin. The benefits of this new contract will include a further reduction in leakage from pipes, improved water pressure to homes and businesses, and improved levels of service and security of supply,' according to John Butler, manager of Water Services Ltd.

The project team is working closely with businesses and An Garda Síochána to manage traffic while the works are underway and delays will be kept to a minimum. People are advised to plan their journeys and give themselves enough time if they have to cross the works.

Regular updates and maps outlining where and when work is taking place are available at www.watermains.com.

People can contact the project's customer communications team on lo-call 1890 99 77 66 (Monday to Friday, 9 am to 5 pm) for more information.

Example 3: Exhibition Launch

CORK DOCKWORKERS PHOTOGRAPHIC EXHIBITION LAUNCH IN LIBERTY HALL

Date released: 20 July 2015

SIPTU general president, Sheila Doherty, will launch the Cork Dockworkers Preservation Society photographic exhibition in Liberty Hall on Wednesday, 6 August, at 7.00 pm. SIPTU is hosting the photographic exhibition from Wednesday, 6 August to Wednesday, 13 August.

The exhibition of 50 photographs and over 400 slides features images of life and work on the docks from 1900 to 1960.

Also speaking at the launch is Cork Dockworkers Preservation Society spokesman David Jones and labour historian Pamela O'Brien.

All are encouraged to come along and enjoy this unique celebration of Cork's working-class history.

Further information from Denis Leahy at 021-654-777 or e-mail dleahy@siptu.ie.

Writing Task – Press Release

Using the layout in the examples above, write a press release in your **PORTFOLIO** announcing a fundraising fashion show. Put your main news in a big, bold font at the top of the page. Use the details below (make sure you cover the 5 Ws):

- Name of event organisers/company
- Date of press release
- Name of charity to benefit from event
- Date and time of event
- Place of event
- Cost per ticket
- Sponsors of event
- Samples of raffle prizes
- List famous or well-known local supporters of event
- Contact details for further information

ACE this task! Remember RAFT.

Proofread your press release and correct any mistakes.

Petitions

Some people who feel strongly about a particular issue and want to raise awareness of and gain support for it, set up a **campaign** to put pressure on other people to act regarding the issue.

To show that many people support the issue, a **petition** may be written for supporters to sign. This document sets out what the supporters want to do or change. For example, some primary schools in Ireland have been involved in organising petitions against cutbacks (receiving less money from the Government) in education. They have asked parents to sign postcards and post these to government ministers.

If you wish to support an issue, you can sign online petitions, or you can sign a petition page which may be distributed in your local area or community by people involved in the particular campaign.

Example: Online Petitions

http://www.petition.com

Sign up for a petition NOW!

Click on whichever petition you support and follow the links and instructions. Petitions are subject to change and new petitions will be added, so keep in touch with this page.

> SAVE OUR SHORELINES FROM POLLUTION
>
> END CUTS IN EDUCATION
>
> STOP CRUEL HARE COURSING
>
> STOP GREYHOUND RACING
>
> KEEP DUBLIN BAY OIL FREE

 **Pairwork**

In pairs or groups, discuss any petitions that you, your family, your school or your community have been involved in. Was it worthwhile? Why?

Memos

Memos are short pieces of writing that communicate information. They are usually internal pieces of communication from one worker to another in a company or organisation. For example, the accounts department might send a memo to the purchasing department.

They are quick, concise pieces of text. If they are too long, they lose their impact. People are more likely to read a short message when they first receive it, whereas they tend to put away a long one for later (when they have more time). Therefore, keep memos short.

BACK IN 10

For _____ A.M. P.M.
Date _____ Time _____

WHILE YOU WERE OUT

M _____
Of _____
☐ Phone _____
☐ Fax _____
☐ Mobile _____
Area Code   Number   Extension

TELEPHONED		PLEASE CALL	
CAME TO SEE YOU		WILL CALL AGAIN	
WANTS TO SEE YOU		URGENT	
RETURNED YOUR CALL		SPECIAL ATTENTION	

Message _____
_____
_____
_____
_____
_____

Signed _____

Example 1: Closure of Library

Closure of the School Library Due to Renovations

To: Students and staff of Glenties Comprehensive School
From: Margaret Byrne (Principal)
Date: 09/03/2015
Re: Closure of the School Library Due to Renovations

The library will close from Thursday, 12 March 2015 for one week while it is being refurbished.

I apologise for the inconvenience that this closure will cause. The facility will be improved afterwards with a new layout, new furniture, new lighting, new books and new computers.

Students and staff may use the library in the neighbouring Education Centre for research and study purposes.

Thank you for your cooperation.

Example 2: Launch of Report

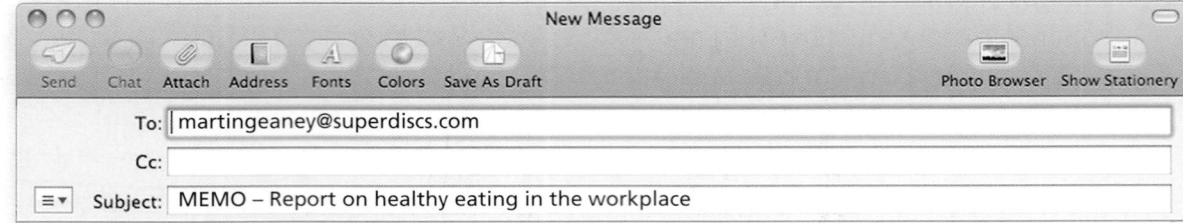

New Message

To: martingeaney@superdiscs.com

Cc:

Subject: MEMO – Report on healthy eating in the workplace

To: The Managing Director, Super Discs Ltd
From: Jennifer Corcoran
Date: 1/5/2015

Re: Report on healthy eating in the workplace

The report on healthy eating in the workplace is almost complete. It is being edited and proofread this week and will be ready for publication as intended on 8 May. Two interesting findings from the survey were the desire to remove the vending machines completely from the building and to install water fountains at a number of locations.

The Healthy Eating Committee wish to formally invite you and the management team to attend the launch of the report on Friday, 8 May in the Clarion Hotel at 10 am.

Thank you,

Jennifer Corcoran

Writing Task – Memo

In your **PORTFOLIO**, write a memo based on the following details:

To: Manager, Excel Sports

From: Deputy Manager

Re: Stock check of goods in the store on 31 July 2015

- Team completed the stock check and found the following issues of concern:
  - Two boxes of water-damaged Puma Tracksuits (50 pieces) that had been stored near a leaking radiator.
  - Four boxes of nutrition bars that were past their best-before date (400 pieces).
  - Three boxes of hurleys imported from abroad infested with woodworm.
- Advice required about what to do with each of these problems.
- An early response would be appreciated.

Try using the memo template in Microsoft Word.

ACE this task! Remember RAFT.

Proofread your memo and correct any mistakes.

More Adjectives

Regular adjectives describe nouns: the *steep*, *lofty* cliffs, the *crystal-clear* stream, the *orange* sunset, the *red* leaves.

Comparative adjectives compare nouns: the *bigger* tree, the *longer* straw, the *brighter* light.

Superlative adjectives are *super* adjectives: the *highest* mountain, the *most beautiful* view, the *oldest* castle, the *longest* river, the *quickest* route, the *latest* gadgets.

Here are some more examples:

Regular	Comparative	Superlative
sweet	sweeter	sweetest
angry	angrier	angriest
bright	brighter	brightest
calm	calmer	calmest
cold	colder	coldest
cool	cooler	coolest
curly	curlier	curliest
early	earlier	earliest
rich	richer	richest
lovely	lovelier	loveliest
smart	smarter	smartest
simple	simpler	simplest
famous	more famous	most famous
immense	more immense	most immense
long	longer	longest
perfect	more perfect	most perfect
quick	quicker	quickest
thin	thinner	thinnest

It is important to remember that adjectives do not always appear beside the noun, for example:

- His handwriting was *awful*.
- He had *awful* handwriting.
- It was a *fantastic* concert.
- The concert was *fantastic*.
- It was the *best* view ever.
- The view was the *best* ever.

Writing

1. Rewrite the following sentences so that the adjective is not beside the noun. Change the order of the words and add in more words if necessary. The first one has been done for you.

   i. Powerful sunshine flooded the room.
   The sunshine that flooded the room was powerful.

   ii. The dark, dull day dawned.

   iii. She had beautiful, green eyes.

   iv. He had lean, lanky features.

   v. The cranky children wanted a nap.

   vi. The tired, old woman walked wearily home.

2. Rewrite the following sentences inserting superlative adjectives to replace the ordinary adjectives. Change the order of words or add in more words if necessary. The first one has been done for you.

   i. It was a high mountain with a steep drop.
   It was the highest mountain with the steepest drop.

   ii. The beautiful temple was flooded with natural light.

   iii. The old cathedral dated back to 1233.

   iv. The tall tower gave great views of the surrounding countryside.

   v. The food was magnificent.

   vi. She spoke in a gentle voice and mesmerised the audience.

Peer Assessment – *Swap copies and correct each other's work*

Reviews

A **review** is one person's opinion, assessment or critique of a film, book, TV show, game, CD, musical, concert, etc. Reviews can be formal or informal or a combination of both types of writing. Read the following reviews and notice the type of language used in them.

Example 1: Film Review

http://www.filmreview.com

How I Live Now

Name of film
Name of director
Recommendation

How I Live Now, directed by Kevin McDonald, has just been released and is well worth seeing.

Brief description

The film is an adaptation of Meg Rosoff's award-winning book, which scooped the Guardian Children's Fiction Prize in 2004. It tells the story of American 'cool kid' Daisy (Saoirse Ronan) visiting her distant country cousins in England and remaining aloof until her heart is captured by handsome cousin Edmond (George MacKay). Unexpectedly, the Third World War breaks out. A nuclear explosion flattens London and their struggle for survival is gripping. When war tears the boys and girls apart, Daisy must discover previously hidden strengths in order to survive and to find her lost love.

*Good and
bad points*

Saoirse is superb as the confused, yet arrogant, know-it-all superior cousin. She gains our admiration for her selfless care of the others and her determination to reach Edmond. Edmond is a deep, pensive, attractive character easily endeared to the viewer. The plot is unpredictable, with startling twists and an ambiguous, thoughtful ending. If there is any weakness, it is in the character of Daisy, who has a stronger presence in the book than she has in the film. Worth seeing. Rated 15 due to squeamish bits!

GLOSSARY

Adaptation: Created from a different work, e.g. a book made into a film.
Aloof: Unfriendly, cool, distant.
Selfless: Not thinking about yourself.
Pensive: Thinking deeply or seriously.
Endeared: To be loved or liked.
Ambiguous: Can have more than one explanation.

Listening

 Listen to Dave Fanning of RTÉ 2FM radio interviewing the director of *How I Live Now*, Kevin McDonald, and answer the following questions.

1. Where was Saoirse Ronan born?
2. What is the job of a casting director?
3. What does it mean to communicate 'non-verbally'?
4. What kind of person do you think Saoirse is?
5. Name two other films which Kevin McDonald has directed.
6. Name two documentaries which Kevin has made.
7. Where is the film *How I Live Now* set/located and in what time period?
8. Explain briefly what the film is about; what is the story/plot?
9. Do you think that this is a formal or an informal interview? Explain your answer.

Example 2: Book Review

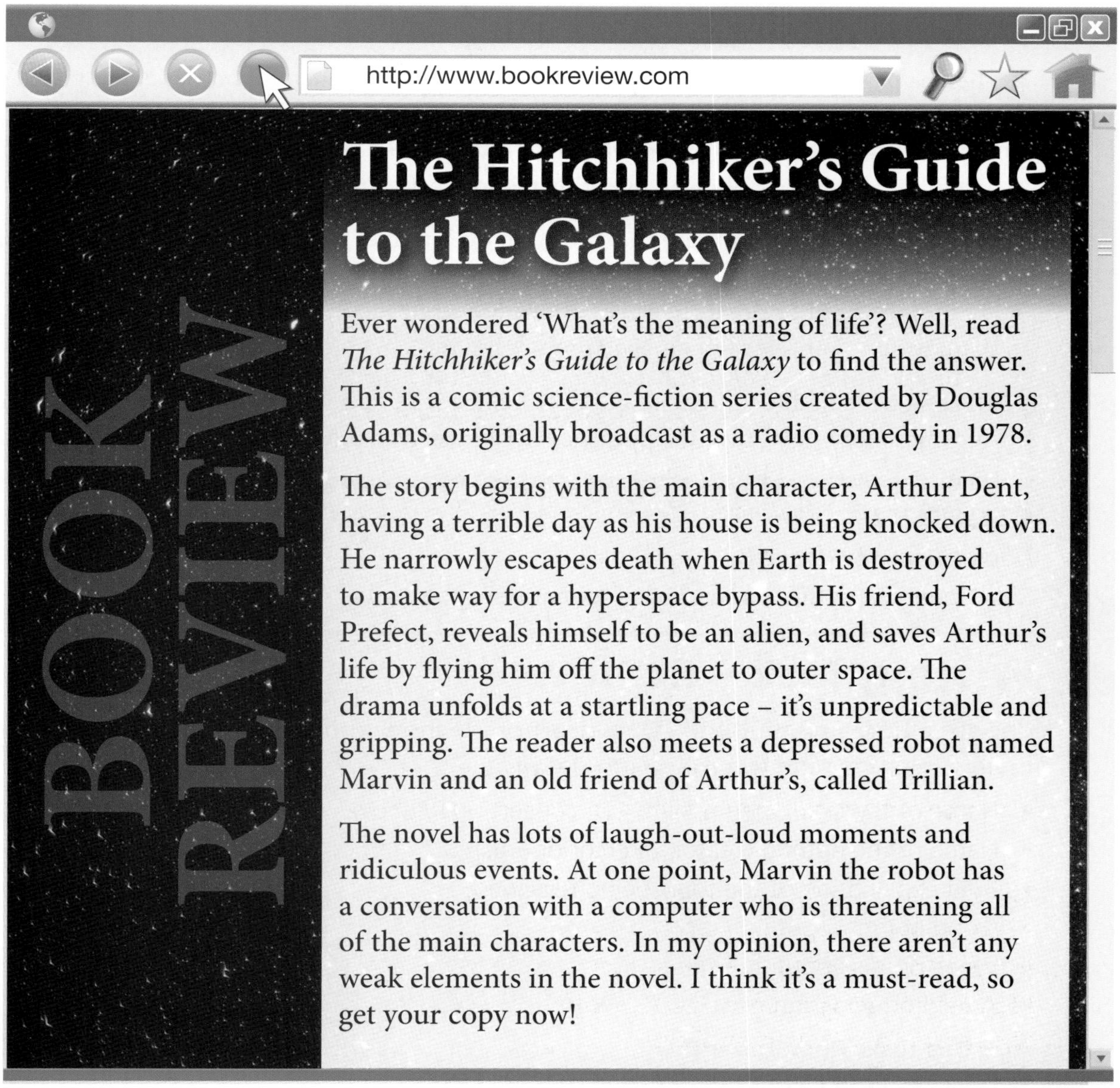

http://www.bookreview.com

The Hitchhiker's Guide to the Galaxy

BOOK REVIEW

Ever wondered 'What's the meaning of life'? Well, read *The Hitchhiker's Guide to the Galaxy* to find the answer. This is a comic science-fiction series created by Douglas Adams, originally broadcast as a radio comedy in 1978.

The story begins with the main character, Arthur Dent, having a terrible day as his house is being knocked down. He narrowly escapes death when Earth is destroyed to make way for a hyperspace bypass. His friend, Ford Prefect, reveals himself to be an alien, and saves Arthur's life by flying him off the planet to outer space. The drama unfolds at a startling pace – it's unpredictable and gripping. The reader also meets a depressed robot named Marvin and an old friend of Arthur's, called Trillian.

The novel has lots of laugh-out-loud moments and ridiculous events. At one point, Marvin the robot has a conversation with a computer who is threatening all of the main characters. In my opinion, there aren't any weak elements in the novel. I think it's a must-read, so get your copy now!

Example 3: Game Review

http://www.gamereview.com

Nintendo 3DS: Professor Layton and the Miracle Mask

Rating: ★ ★ ★ ★ ★

Professor Layton and the Miracle Mask is a game consisting of more than 100 puzzles. Players must use logic and apply basic maths skills to solve problems. The calm, wise and reasonable Professor Layton is a good role model, as are his young apprentices, Emmy and Luke. They never lose their cool, are always kind, and repeatedly show that logic is the greatest tool when it comes to solving difficult problems.

There is hardly any violence. The game's generous, smart, helpful heroes act as proof that calm reasoning and kindness are the best tools for tackling tough mysteries. The game suggests that most of the crises and mysteries in our lives can be solved through careful investigation followed by rational and creative thought.

One of the mini-games is about retail strategy. It makes players think about how shops arrange their products to entice people to buy more. It may make teenagers think about how the shops that they visit in real life strategically arrange products to make them want to buy extra items (i.e. impulse buying).

The game is suitable for age 12 and up. Luckily, it has a hint system that provides bits of information to help solve the puzzles. Highly recommended. Put it on the birthday list!

GLOSSARY

Depict: Show or describe.

Rational: Able to think sensibly, reasonably or logically.

Writing Task – Review

Choose a book, game, film, CD, concert or TV show and write a review of it. Your review must include the following details:

- Name of the book, game, film, CD, concert or TV show
- Name of the author, creator, director or artist
- Brief explanation of the topic being reviewed
- Good points about it
- Weak points about it
- A recommendation on it

ACE this task! Remember RAFT.

Proofread your review and correct any mistakes.

Debates

A **debate** is a formal argument or discussion about a particular topic. Debates usually take place in public, for example, there are debates in the Dáil, debates on television, debating competitions between schools.

In debating competitions, there are two teams and each team usually has four speakers. One team, the **proposition**, supports (is in favour of) the **motion**. The other team, the **opposition**, opposes (is not in favour of) the motion.

 **Pairwork**

Organise a debate in your English class. Choose a motion such as:

• Teenagers today watch too much television
• Junk food is too popular and is ruining our health
• Technology does more harm than good
• Homework should be done during school time
• It is possible to live in a paperless world: ban printers, photocopiers and paper

Follow these rules:

• Organise two teams with four speakers in each.
• Allocate each speaker 2/3 minutes per speech.
• Choose a Timekeeper to time each speaker and record their time.
• Choose a Chairperson to introduce the debate and introduce each speaker.
• Choose two adjudicators (judges) to evaluate each speaker, award scores and announce the winning team.

Letters and E-mails

Letter writing has been replaced in a lot of instances by e-mails, text messages, Facebook messaging, etc. However, many people still type up letters and either e-mail them or print and post them, so it is important to know how to structure a letter. You can write informal or formal letters.

Informal Letters

An **informal letter** is written to someone you know, for example a thank you letter to a relative for a gift, or a 'newsy' letter to a family member or friend living far away, telling them about what's happening in your life, family and school. Informal letters are not very common now due to social networking.

How to Write an Informal Letter

1. Write your own address in the top right-hand corner.
2. Write your address neatly, with correct capital letters and spelling. Punctuation is optional, you can choose if you want to use commas and full stops in the address.
3. Skip a line and write the date.
4. Skip a line and write the greeting. Put a comma after it.
5. Use separate paragraphs for each point in your letter.
6. Sign off in a suitable way, for example, 'Love you', 'Bye for now', 'See you soon'.
7. Sign your name in joined writing on the line.

Example: Letter to a Friend

4 Oak Lane,
Enniscorthy,
Co. Wexford.

12/9/2017

Hi Trish,

How are things? How's the new puppy settling in? Bet he's peeing everywhere, like ours did at first! Have you thought of a name for him yet? Text me as soon as you have all stopped arguing. I'm dying to know what ye pick.

Well, school is the same as ever, with tons of homework, but I joined the basketball team and the choir so at least I'll get time off classes here and there for matches and events. Then there's the Halloween fancy dress disco to look forward to! Have to find a silvery, sparkly dress and a sweeping black cloak or cape and a mask!

What are you doing for Halloween and for the mid-term? We might go to Dublin to visit ye or else ye could come down here to us to escape the madness of the city!

OK, no more news. Am off to pick blackberries now, there are tons of them in the lane outside. The bushes are bursting with them this year 'cos of all the sun we had and it would be a pity to let them go to waste.

Talk soon, text me the dog's name.

Bye for now,

Kate

Writing

Write an informal letter and post it. Write it to a friend or relative telling him or her about life in school and at home. Ask them about their own experiences. Make sure you tell them to reply by post so that you can look forward to getting a letter.

Now write the address on the envelope, like this:

ACE this task! Remember RAFT.

Proofread your letter and correct any mistakes.

Ms Trisha Mooney,
7 Killiney Terrace,
Dublin 3.

Formal Letters

A formal letter is a serious letter written in a formal, polite, writing style. They are generally written to people you do not know. Formal letters are written for a number of reasons, for example:

- To ask for information
- To complain about a service or a product
- To praise a company or organisation
- To apply for a job

How to Write a Formal Letter

1. Write your own address in the top right-hand corner. Write your address neatly, with correct capital letters and spelling.

2. Skip a line and write the receiver's title/name and address on the left. Punctuation is optional, you will see some formal letters with commas and full stops in the addresses and some without.

3. Skip a line and write the date under the receiver's address. Some formal letters have the date on the right, some have it on the left.

4. Skip a line and write the greeting. Put a comma after it.

5. Skip a line and explain why you are writing.

6. Use separate paragraphs for each point in your letter.

7. Skip a line. Write 'Thank you for your help in this matter.'

8. Skip two lines and write 'Yours faithfully' (with a small 'f') if you do not know the name of the person to whom you are writing (so you write 'The Manager' etc.). Write 'Yours sincerely' (with a small 's') if you know the name of the person.

9. Sign your name in joined writing on a line.

10. Write your name in unjoined, clear writing underneath.

Example 1: Request for Information from a Theatre

(1) 4 Oak Lane,
Enniscorthy,
Co. Wexford.

(2) The Manager,
Lemon Tree Theatre,
Bunclody,
Co. Wexford.

(3) 12/2/2015

(4) Dear Sir/Madam,

(5) I am writing to you to request information. I am a transition year student in Coláiste Mhuire and am involved in organising a drama production. We are performing a mini version of Brian Friel's play *Dancing at Lughnasa*.

(6) We attended your production of the play last October and thoroughly enjoyed it. We were wondering if you could give us some assistance with our own production. In particular, if you had posters, props or costumes that you may not be using, we would be grateful if we could borrow them. Even a phone call from your director to give us advice on how best to stage our play would be much appreciated.

(6) We would acknowledge your assistance in our drama programme and give your theatre a free advertisement in our school magazine, due out in April.

(7) Thank you for your help in this matter.

(8) Yours faithfully,

(9) *Kate O'Brien*

(10) Kate O'Brien.

Example 2: Request for Information from an Activity Centre

'Lissadell'
Seaview
Sligo

The Manager
Westport Activity Centre
Westport
Co. Mayo

22 September 2016

Dear Sir/Madam,

I am writing to request information. I am a second year student in Summerhill Educate Together School and we are participating in the Bronze Gaisce Award programme.

As part of this programme we must complete a challenge and spend a few nights away, so I would like information on the activities or challenges available in your centre.

I would be grateful if you could please send me brochures and perhaps advise me on what our group of twelve could do in your centre to fulfil the Gaisce criteria.

Thank you for your help in this matter.

Yours faithfully,

Joseph Sweeney

Joseph Sweeney

Writing Task – Formal Letter

Imagine you are doing a CSPE project about services for the homeless in Waterford. Write a formal letter requesting information from the local Simon Community. Follow the instructions below:

- Address the letter to The Manager, Simon Community, Bridge Street, Waterford.
- Request information about what services are provided for the homeless.
- Request posters for your school so that you can raise awareness of the service.
- Ask if it would be possible for a guest speaker to come to your CSPE class to talk about the service.

Now write the address on the envelope:

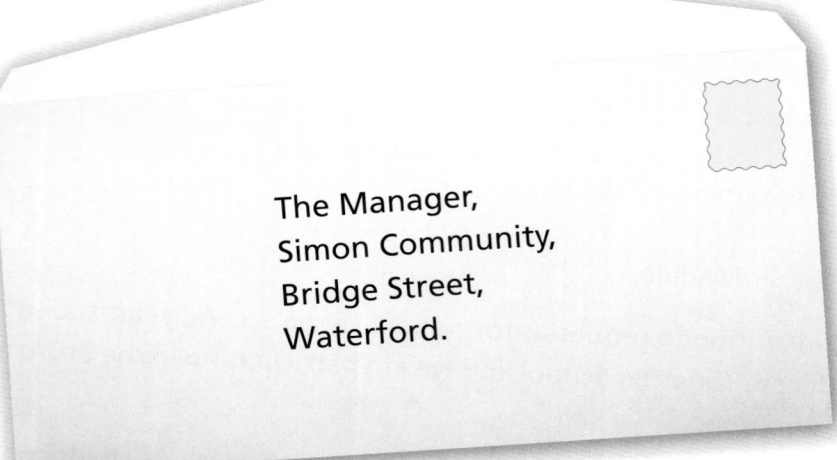

The Manager,
Simon Community,
Bridge Street,
Waterford.

ACE this task! Remember RAFT.

Proofread your letter and correct any mistakes.

E-mails

An **e-mail** is a message sent digitally using a PC, tablet, smartphone, etc. E-mails, like letters, can be formal or informal depending on their purpose. They can generally follow the same format as the letters above, except there is generally no need to right-align anything or write the receiver's address in an e-mail.

Newsletters

Newsletters are short documents often 2–4 pages long, informing people about events/activities happening in an organisation/company/workplace/school. Newsletters appear regularly, which could mean once a month, every six months (bi-annually), or in the case of a school, at the end of each term. You may have had to bring home your school newsletter for everyone to read. Can you remember what kind of news was in it? Newsletters are printed in hard copy (paper) or are available online as an e-newsletter that can be e-mailed.

Creative Project – Write the Front Page of a Newsletter

Your English teacher has asked your group to create the front page for the school newsletter – the real one!

1. Draw a blank **template** of a newsletter page.

2. Decide what **topics/activities/events/photos** you will include. Think about the activities that go on in the school, for example sport, drama, school tours, field trips, competitions, music, choir, debates, library news, guest speakers.

3. Each person in the group can write a **piece/article**. Four or five sentences on each topic is fine. Choose your article headings.

4. Work together designing the **layout** of your text and photos/images.

5. You can **handwrite** the task and paste in actual images or you can do it on the **computer**.

6. Why not be competitive? See which group designs the most interesting and attractive newsletter?

ACE this project!
Remember to brainstorm.

Proofread your newsletter and correct any mistakes.

Blogs

A **blog** (from web log) is a website containing short articles called **posts** that are changed regularly. Some blogs are written by one person about their own opinions, interests and experiences. Others are written by many different people, such as a blog set up by an English class.

A blog can be about anything, as it simply reflects the interests of the writer. There are blogs about fashion, food, games, films, books, parenting, home décor – the list is endless!

People with the same interest as the blogger might choose to '**follow'** that blog by checking in often to see what has been written. They can leave **comments**, questions or suggest links to related material.

Bloggers (the people who write blogs) can be very passionate about their subject. Some bloggers have been contacted by people and companies to do work for them; for example some fashion bloggers have become stylists or magazine writers.

Here is a sample of a page from a blog set up by an English teacher for his class:

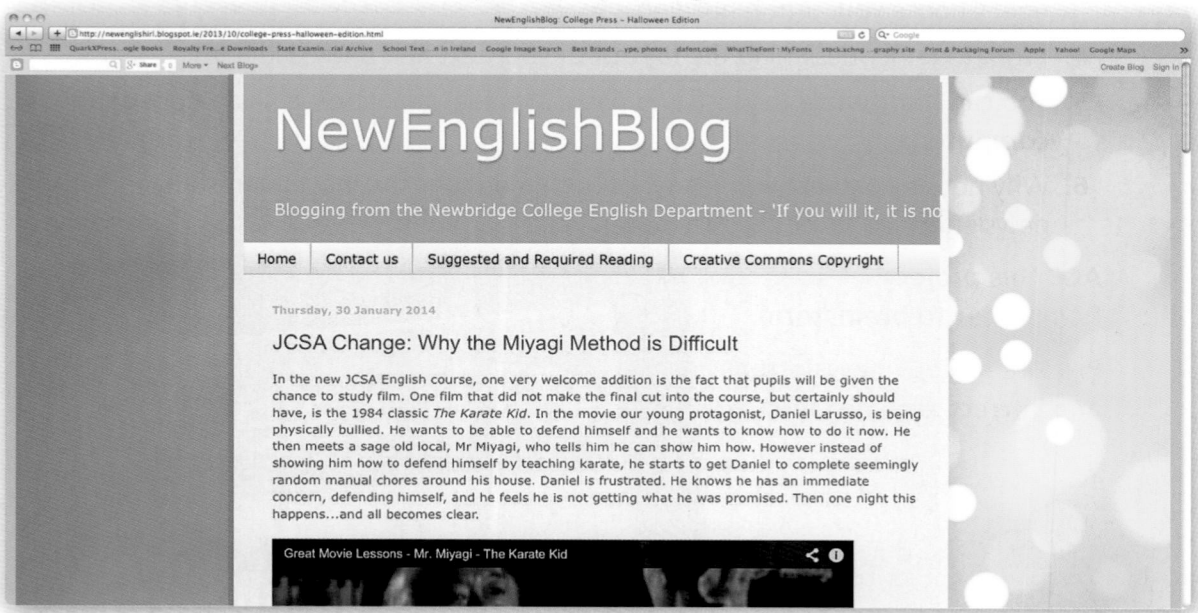

A. Oral Language

Have you any experience of blogging? Discuss this with the person beside you. If you were to write a blog, what would the subject be? Why?

B. Creative Project – Write a Blog Post

Write a paragraph on something you feel passionate about.
Log on to *www.kidblog.com* to set up your own blog and post your article.

ACE this question! Remember RAFT.
Proofread your blog post and correct any mistakes.

Application Forms

An **application form** is a document that you fill in giving personal and specific information because you want to apply for something. There are many kinds of application forms, since there are many reasons for applying to places and things. Here are some examples:

- School application form
- Sports club membership application form
- Girl Guides/Scouts membership application form
- Summer camp application form
- Competition application form
- Passport application form
- Driver's licence application form
- Application form for transition year (in some schools)

Example: Join the Library

LIBRARY MEMBERSHIP

Louth County Library
Junior Membership Application Form

Name ....

Address ....

....

Date of birth ....

Name of parent/guardian ....

Address ....

Telephone ....

E-mail ....

Declaration: I, the undersigned, agree to replace/pay for any lost/mislaid books/ CDs/DVDs/materials borrowed by my son/daughter.

Signature of parent/guardian ....

Writing Task – Application Form

Fill in the application form in your **PORTFOLIO**.
Proofread your answers and correct any mistakes.

Brochures, Pamphlets and Leaflets

Brochures, pamphlets and leaflets are all used to pass on information about a product or service to **persuade** the reader to buy or use that product or service. They are the **promotional** material used by companies/organisations to get their message to the public.

A **brochure** is a short booklet with a cover. A **pamphlet** is also a booklet but it doesn't have a cover and a **leaflet** is one sheet of paper, which may be folded.

Essential features

To create good promotional material you need to ensure the following are included:

1. Interesting text
2. Vibrant pictures
3. Good layout and spacing
4. Attractive colour
5. Concise information
6. Unique features of the product or service
7. Contact details, e-mail/telephone

Health pamphlets in Boots chemist.

Creative Project – Design a Leaflet

Design a leaflet advertising a new canteen in your school. Include the following information:

- Where the canteen is located in the building
- Range of hot food available and prices
- Range of cold food available and prices
- Types of drinks available and prices
- Prices for meal and drink combinations
- Range of snacks, fruit and healthy options (nuts, seeds, salads) available and prices
- Contact details of the service provider (i.e. manager of the canteen)

Tourist brochures for Northern Ireland.

Use the leaflet template in Microsoft Word/Office, or follow the simple instructions below:

1. Hold an A4 page in landscape (sideways) rather than portrait (upright) format. Fold it. You now have a front cover, inside left page, inside right page and back page. Number or label the pages as 1, 2, 3 and 4.

2. Use this as your hard copy guide or sample. Decide what information is going on each page. Jot this down briefly on each page. For example:
   - Front page 1: Picture of the school and a slogan or headline about the new canteen
   - Inside left page 2: Picture of canteen and bullet points on hot and cold food available
   - Inside right page 3: Picture of food products and bullet points on drinks, snacks, healthy options
   - Back page 4: Picture of smiling canteen staff serving happy students, bullet points on special offers, meal deals, meal combos, etc.

3. Now do it for real on a new page!

Proofread your leaflet and correct any mistakes.

Invitations

An **invitation** can be a formal or informal document asking someone to attend a certain event. We send invitations for:

- Birthdays
- Weddings
- Christenings
- Engagements
- Christmas parties
- Other special occasions

 Drawing

Design your own birthday party invitation. Consider having a competition in the class for the best design.

Include the following details:

- Type of event
- Date
- Time
- Place
- Your contact details to RSVP (RSVP means *répondez s'il vous plait*, 'reply if you please', i.e. please reply)

It's .... Party!

Date: ....

Time: ....

Place: ....

....

R.S.V.P. ....

Tel.: ....

Multimodal Texts

'Multi' means *many* and 'modal' means '*way of doing something*'. A **multimodal** text communicates information using more than one method, such as **paper** (book, comic, poster, etc.), **audio** (sound), **digital** (animation, film, video games, etc.) or a **live** performance or event. With the increased use of digital technology, multimodal is usually associated with digital presentation. You may have created multimodal texts in primary school doing projects and presentations using a mix of pictures, words, animation, sound, etc.

When an image is used to convey information, a person uses their **visual** (seeing) literacy to understand the meaning. So when you look at photos, illustrations, films, etc. you figure them out from what you see. Visual literacy can be used where people may speak different languages but need to understand the same things. Here are some examples where images are used to show meaning:

Airport signs

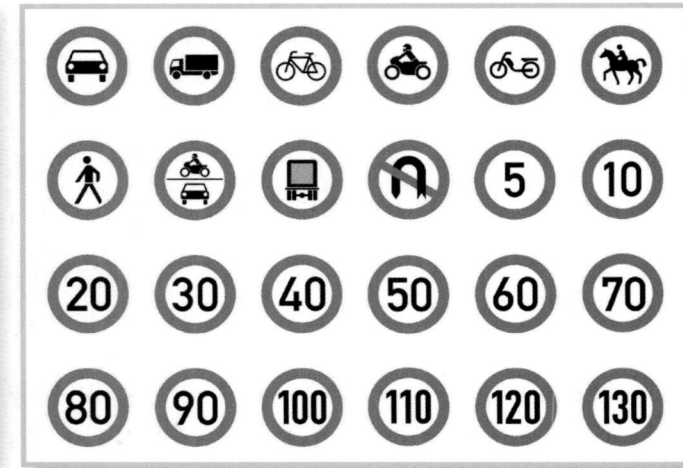

Road signs

Weather symbols

 ## A. Pairwork

Brainstorm other examples of visual literacy signs, symbols and icons. Collect examples and paste them onto a chart that you can display in your classroom.

 ## B. Creative Project – Create a Multimodal Text

Create a multimodal text on a topic of your choice and present it to the class. It can include some or all of the following: text, pictures, video, sound, symbols.

Travel Writing

Travel writing records the experiences of a person while travelling. The person can be travelling for pleasure or as part of their job. Someone travelling for pleasure might decide to write about their experience in a blog or magazine article, or they might write a book. A working travel writer might be employed by a TV or publishing company to record their travel experiences for a TV programme or travel book. Michael Palin has travelled all over the world to make TV programmes for the BBC and he has written books about all of those journeys.

The author might write in an informal, personal, narrative style or in a diary style, as you saw in Chapter 1. They usually include formal facts about the place, the journey, the costs involved, places to visit, etc. Travel writing therefore can be a mix of formal and informal writing.

If the writer has enjoyed their experience, they often try to **persuade** the reader to holiday in the places they have visited.

On Two Wheels in Magical Madagascar

by Donal Cronin

Donal Cronin is a teacher and a travel writer. He travels to various places in the world and keeps a journal of his experiences. He then writes about his experiences in newspaper articles. This article is about his trip to the island of Madagascar. The writing style is a mix of plain, direct and straightforward, e.g. 'I pack my small bag and am ready to go' and descriptive, e.g. 'The majestic mango tree... is struggling to wring a shape from charcoal grey light'.

A 1,100 km motorbike trip across the Indian Ocean island was the perfect way to savour its stunning landscape.

1. It is 6 am. The majestic mango tree in front of my door is struggling to wring shape from charcoal grey light. In the shower the water is refreshingly cold. The small wooden bungalow – with its bed, mosquito net, one-channel ancient TV set – has been comfortable enough. With dinner and a large beer it has cost me all of €10. It's expensive to get to Madagascar but cheap when you get here. I pack my small bag and am ready to go.

2. The caretaker is wiping down my motorbike, he's hoping for a small tip which he gets. I strap my bag to the carrier, the bike is reluctant to start the day. I don't mind, I need a little more light before I face the road – 300 km today. The gate of the compound is opened, the streets of the small town are already busy with school-going children and people heading for the market.

3. It's cool and fresh – the nicest part of the day to ride. A traffic policeman on the outskirts of town has his hand up. I speak only 'un peu' French, I say and he is forced into his little English. He's courteous, though, and seems to like it when I say I'm a teacher. He smiles and shakes my hand and wishes me goodbye.

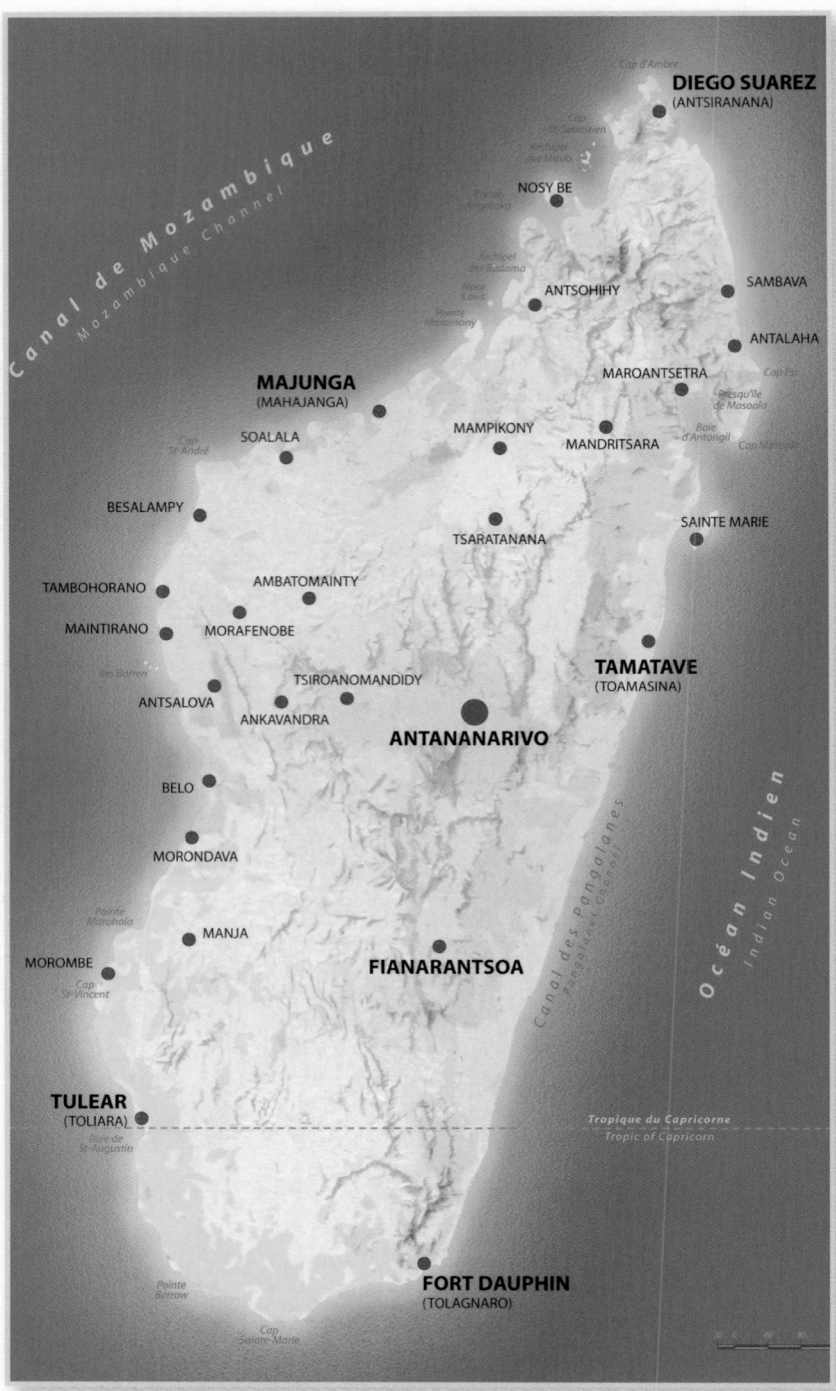

4. In my 1,100 km trip to the north of the island I pass through 20 checkpoints. There are police, traffic police, gendarmerie, military, all with different uniforms. Some lay spikes across the road, some booms. I don't get stopped at all of them, just enough to make me slightly paranoid of uniforms.

5. A little outside the small town I stop for breakfast at a small wooden shack with a raffia roof and a small bench for customers. The woman gives a surprised smile to see a white client. I have two strong black coffees and small cakes she had gotten up at 4 am to bake. I say goodbye in Malagasy which brings a delighted chuckle. Breakfast has cost all of 35 cents. I feel slightly guilty that she works so hard for so little.

6. The landscape is stunning – I've been through plains and high plateaus. I keep lifting my eyes to the vast dome of sky which is now turning little by little from pale to deep blue. The mountains are shrouded in hazy distance and I feel a great liberty as I ride towards them, free at last. The delicate green of rice fields is everywhere, on the plains, in clefts in the hills, on terraces stepping up the mountains.

7. There are dangers on the trip that often force you to ignore this beauty. There are huge potholes and one-time sealed roads that have taken on strange and grotesque shapes as if minor volcanoes were alive under them, many bridges with missing pieces, skittish or uncontrollable zebus with huge pointed horns, the swish of an occasional huge lorry on a narrow road, a sporadic snake. I stop on the high plateau and switch off the noise. The silence is broken by an infrequent gust of wind. I watch a kestrel hovering before a strike. I can see, far away, the highest point of the highest mountain in Madagascar.

8. I am riding through the heart of the Sakalava Kingdom in north-west Madagascar – once independent, they no longer have their kings or queens but have their pride. Dark skinned and curly-haired, they are one of the many ethnic groups on the island with different cultures and taboos. Taboos differ wildly among ethnic groups – a pregnant Sakalava woman should not sit in a doorway or eat fish. Some of the taboos stretch the imagination further.

9. I take a break. I sit in a local market and have a cold drink. I am happy to watch these people from my corner. A man with oxen is delivering charcoal to the little shanty restaurants, a woman is carrying some coals to light her neighbour's charcoal, an old man plies bottles of honey. A girl of six or seven comes to where I sit, gazing at me intently and says, 'I'm going to dance *vahaza* [a friendly term for foreigner], watch me.' And she does.

10. There is no existential questioning of the meaning of life. There is the daily struggle for survival but there is some grace and dignity in that struggle. Add much good humour and stoicism, laughter and banter – an envious mix. It is one of the reasons I travel to these places, a gentle going back to a less complicated time.

11. When I reach the tip of The Big Red Island, as the inhabitants call it, I feel a sense of achievement as I admire the three-pronged beautiful Diego bay.

12. I was nervous starting out, the first three-day trip on a motor bike I'd done. I pat my machine affectionately, then, optimistically I take out my map of the island and begin to look at another line on it, a more challenging line perhaps.

GLOSSARY

Un peu: French for 'a little'.

Gendarmerie: Soldiers who perform police duties.

Booms: Beams used as barriers on the road.

Paranoid: Unfounded fear that someone is going to harm you.

Raffia: A palm tree native to tropical Africa and Madagascar.

Malagasy: The language of Madagascar.

Plateaus: Areas of flat land higher than surrounding areas.

Shrouded: Covered, as in keeping a secret.

Clefts: Cracks in the rock.

Terraces: A series of flat areas like steps on a slope, usually to help crops grow.

Grotesque: Horrible and weird.

Skittish: Nervous and jumpy.

Zebus: A breed of domesticated ox with a humped back.

Sporadic: Happens only very occasionally.

Ethnic: A group of people who have a common national or cultural tradition.

Taboos: A social or religious custom that bans something.

Oxen: Cows, bulls.

Plies: Persuades people to buy.

Existential: Relating to how and whether life has meaning, and why we exist.

Stoicism: Suffering pain without showing any feeling.

 ## A. Reading

Rate this text for 'readability'. Write the word/phrase of your choice into your copy.

VERY EASY ☐   EASY ☐   OKAY ☐   HARD ☐   VERY HARD ☐

 ## B. Literacy Questions

1. Find two examples of the writer's plain, simple style of writing.
2. What form of transport is the writer using to travel around the island?
3. What languages do the islanders speak?
4. Where does the writer stop for breakfast? What does he have?
5. Describe the landscape on the island. Include quotes from the text to support your points.
6. List the dangers of his journey.
7. Explain what the writer means when he says that one of the reasons he goes to Madagascar is because it allows him to go 'back to a less complicated time'.

Proofread your answers and correct any mistakes.

 ## C. Research

Do some research on taboos in Irish culture. Ask your parents or grandparents about them or use the internet to find some.

In Japan, it is taboo to sneeze in public!

Writing Style: Persuasive

Persuasive language is often used in travel writing articles and tourist brochures, to encourage and persuade people to buy into the travel experience or to visit a particular place. Read the following extracts and notice where the author tries to *persuade* you.

Hanging with Hemingway *by Gary Quinn*

Ernest Hemingway was a famous American novelist. He was born in 1899 and died in 1961. Here, travel writer Gary Quinn travels to what was Hemingway's home in Key West in Florida.

1. There's a touch of voodoo about Key West, this subtropical island basking at the foot of Florida. It's famously closer to Havana than Miami, but stepping off my bus I know I'm deep in the heart of America. Chickens wander freely in the streets and at this early hour my only companions are slow-moving families. Key West is a party town and is the location of America's best-known literary festival – Hemingway Days. Ernest Hemingway stumbled on Key West by accident, arriving there from Havana to pick up a new car in 1928. The car was late and so the writer was put up in an apartment above the car dealership to wait for it.

2. Its arrival took just long enough for the town to weave its spell. Like many who testify to have washed up there, a decade quickly passed and Hemingway and Key West were like brother and sister. He finished *Death in the Afternoon* there, *For Whom the Bell Tolls*, 'The Snows of Kilimanjaro' and 'The Short Happy Life of Francis Macomber'. 907 Whitehead Street was Hemingway's home. It's a museum now and the tours that take place there bring you face-to-face with this literary landmark. His writing studio, his living areas, the fantastic outdoor pool and even the living descendants of his famous six-toed cat. The house is a national historic landmark and well worth visiting.

3. Key West is fantastic for families. It's surrounded by the Atlantic Ocean and the Gulf of Mexico with the point at which the two bodies of water meet being the Florida Straits. The waters here are renowned for their sea life and there are many great and safe trips to be taken. Fury Water Adventures took me out into the Gulf of Mexico on a dolphin safari, followed by a great snorkelling session in the Key West wildlife refuge. Back on land, the Key West Butterfly and Nature Conservatory is a beautiful experience with its glass house full of hundreds of tropical butterflies that flutter around and alight on your hands and feet. You can learn about the journey a butterfly makes from cocoon to adult butterfly and get up close and personal with these delicate insects – just make sure there aren't any hitching a ride when you leave.

4. Families will also love the aquarium, the Shipwreck Museum, the Eco-Discovery Centre and of course the Sunset Celebration – a nightly event at Mallory Square in the old town to watch the sun slip slowly into the sea surrounded by fire eaters, jugglers and musicians. Key West has lots of accommodation of all types – historic guest-houses, bed & breakfasts and five-star resorts.

GLOSSARY

Subtropical: Close to the Tropics, which are near the equator, the hottest area on earth.

Basking: Lying exposed to warmth or sun typically for relaxation.

Descendants: Living animals/people are descendants of the animals/people that they are related to that lived in the past.

A. Literacy Questions

1. List any examples of persuasive words or sentences that you find in the above text.
2. How did the writer Ernest Hemingway come to live in Key West?
3. List some of the texts he wrote while he lived there?
4. List three activities that families can avail of in Key West.
5. The description of the sunset – 'watch the sun slip slowly into the sea surrounded by…' is a very good example of alliteration and sibilance. Write three long sentences with lots of alliteration and sibilance.

Proofread your answers and correct any mistakes.

B. Listening

Listen to 'Sharks in South Africa' by Kevin Dawson as read on the RTÉ Radio 1 programme *Sunday Miscellany*.

1. What bait do they use to draw the sharks?
2. How are they protected when they are in the cage?
3. List one example of good description in the podcast.
4. How does the narrator create tension and suspense?
5. What impacts the narrator most about the sharks?
6. Do you agree that it was 'an extraordinary way to spend a Sunday morning'? Would it appeal to you?

A Clare Island Escape *by Audrey Kane*

Irish Daily Star, Tuesday, August 15, 2013

JUST when you think there are no more surprises left on this beautiful island of ours, you come across a little gem, and earlier this month in the blistering heat, myself and my sister's family did just that on Clare Island writes Audrey Kane.

Clare Island, the largest island in Clew Bay, is not actually in Co Clare but in Co Mayo, and the stunning island is only three and a half miles from the nearest mainland harbour at Roonagh in County Mayo and only 18 miles from Westport. So now you know where it is, let me tell why you should go. The ferry only takes 25 minutes across to the island and the view is breath-taking as you pass a maze of little islands until Clare rears up on the horizon to a height of 500 metres.

Once there, we were greeted by the very lovely Helen O'Grady from O'Grady's B&B who collected our luggage even though the B&B was a five-minute walk. This show of kindness and friendliness was something that was consistent throughout our weekend from the islanders. Myself and the gang were thrilled when we reached the guesthouse to find we were right on the beach's doorstep. With a bright interior and sweeping stairway leading up to the luxury en-suite bedrooms with tea/coffee and TV and all with beautiful sea views, you would be forgiven for thinking you were in a five-star hotel, but the only difference you'll find here is the price.

B&B singles start at €40 and twin/doubles at €70. The breakfast is to die for with Helen's freshly baked brown bread, full and mini Irish breakfasts. Contact Helen at 098 22991 or e-mail info@ogradysguesthouse.com or view more information on www.ogradysguesthouse.com.

After we had settled in to our rooms and admired the view, Helen arranged a speed boat trip around the island with amazing views everywhere we looked. With our sea legs firmly back on land, it was time for a stroll to visit to Anna's Coffee Shop (annascoffeeshop@gmail.com) for her famous chocolate cake and it certainly didn't disappoint. The cozy atmosphere of her cottage at the Mill makes it the perfect place to stop on the road to the island's spectacular lighthouse. It was a much-needed break from the blistering sun outside. The next stop was the lighthouse. This architecturally majestic, listed building has been lovingly transformed into fully catered, luxury accommodation, complemented by magnificent sea views and an inspiring, natural environment (www.clareislandlighthouse.com).

With so much to do on the island, it was hard to fit everything we wanted to do in two days, so I would recommend staying for a little longer. So after an action-packed day, we headed up to Sailor's Bar and Restaurant for dinner. The newly renovated hostel run by Carl O'Brady with bar and restaurant is nestled on top of a small cliff, surrounded by open Atlantic waters. The bar prides itself on serving freshly caught pollock and mackerel so it would have been rude not to order it for dinner – and it was delicious. The restaurant is spectacular, welcoming and above all reasonably priced.

If you're looking for something with a bit of adventure, then book yourself in here as there's a wide range of activities, such as angling, scuba diving, kayaking, surfing, cookery classes and more. There is also the famous Bard Summer School and Singles Adventure Weekend (www.goexplorehostel.ie). The following day, my sister's kids enjoyed a visit to the equestrian centre. At Macalla Horse Farm, guests can partake in Natural Horsemanship lessons, which are an exciting way to pass the day for all the family. E-mail christophe@ecofarm.ie for more information, call him on 087 2621832 or see www.ecofarm.ie.

On our way back, we stopped off at the Community Centre and Bar for some light lunch and refreshment. The community centre is a vital part of the island and hosts many trad sessions, which brings the islanders and visitors together to share their love of music.

There is plenty to do on the island, including a visit to Grace O'Malley's 15th-century castle, a 12th-century Cistercian abbey and rare medieval wall and ceiling paintings. Or try angling and boat trips or a family-run yoga and meditation retreat centre located on a large farm. The island also has one of the most diverse geologies in Europe. The best way to get around the island is by bike, and for €10 a day you can hire a bike from Mountain Bike Hire.

To get to Clare Island, take O'Grady's Ferry across from Roonagh Quay (you can't take your car, so pack wisely). For a list of ferry prices and times, see www.clareislandferry.com.

GLOSSARY

Architecturally majestic: Beautifully designed building.
Diverse geology: Varied landscape.

A. Literacy Questions

1. List any examples of persuasive words or sentences that you find in the above text.
2. Why do think there might be a little confusion over the name and location of Clare Island?
3. From the list of activities available to do on the island, what appeals to you and why?
4. Would you like to visit the island? Explain your answer.

Proofread your answers and correct any mistakes.

B. Writing Task – Write a Persuasive Article

Think about a place that you would encourage tourists to visit in your area. In your **PORTFOLIO**, write a persuasive and informative article on this place.

- Persuasive: How will you persuade people to go there? What language will you use to encourage visitors to go there?
- Informative: What information will you give on the place that is factual and appealing?

Read the two examples on the next page to help you come up with ideas.

ACE this task! Remember to brainstorm.

Kilkee, Co. Clare, Ireland

Kilkee is a small seaside resort on the mid-west coast of Ireland. The beach is horseshoe shaped and beautiful. Walk from one side of the bay to the other and gaze out at the gorgeous blue sea and bobbing boats – your own little piece of the French Riviera! The main street is dotted with small, quaint shops, a  few pubs, cafés and the essential ice-cream parlour. For breath-taking cliff views, scenic drives and gorgeous, safe beaches, go west to Kilkee, Co. Clare. You won't be disappointed!

Coole Park, Gort, Co. Galway

The trees are in their autumn beauty,
The woodland paths are dry,
Under the October twilight
The water mirrors a still sky

from 'The Wild Swans at Coole' by
W.B. Yeats

W.B. Yeats loved Coole Park and once described it as 'the most beautiful place in the world'.

He spent many happy times in Coole Park with his dear friend, Lady Gregory. They both wrote poetry and together they founded the Abbey Theatre in Dublin in 1904.

Coole Park is 3 km north of Gort, Co. Galway, on the N18. Admission to the park is free and it is open year round, but the visitor centre in it is open only during peak tourist season, from Easter to the end of September.

The park is situated on a thousand acres, encompassing gorgeous, verdant walkways, whispering trees and tranquil lakes. It is more than simply a park – it is a nature reserve with a beautiful, walled garden and a modern visitor centre. Learn about the history of the park from the audio-visual presentation in the visitor centre, then explore magical woodland walks, admire the swans, ducks, squirrels and otters and watch the deer in their own enclosure.

Escape from the stress of modern life by losing yourself in the peace and tranquillity of Coole. Enjoy the lush lawns and gently lapping lakes, 'where midnight's all a-glimmer and noon a purple glow' and 'evening full of the linnet's wings'. Be inspired as Yeats and Lady Gregory were by the breathtaking beauty of Coole, and you may even write a poem yourself.

For more information e-mail info@coolepark.ie or telephone 091-631-804.

 ## C. Oral Language

Give a short talk to your class based on the article you wrote in task B on p. 190.

Advertisements

An **advertisement** (advert or ad) is a notice, picture or film telling people about a product, job, service, etc. Ads are placed where the target audience can see/hear them, for example:

- Radio
- Television
- Online
- Magazines
- Newspapers

To catch attention, many adverts have **slogans**. An advertising slogan is a short, memorable group of words used in an advertising campaign. Can you explain why this slogan from Independent Newspapers is so effective?

Before you make up your mind, open it.

Companies usually establish a **brand** so that potential customers recognise their ads immediately. They do this by creating **logos** and using particular colours and images, for example the Aer Lingus logo is green and features a shamrock.

Ad makers consider the following kinds of questions:

- What is the **budget** (amount of money) to spend on advertising?
- Who is the **target audience** (young children, parents of babies/toddlers, teenagers, young adults, middle-aged people, older people)?
- Is the product/service more suited to a **certain type of ad** (TV, radio, newspaper, magazine, etc.)?
- **When** should the ad appear on TV/radio (before a certain programme, after the programme or during the break, etc.)?
- **Who** should play the parts in the ad; would a certain celebrity suit the part?
- If it's a charitable organisation; which **celebrities** support the charity?
- **How long** does an average TV ad play for and how long will this ad be?
- **How much** does it cost to place an ad in the different media?
- Will this be **a one-off** ad or will it be repeated regularly. Some companies challenge themselves to improve their ads all the time. For example, Marks & Spencer recreate their ads regularly using different themes, and Specsavers change the story to match their slogan 'Should've gone to Specsavers'.
- Should it be **funny/serious**, etc.?
- Will it have a **narrative/story** that continues in other ads? Check out *http://www. postadvertising.com/2013/05/tv-ads-brand-storytelling/* to see some ads that have great stories.
- Will it be **shown in parts?** Some ads have a part 1, then a few seconds later, a part 2 in their ad.

Radio

Radio is a form of **aural** (listening) communication. The **listener** cannot see anything; they have to tune in to hear the broadcast. The radio listener uses their imagination to put pictures to the words that they hear. For this reason, words and music are very important on radio. Radio ads need to be:

- **Appealing to the ear:** using clever words/phrases/dialogue, catchy/beautiful/powerful music, etc.

- **Short:** Listeners might tune out if the advertisement is too long or if it is boring.

 ## A. Listening

Copy the headings from the following table into your copy. In class or at home, listen to three radio ads and write down information under each heading. Some examples have been filled in for you.

Product/ service	Company name	Persuasive words	Slogan	Music, jingle, drama scene
Family car	Nissan	Big Bonus Week	Innovation that excites	Mum and children getting out of car
Washing machine	Harvey Norman	10th birthday bargains Save 40–50% Sale must end Sunday	Go Harvey Norman, go!!	Man shouting about the sale
RTÉ National Symphony Orchestra	RTÉ	Best performance ever. Not to be missed.	Love your orchestra	Classical music playing

 ## B. Oral Language

Read the following ad out loud the way you think it would be read on radio. If you can, add music to it.

Ad for Jolly Zingy Jellies

Need an instant energy boost? Try Jolly Zingy Jellies, the newest, chewiest, juiciest jellies ever. Five fantastic new zingy flavours combine to give you whizz and fizz: lime, raspberry, mango, orange and pineapple. Only Jolly Zingy Jellies for the real zing! Buy one get one free for a limited time only.

C. Creative Project – Create a Radio ad

Invent a new product or service and create a radio ad for it. Use the above example for ideas.

- Read your ad aloud.
- Add music to it.

- Record it.
- Time it.

Television

Television ads are a form of both **visual** and **aural** communication. In addition to the words and music, the **viewer** needs to find the images, colours, action, etc. appealing/striking.

 ## Research Project

1. Watch some TV ads and try to match up the ads to the approaches/features in the list below.

   i. Some ads use cuddly animals to appeal to our emotions, for example, the puppy in the Andrex ad.

   ii. The people in ads can often be beautiful and seem perfect.

   iii. Many ads use superlatives to claim that the product or service is newest, best, safest, healthiest, tastiest, freshest, brightest, etc.

   iv. Ads often appeal to our sense of humour.

   v. Serious information ads warn us about road safety/ ESB power lines/gas leaks, etc.

   vi. It can be obvious that some ads are aimed at either males or females.

2. Do some research on the ads which are on when you and your family are watching TV. Copy the following table and fill in the details based on what you watch. Some examples are done for you.

TV Channel	Time of Day/ Night	Programme	Ads at this time	Comment
RTÉ 1	Fri 9.30 pm	The Late Late Show	Insurance ads	Aimed at adults
RTÉ 2	Sat 6.30 pm	Horrible Histories	Anti-smoking ad	Aimed at young children

Online

Online ads are **visual** and **aural**; they can include text, pictures, moving images and sound. When you are looking at different websites, there can be ads placed anywhere on the screen; at the top, bottom, sides and even the centre of the screen. Often the ads are moving and flashing and demanding your attention.

Ads on webpages can also take the form of **sponsored links**. This means a company pays a fee to place a link to their website on the page.

You cannot avoid ads when you are online. When you are about to watch a clip on YouTube, an ad may pop up just before you watch. Other ads begin playing and you have the option to 'skip ad' after a certain amount of time.

When online, you should be very careful about following certain links in ads as they may lead to inappropriate content.

 ## Research Project

Make a list of the ads which you come across in your online activity. Make a note of the details of the ads, such as:

- Colour
- Logo
- Flashing
- Moving images/text
- Persuasive: Buy now/Find out more
- Effective/good
- Annoying/bad

Magazines

Without the option of sound or moving images, magazine ads rely on their **image/visual** and on the **text** to make the impact.

Magazines are aimed at particular target groups and ages, for example *Kiss* magazine is for pre-teen and teenage girls while *Hello* and *OK* are for older girls and women.

There is a huge selection of magazines available, on a wide range of topics: sport, cars, wedding/bridal, health/fitness, beauty, parenting, home décor, politics, economics, cartoon TV shows, comics, etc. The ads in magazines target particular readers, so a parenting magazine will have ads for baby and toddler products, while a fishing magazine will have ads for fishing gear and fishing holidays, etc.

Irresistibly snuggly duvets & pillows. Let **battle** commence.

The extra springy, twisty fibres in our duvets and pillows trap the air inside making them super-soft, toasty-warm and feather-light. It's no wonder they are so huggable. For stockists and details of our whole range visit www.silentnight.co.uk

All Silentnight bedding accessories are sold under licence by Comfy Quilts Ltd.

Silentnight

 ## A. Research Project

Find some magazines at home. Copy the following table and fill in the information for each magazine. A sample has been done for you:

Name of magazine	Target reader	List 5 ads in the magazine	Comment on ad
Match of the Day	Pre-teen and teenage football fans	Wicked Lego Mixels Figures	Good images
		Air Storm Pop Rocket	Bad explanation
		XBox One	Great competition
		FIFA 1	Terrible images
		Adidas boots	Cool colours

 ## B. Pairwork

Bring the magazines into class. In pairs, look at the ads and list the features which make the ads good or bad.

You could consider the following:

* Picture/visual
* Colour/branding
* Clever 'story' in the ad
* Good slogan/headline/caption
* Unusual/interesting feature/angle in the ad

Newspapers

Newspapers, like magazines, must rely on the printed, **visual** word and image to get the message across.

There are different types of newspapers; there are weekly local papers such as the *Drogheda Independent* and daily or weekly national papers, such as the *Irish Independent* or *Sunday Independent*. Weekly papers usually publish at weekends with extra magazines and **supplements** (separate smaller papers) on property, motoring, travel, health, etc. Advertisers can target a specific market with such supplements.

There are also free local newspapers that contain lots of ads about products or services in the area, such as the *Tralee Outlook*. Local traders can get their message to customers without paying the high prices charged by the national papers.

Newspapers come in two different formats: **broadsheet** (with a large page) or **tabloid** (with a smaller page). *The Irish Times* is a broadsheet and the *Irish Daily Star* is a tabloid. The *Irish Independent* is sold in both formats, so readers have a choice.

Notice the newspapers which come into your house. Are they local or national, broadsheet or tabloid? See what articles you'd like to read in them.

 ## A. Pairwork

Chat about the differences between ads in newspapers and ads in magazines. List five difference you have noticed.

 ## B. Oral Language

Cut out and bring in three ads from a newspaper. Show these to the class and explain what is being advertised. As a class, decide on the best and worst ad of all.

Direct Speech

Quotation marks/inverted commas are used for a number of reasons:

Direct Speech

If you are quoting exactly, word for word from the source, you must use inverted commas.
'It's all over. I'm leaving now,' said Sheila.

If you quote exactly what Sheila said, you must use quotation marks/ inverted commas.
I heard Sheila say 'It's all over. I'm leaving now.'

If you are simply reporting on or recounting what was said you don't use quotation marks.
Sheila said that it was all over, and that she was leaving.

This is reported speech.

When used for direct speech, quotation marks are used at the opening and closing of the sentence. Single or double quotation marks can be used. Single are more commonly used in Ireland, whereas double are more commonly used in America.

 Single

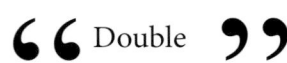 Double

Dialogue/conversation

In fiction, the writer often writes exactly what the characters said.

'Look here,' he said. 'How long does this tunnel go on for? I mean, does it stop where your house ends?'

If a person is being quoted, and that person is quoting another person then quotes within quotes are used. In this example single quotes are used for the overall quote and double quotes for the quote within.

'So, Polly said, "No, the walls don't go out to the roof." That's what she said,' recalled Tom.

Quotations

If you **quote** directly from another person's work (taking a line/lines from a poem, novel, drama, speech) you must use quotation marks.

In the poem *Boy at the Window*, the poet Richard Wilbur explains that the boy feels sad for the snowman: 'The small boy weeps to hear the wind prepare / A night of gnashings and enormous moan.'

Irony and Sarcasm

Quotation marks can be used to indicate **irony** (saying one thing but meaning the opposite) or **sarcasm** (using irony to make fun of someone/something).

This lesson on quotation marks is so 'exciting' I think I'm going to explode!

Titles

Quotation marks can also be used to indicate the title of a song, poem, book, play etc.

Chris Rea's song 'Driving Home for Christmas' is a much loved favourite at this time of year.

Research

Check the novels you are reading to see examples of conversation/dialogue in inverted commas. Notice if double or single quotation marks are used and think about where the author is from. Are there any examples of speech within speech?

Articles

Unlike ads, **articles** are not trying to sell you anything. They are generally written to inform and/or entertain.

Newspapers give us the news and information about events which are happening each day, but they also have articles written on specific topics, such as health, education, parenting, technology, entertainment, science, etc.

Newspaper articles can be written using formal or informal language. Formal articles are more usually found in **broadsheet** newspapers. **Tabloid** newspapers use informal and sometimes **sensationalist** (shocking) language that is easier to read and understand. They present news in a dramatic way and also focus on celebrity news and gossip.

Read the following articles to see examples of both kinds of writing.

Formal Articles

Teens get €30 pocket money and use it to shop online *by Charlie Weston*

The following newspaper article is from the Irish Independent, August 2013. Charlie Weston is the Personal Finance Editor with the Irish Independent.

The majority of teenagers are shopping online. And most of those between the ages of 12 and 15 get almost €30 every month in pocket money, a new survey shows. But only half of parents talk regularly to their children on how to manage money and spend wisely.

Most parents are giving an average of €27 a month in pocket money to children between the ages of 12 and 15, the new research commissioned by Danske Bank shows. Most save €10 of this, with the rest of the money mostly spent online buying music downloads and books.

A little over one-third of parents give their teen children less than €20 a month in pocket money, while another third of parents are handing over between €21 and €50 a month in pocket money.

Online purchases are taking place without regular help from parents, the research carried out by iReach shows.

Nine out of 10 young teenagers and pre-teens shop online. And the vast majority of secondary school children own a mobile phone. Average spending on bills and credit is €12 a month.

The survey also found that just one-third of parents are confident that their secondary-school-going children understand financial terms like interest rate and fixed rate. Parents feel youngsters should learn more about money at school.

The bank has launched *www.controlyourmoney.ie* to help pupils and teachers manage their money.

Danske bank's Maria Sheehan said financial literacy was an important part of a child's general education.

Understanding

'Our research shows that parents want their children to have a strong understanding of their own money and personal finance and that they would like their children to learn these skills as part of their school curriculum,' she said.

She said that a high level of financial literacy not only enriched the lives of individuals but also contributed to healthy economic growth in society.

'Improving the financial skills and knowledge of money and personal finance among our teenagers will ensure that they are better positioned for their own future in society,' Ms Sheehan said.

A. Literacy Questions

1. Name the organisation which commissioned (asked for) the research to be carried out on teenagers and pocket money.
2. Name the company who carried out the research.
3. What is the purpose of the website *www.controlyourmoney.ie*?
4. Why did the journalist write this article?

Proofread your answers and correct any mistakes.

B. Numeracy Questions

1. What is the average monthly pocket money given to 12-15 year olds?
2. What percentage of teens gets less than €20 and what percentage get between €21 and €50?
3. Draw a Pie Chart showing monthly pocket money amounts given to teens.
4. How do you think you could manage your money better?

Tragedy Gives Hope to Leather Workers

by Jason Burke

The following newspaper article is from *The Guardian*, July 2013. It is written in a formal, serious style. The writer explains the problems with the factories in Bangladesh. Viewpoints of the workers and the employers are given. Local workers are interviewed and their opinions are quoted. Facts and figures are included in the article to support the points being made. Read the article and see if you think it is balanced and fair to each side.

Note: Tanneries are places where animal hides (skins) are processed and turned into leather.

Factory collapse may throw spotlight on notorious Bangladeshi tanneries.

Part 1

The gutters run blue and red, contaminated by chemicals; the air is acrid with fumes; the white midday sun bleaches the dirt of the busy thoroughfare. Mohammed Jalal, 42, is sitting under a ragged awning. He sips tea served scalding hot, despite the 45°C temperature. Soon he will return to work in one of the 185 tanneries that dominate this choked, congested neighbourhood of Dhaka, the capital of Bangladesh.

'If there was any other job, I'd do it,' Jalal says, shaking his head. Bangladesh has been under a spotlight since the deaths in April of 1,130 workers in the collapse of a factory in Dhaka, which produced cheap garments for western high street retailers. In the tragedy's aftermath, politicians in the chaotic south Asian state promised reforms and companies such as Primark, Matalan and Gap scrambled to repair battered reputations.

Many western firms have signed up to an agreement that legally binds them to source garments from factories in Bangladesh with safe working conditions and to contribute to the cost of improvements. Others are negotiating a separate accord.

But Bangladesh is also a major supplier of leather for shoes, handbags, belts, jackets and suitcases used in Britain, other European countries and south-east Asia. This booming trade – predicted to soon be worth more than £700m annually but notorious for its harsh conditions and pollution – has received less attention. Almost all Bangladeshi leather is produced from local animal hides by about 15,000 labourers in the small Dhaka neighbourhood of Hazaribagh. A recent report from international campaign group Human Rights Watch (HRW) described 'systemic human rights violations' in the industry. They also warn over a catastrophic environmental impact as tanneries dishcarge huge quantities of toxic waste into the Buriganga River, which flows through Dhaka.

201

GLOSSARY

Notorious: Famous or well known (usually for something bad or negative).
Contaminated: Made unsafe due to the addition of a harmful substance.
Acrid: Unpleasant to smell or taste.
Awning: A roof of canvas or other material supported by a frame to provide protection from the weather.
Congested: Crowded, overfull.
Accord: An agreement.
Systemic: Refers to something that is spread throughout a group or system.
Human rights violations: Stopping people from having their basic rights and freedoms.
Catastrophic: Sudden and large-scale damage/suffering/injury.
Discharge: Release, emit.

 ## A. Literacy Questions

1. On which continent is Bangladesh?
2. What is the capital of Bangladesh?
3. Name the river running through the capital city of Bangladesh.
4. What are the main industries in Bangladesh?
5. Name three large western companies that buy goods from the factories.
6. List two problems that the industries/factories are responsible for.
7. Pick out some examples of effective verbs (remember verbs are action words) from the above extract.

Proofread your answers and correct any mistakes.

 ## B. Numeracy Questions

1. In what temperature is Mohammed Jalal working?
2. What age is he?
3. How many workers died in the clothing factory collapse in April 2013?
4. How much money is the leather trade worth annually?
5. How many labourers work in Hazaribagh to produce leather?

Part 2

Residents and workers in Hazaribagh are hoping they may see some benefits from the global outrage that followed the Rana Plaza factory collapse. 'We know what happened to those poor people and have heard that the whole world was angry. Maybe this can help us too,' said Jalal, who has worked in the tanneries for 30 years. Mohammed Abdul Hai, head of the Bangladesh Traders Association, said he had allayed European concern by reassuring them that the tanneries would move to a new purpose-built complex on the outskirts of the city next year. The zone will be equipped with a waste treatment plant and conditions for workers will be hugely improved. Activists and workers express doubt that after decades of delays the move will happen soon. There is little sign that land allocated for the new factories is being prepared. 'The tanneries are horrible. I worry it may be a lost cause. The courts have ordered relocation again and again but each successive government had demanded more time,' said Syeda Rizwana Hasan, chief executive of the Bangladesh Environmental Lawyers Association.

Two main concerns are the health of workers and child labour. Conditions vary but in several factories visited by the *Guardian*, men could be seen working with minimal or no protection from the range of corrosive chemicals used in the tanning process. While some had been equipped with cheap rubber boots, none was wearing a face mask or eye protection. The heat in many tanneries is intense. In some, saline solution is distributed to workers to prevent dehydration. Teenagers were also present in several tanneries, in breach of the UN Convention on the Rights of the Child, which prohibits hazardous work for under-18s.

In the MB Tannery, one 15-year-old said he was paid 3,500 taka (£30) a month to cut and shape leather six, or sometimes seven, days a week. One boy, who said he was 13, said he was paid 4,000 taka for a 12-hour shift as a general helper. Habibur Rahman, the managing director of the tannery, said he employed about 125 labourers 'but no children'. Most of the workers in Hazaribagh are paid monthly wages of between 6,000 taka to 25,000 taka for eight- to 14-hour days, six or even seven days a week. Such salaries mean labour costs in Bangladesh can be up to half of those in China, the major competitor, and are one reason for the boom in leather production in the south Asian state.

The long hours among machinery and toxic chemicals – some workers sleep in the factories – take their toll. Most complain of eye, respiratory, cardiac and skin problems, as well as frequent accidents. It is not just the workers who suffer. The tanneries are flanked by slums and crowded residential streets with schools, mosques and shops. Space is so limited that some homes are built on stilts over stinking waste outflows. 'It's a terrible place for kids. They cough, vomit because of the stench,' said Hamida Akhter, a health-worker. She is sceptical of the claims of officials that the tanneries will be relocated soon. 'They've been saying they will soon be gone for 13 years and it has not happened. I don't think much is likely to change round here soon,' Akhter, 29, said.

GLOSSARY

Allayed... concern: Reduced or lessened fears/worries.

Activists: People taking parts in activities designed to achieve a political or social goal.

Successive: One after the other, each one succeeding the previous one.

Corrosive: Tends to cause the gradual destruction of materials.

Saline: Contains salt.

In breach of: Have failed to do what is required by a law, an agreement or a duty.

Prohibits: Says something is not allowed by law or rule.

Hazardous: Dangerous.

Toxic: Poisonous.

Respiratory: Relating to the breathing system in the body.

Cardiac: Relating to the heart.

Flanked by: At the side of.

Sceptical: Having doubts, not convinced.

 A. Literacy Questions

1. What improvements have been promised by the Traders Association?
2. Why are the lawyers, health workers and ordinary workers not convinced the improvements will take place?
3. List the medical problems that tannery workers suffer from.
4. List some examples of effective verbs used in the above extract.
5. What country is Bangladesh's main competitor in the tannery industry?

Proofread your answers and correct any mistakes.

B. Numeracy Questions

1. How much money did the teenage boys earn per month?

2. How many hours a day and how many days a week did they work?

3. How many hours do the adults work? What is their range of pay?

C. Writing Task – Write a Formal Article

Do some research on the Rana Plaza factory collapse in Bangladesh and write your own short article on what happened. Think about the five Ws (Who, What, When, Where, Why) when preparing the article:

Alternatively write an article on your own experiences of pocket money, your spending/saving habits, your own views or opinions on the topic etc.

ACE this task! Remember RAFT.

Proofread your article and correct any mistakes.

Informal Articles

The media often use **sensationalist** and **emotive** (bringing out emotions in people) language to grab attention. In some newspapers, especially tabloids, dramatic and powerful headlines might be used, for example:

> Agonising injury for O'Driscoll

> *Terrified pensioner robbed*

> Death trap apartment collapses

> **Mass murderer on the loose**

> SHOCK AS MANAGER FIRED

> **THUGS RIP UP TRAIN TRACKS**

The extracts in the previous pages were formal, serious, factual articles; the following articles are less serious and are taken from the *Irish Daily Star* newspaper.

Russell Brand's new crush on Cheryl Cole

This newspaper article is from The *Irish Daily Star*, 15 October 2013.

No sooner has Cheryl Cole confirmed she is back on the market than Randy Russell's trying to work his magic on the Fight for This Love star. Russell (38) has invited the gorgeous singer to watch him perform at the Hammersmith Apollo in London tonight – where he plans to woo her with his outrageous stand-up routine.

Cheeky Russ must be hoping Cheryl (30) is already over her break-up with dancer Tre Holloway (28).

A friend of the lanky Lothario said: 'Russell asked staff to send Cheryl two tickets for tonight's Messiah Complex stand-up show in London. He even said he hopes she will bring her mum Joan Callaghan along too because he thinks she's the key to winning Cheryl over. Russell reckons if she enjoys the show enough, she might consider going out on a date with him.'

Jan' of the moment

This newspaper article is from The *Irish Daily Star*, 8 October 2013.

Manchester United sensation Adnan Januzaj insists he will take his time before deciding on his international future.

Januzaj has become the talk of the Premier League following his stunning full debut for United at Sunderland on Saturday.

The midfielder scored twice to inspire United to a 2–1 win and is seen as potentially one of the brightest talents in Europe.

Januzaj was born in Brussels and qualifies for Belgium, but could also turn out for Albania because his father was born there.

But he could also qualify for England in 2017 once he secures residency here and Three Lions boss Roy Hodgson is keen to secure his services.

Januzaj has rejected the chance to play for Belgium at youth level and insists publicly his preferred choice would be Albania.

The FA and Hodgson have made enquiries about his future availability but the 18-year-old is happy to bide his time.

Quiet

Januzaj admits he's more interested in doing well for United and said: 'At the moment international football isn't something that I've thought a lot about.

'I know that first I have to concentrate on what I do for United because that is the most important part of my career right now.

'I want to play well for United and give everything for my club.' His agent Dirk De Vriese has also told England they will have to wait for a decision.

He said: 'The priority is to break into the first team at Manchester United. Like Adnan himself, his father remains very quiet. They are in no hurry to choose.'

Januzaj, meanwhile, has revealed his mentors at Old Trafford are veteran stars Ryan Giggs and Patrice Evra.

He said: 'Everyone gives me advice, that's the great thing here at United. I speak a lot with Patrice and Giggsy.

They have great experience, they're big players at the club and have gone through everything I'm going through.

Position

'Their advice is important. If I play on the left Patrice is just behind me so he helps me, and I'm playing in a similar position to Giggsy.

'I ask him questions all the time as he's been a top, top player for so long. He's a good teacher.'

Wayne Rooney admits that throwing the 18-year-old into the struggling United team could have been considered a risk, but was pleased that the decision paid dividends.

'There was big pressure on us, but the manager has trusted him and he has repaid that,' said the United striker.

'He's very confident, that's great to see. A lot of the young players who come through are a little bit timid and shy, but he looks comfortable and he's confident in his own ability, which you need to be.

'It was a brave move to play him in the circumstances and we're delighted it's paid off.'

Rooney has also declared himself fighting fit for England's upcoming games against Montenegro and Poland after sustaining a minor injury while playing for United on Saturday.

'I've got a little knock but I'll be fine for England,' he said.

Honest

'I can't wait to be honest. As soon as the Sunderland game had finished, I started to think about England.'

Striker Wayne Rooney is certain England will qualify for the World Cup but has warned against complacency.

'We're going to do it. We're going to get to the World Cup,' he said.

' I'm confident, we're confident, but you always have to be sure you're not over-confident. These are going to be two tough games for us, but we're good enough to do it.'

GLOSSARY

Complacency: Being satisfied enough with something not to try harder.

A. Literacy Questions

1. Read the two articles from the *Irish Daily Star*. Pick out two examples of simple, straightforward language that is easy to read and understand.

2. Why do you think the articles use a lot of quotes?

3. In your opinion, what kind of a person is Adnan Januzaj?

4. In what other ways does the article make it easy for the reader to follow (Hint: paragraphs and headings)?

Proofread your answers and correct any mistakes.

B. Pairwork

In pairs, rewrite the following headlines to make them emotive and sensational.

- School fire damages classrooms
- Heavy rain floods Cork
- Player hits referee
- Protestors delay Dáil meeting
- Car crash kills two
- Strike disrupts train service

Not all pets are perfect but they still need to be loved *by Sinéad Moriarty*

The following newspaper article is from *The Irish Independent, August 2013*. It is written in a style somewhere between formal and informal. It is not sensationalist, but it does contain language and phrasing that makes it less serious than other articles.

The story of Mick, the six-week-old Boston Terrier, has been warming the hearts of animal lovers around the globe. Mick was born with 'Swimmer Puppy Syndrome'. This condition meant that he was unable to walk, stand or even sit because all four of his legs were splayed out. The poor thing could only lie on his stomach. Thankfully for him, the Mia Foundation in Rochester, New York, took him in. It was this little puppy's lucky day when the foundation, which takes in animals with birth defects that might otherwise be put down, agreed to help him.

And so began his journey to recovery. To begin with, they propped him up to take the weight off his chest. They then placed him in a harness to put his legs, which were also taped, into the correct resting position. Then he was taken to swim therapy where he was made to swim in a mini-pool to build up the muscles in his legs. The results were almost immediate. After a few days he was sleeping on his side and after only two weeks, he was able to sit up and walk. Granted he walks like a man with 10 pints on him, but it's a miracle that he's walking at all.

This little pup may never win any gold medals at the Crufts dog show, but I defy anyone to watch the YouTube video of him stumbling about, delighted with life, and not have a tear in their eye. Mick's story reminded me of my own experience of growing up with a dog that was less than perfect. When I was 10, my blood turned cold as I heard a high-pitched shriek outside the front door. I knew it was our dog, a golden cocker spaniel called Murph. I ran out to see her poor body lying on the side of the road and a distraught woman standing over her. The woman's car was askew and she just kept saying, 'I'm so sorry, I didn't see her'.

The woman's car had hit Murph and my poor dog was in a bad way. My mother came out and we gently carried the whimpering dog into the house and called the vet. Even at that age, I knew it didn't look good. The vet called to the house and after examining her, he suggested gently that we put Murph out of her misery. He explained that she'd never be the same again. She'd never walk again, run again or have any quality of life. I was beside myself. Then I heard my mother say, 'I think we'll give her a few days and see how she gets on'.

And so we did. The poor thing could only drag herself around by her front legs. Murph's back legs and coccyx had been crushed in the crash. But my mother nursed her back to health and slowly began to put her up on her back legs to regain her balance and strengthen the muscles. Over many weeks, with a lot of love, attention and patience, Murph began to regain her strength until one day she took a step unaided. Within two weeks she was running – granted she was running diagonally, but what did we care.

Like Mick, our dog was crooked, and walked with a limp. But she was alive, she was happy and she lived for another six years. I don't doubt that the vet gave us what he thought was good advice, but pets aren't just animals, they're family members. And when it comes to family, you don't give up until you've explored every avenue. The next time you decide to get a puppy, perhaps you should choose the one that looks 'different'. After all, they're the ones you'll love the most.

A. Literacy Questions

1. What was wrong with Mick?
2. List two ways that the Mia Foundation helped him?
3. What did Mick's story remind the writer about?
4. Give three examples of phrases that make this article less serious that the articles in the previous section.
5. Why do you think the writer wrote this article?

Proofread your answers and correct any mistakes.

B. Research

Read the tabloid newspapers online to get ideas for your article below.

C. Writing Task – Write an Informal Article

Imagine you are a journalist writing for the *Irish Daily Star* newspaper.
Write an article on one of the following incidents:

- Runaway bus crashes into busy department shop
- Lotto windfall for small farmer
- Tornado hits Mayo coast

Alternatively write an article about your own experiences, good or bad with family pets.

ACE this task! Remember RAFT.

Focus on Radio

Do you listen to the radio? Once upon a time, before the world-wide web, before 157 TV channels, before Facebook... most people listened to the radio each week. Today, despite the massive growth of media options, most people still use and love radio.

Why is this? Radio has an advantage over TV and newspapers/magazines as it can be enjoyed while **on the move**, in particular while walking or driving. Some people can even listen to the radio while they work. Many people listen to radio in the morning at home while having breakfast, making lunches, etc. and then on the way to work on the bus or in the car. It can give a feeling of companionship and can offer an escape from everyday life.

A. Pairwork

Working in pairs, answer the following questions.

- Do you listen to the radio?
- What radio stations or presenters do you listen to?
- Why?
- Who is your favourite presenter?
- Who is your least favourite?
- When do you listen to the radio?

B. Listening Project

Listen to the introduction to a radio show and complete the following checklist in your copy. Write out the list of topics that will be on the show.

Feature/Aspect	Tick
Greeting to listeners	
Tells us the date	
Tells us the time	
Tells us the name of the show	
Tells us his or her name	
Tells us the list of topics on today's show	
Tells us the duration of the show	
Encourages us to contact the show (text number, e-mail address, etc.)	

C. Writing Task – Write a Radio Intro

Imagine you are a radio presenter. Write out the text of the introduction to your show using the following guidelines:

- Invent a name for the radio station and a name for your show.
- What topics would you like to talk about on your show?
- Who would you like to interview?
- Would you like to play music? Choose music that your audience will like as well as your own personal favourites.

ACE this task. Remember RAFT.

D. Oral Language

Deliver your introduction from Task C to the class. If possible, record it and replay it.

Radio Documentaries

A documentary is a **factual film or radio/TV programme** about a real event, issue or experience. The documentary makers investigate the topic and then present their facts and conclusions. You may have your own favourite documentaries about wild animals, zoos, history, geography, astrology, etc.

Radio documentaries need to engage the listener to keep them tuned in. The listener must get all the information they need from just listening – it means the documentary makers need to make sure they hold our attention using interesting scripts, dialogue, sounds and music.

A. Listening

Listen to the documentary from RTÉ Radio 1 about where different people were on the day the US President, John F. Kennedy, was shot in Dallas, Texas in 1963. This is a formal account, so listen to how the events are explained. Then answer the following questions.

1. Name two other major events that have occurred since Kennedy was shot.

2. How do we know that JFK was much loved in Ireland?

3. What time was it in Ireland when the news came in about JFK?

4. What tragedy happened in Kerry to the O'Sullivan family on the same day that JFK was assassinated?

5. Where were they going in the tractor?

6. How many children were in the O'Sullivan family?

7. Who reared Stevie and his older sister after their mother died?

8. Name three popular 1960s bands/singers mentioned by DJ Larry Gogan.

B. Research

1. Find out what showbands, drainpipe trousers and winklepicker shoes were.

2. Why is Gerry and the Pacemakers' hit song, 'You'll Never Walk Alone' famous?

C. Creative Project – Make a Documentary

Working in pairs or groups, make a documentary about a topic which interests you. Choose your topic and research it. Record it as a radio documentary and present it to the class.

ASSESSMENT

Complete this assessment in your **PORTFOLIO**.

Oral Assessment

Imagine you are being interviewed on television by Ryan Tubridy about your favourite hobbies/pastimes. He says; 'Tell me about what you like to do in your spare time, what sport you play or what activities you are involved in after school or at weekends.' (Complete the Oral Assessment Checklist in your **PORTFOLIO**.)   (10 marks)

Written Assessment

A. Formal Writing

Choose two of the following tasks.

Job Interview

Imagine you are an employer preparing to interview a student for a summer job in your Summer Camp Activity Centre for children aged 6–10 years. Write out a list of five questions that you want to ask the job applicant.   (10 marks)

Survey

You have been asked to create a brief five-question survey (for your class) on hobbies and interests, offering suitable response options/choices. List the questions and response options.   (10 marks)

Instructions

Write a brief set of formal instructions (five bullet points) explaining how to care for a pet of your choice.   (10 marks)

Press Release

Imagine your local community centre or school is organising a table quiz to raise funds for charity. Create the details (remember the five Ws) and write the press release which will be given to the local radio and newspaper.   (10 marks)

Memo

Imagine you are a team leader in your local scouts/girl guides. You have been asked to send a memo via e-mail to all members telling them that next weekend's camping trip has been postponed until the good weather returns. Write the memo. Invent the necessary details.

(10 marks)

Debate

'Exercise is boring.' Write two points in favour or against this motion.   (10 marks)

Formal Letters

Write a formal letter to RTÉ complaining that there is too much sport on TV.   (10 marks)

ASSESSMENT

B. Informal Writing

Choose two of the following tasks.

Blog
Write a five sentence blog on your favourite topic.   (10 marks)

Reviews
Write an interesting review (five sentences) of one of the following: film, book, game, musical, concert or theatre show.   (10 marks)

Leaflets
Design the front cover of a leaflet promoting running as a fun activity.   (10 marks)

Invitations
Imagine your 16th birthday is coming up soon and you are having a big party in a hotel. Design your invitation.   (10 marks)

Travel Writing
Imagine you work for a travel agent. You were sent on a weekend trip to a place of your choice and asked to write a short travel article about it. Write five sentences about your location and experiences. It can be factual or persuasive or a mixture of both.   (10 marks)

Advertisements
Design an advertisement for a new type of ice-cream. The ad will be placed in a teenage magazine. Think about colour, image, text, layout, etc.   (10 marks)

Article for a Teenage Magazine
Write a brief (five sentence) article on the topic 'teenagers and technology today'. (10 marks)

C. Superlative Adjectives

Rewrite the following sentences in your copy using superlative adjectives:

1. Peter is the (fast) _____ runner on the relay team.

2. Kasha is the (tall) _____ girl on the basketball team.

3. Gucci is the _____ (expensive) brand in the shop.

4. The President is the _____ (important) person in Ireland.

5. She was wearing the (cool) _____ runners.

6. It was the (cold) _____ of days.

7. Sunrise is the _____ (beautiful) time of the day.

8. Everything went wrong for John last Friday. It was his (bad) _____ day ever.

9. Children find cartoons the _____ (interesting) programmes on television.

10. 'It's the _____ (delicious) soup ever! ' gushed Sophie.   (10 marks)

D. Self Assessment

I did well in _____

The things that I found difficult were _____

The things that I don't fully understand are _____

I would like to improve _____

CHAPTER 5

Drama, Short Story and Film: A Story to Tell

~ *My Learning Expectations* ~

In this chapter, I will:

- Examine how **stories are told through drama** (acts, scenes, stage directions, costumes, props, sets, narrator, lighting, sound)

- Write a **drama scene** (setting, plot, characters, dialogue, action)

- **Perform** parts from some of the extracts

- Read some **short stories** and examine the **key moments**

- Recognise the **descriptive style** of writing in short stories

- Write into my **PORTFOLIO** to keep a record of my creative writing and projects

- Examine how **stories are told through film** (visual impact, opening scene, camera shots and angles, camera movement, soundtrack, voiceover)

- Create a **film poster** (title, text, colour, image, font, symbols)

- Examine the **fairy-tale genre** (good versus evil, character analysis of heroes and villains)

- **Write a story** as a basis for a film script, then act it, film it and show it!

Drama, Short Story and Film: A Story to Tell

Drama

What is drama? The brilliant director Alfred Hitchcock once explained that:

Drama is life with the dull bits cut out.

Think about what we mean when we say 'he's being dramatic' or 'she's a drama queen'? Why do we say this about people; what are they doing to deserve this comment?

A **play/drama** is a piece of writing that uses conversation (**dialogue**) and action between characters to tell a story. Plays were originally written to be performed in front of a live audience, either in the court of the king, or in a field, on a street or in an outdoor theatre. Gradually indoor performances developed and stage sets and theatres were used. Plays are generally intended to be performed live on a stage, but are also performed on radio or television.

Drama also refers to all the elements that turn a play from a piece of writing into a performance, such as acting and using sets, costumes, lighting, etc.

Features of Drama

A **playwright** or dramatist writes a **play script** (**scriptwriting**) to tell the story. Play scripts are generally written in **acts,** which contain a number of **scenes,** where the conversation/dialogue is laid out in a clear format. A scene tells a part of the overall story, like a chapter in a novel or a stanza in a poem.

Play scripts can come from new, original ideas, or they can be created from existing novels, short stories, etc. and changed to suit the intended audience.

The script gives the actors and the director the information they need to stage the play, i.e. the list of **characters**, the **dialogue** and the **stage directions**.

The image of two masks associated with theatre comes from ancient Greece. Known as the 'comedy tragedy theatre masks', the images come from a time when theatrical masks were worn during performances. They show the two main types of drama: comedy (smiling face) and tragedy (frowning face).

Acts

An **act** is a section of the play. For example, there might be three sections to tell the story:

- The introduction/beginning
- The conflict/middle
- The resolution/ending

This could be covered in three acts. Plays can have as many or as few acts as are required to tell the story. Each act is made up of a number of scenes.

Scenes

A **scene** is a particular part of the action in a story. Scenes bring the story forward from one piece of action to the next. For example, in William Shakespeare's play *The Tempest*, a storm wrecks the ship in the first scene. This is followed by a survival scene, where the survivors scramble to land and recover from their ordeal.

Stage Directions

The playwright includes small directions, usually in brackets, directing the tone of voice or the action. These are put in italics beside the dialogue, for example (*angrily*), (*rushes to the door*), (*slams the bag down on the table*).

Other Features of Drama

Dramas also use some or all of the following to tell the story:

- **Costumes** are the clothes worn by the actors. They often tell us a lot about the characters: when the play is set, whether they are rich or poor, etc.
- **Props** are objects used by the actors in the performance: table, book, cup, etc.
- **Sets** are used on stage to show where the play is set: painted cloths hung at the back of the stage (**backdrop**), painted backgrounds (**scenery**), furniture, etc.
- **The narrator** is a speaker on stage who tells the audience more about the story/characters.
- **A voiceover** is a voice heard by the audience, but the speaker cannot be seen. This device is used to give more information about the story or characters.
- **Lighting** refers to the various lights used throughout the play to show daytime, night-time, inside, outside, atmosphere, etc.
- **Sound** refers to the actors' voices, as well as music and other sounds needed for the story: cats wailing outside, guns firing in the distance, etc.

A. Oral Language

In pairs or groups, discuss your experiences of being involved in or of watching a school drama, play, variety show, concert or musical. Then one person has to speak and tell the rest of the class about the experiences of the pair or group.

B. Personal Reflection

Think about your experiences of drama in primary school. Did you act in a drama, help with sets, costumes, etc. or simply watch a performance? In your **PORTFOLIO**, fill in the following drama record sheet about your experiences.

MY PRIMARY SCHOOL EXPERIENCES OF DRAMA

Name **a drama, show, concert or musical** that you experienced in primary school:	Name **another** drama, show, concert or musical that you experienced in primary school:
Props used:	**Props** used:
Costumes used:	**Costumes** used:
My **age** and the **class** I was in at that time:	My **age** and the **class** I was in at that time:
My role in the drama or show (if any):	**My role** in the drama or show (if any):
The impact it had on me as a **participant**: I felt .... I enjoyed .... I didn't like .... My overall feeling was	The impact it had on me as a **participant**: I felt .... I enjoyed .... I didn't like .... My overall feeling was ....
The impact it had on me as a **spectator**: I enjoyed .... I didn't like .... I felt .... Overall, I thought	The impact it had on me as a **spectator**: I enjoyed .... I didn't like .... I felt .... Overall, I thought ....
Skills that you need for drama:	
Problems that you can have with drama:	
Telling a story through **drama is different to telling it through film** because:	
A story told live on **stage is different to reading a book** because:	

Valley Song *by Athol Fugard*

Valley Song was written in 1996 and is set in South Africa. It tells the story of Veronica, who has been raised by her grandparents in a small village. Veronica's mother died while giving birth to her and Veronica never knew her father. When her grandmother died, Veronica had only her grandfather Buks (Oupa). She has grown up now and wants to follow her dream of being a famous singer. This means going to the big city, Johannesburg, and leaving her 76-year-old grandfather all alone. 'Author' is the name of another character in the drama.

Veronica: You must let me go, Oupa, otherwise I will also run away from you.

Buks: No! You mustn't do that! I will let you go. But explain it to me. I want to understand.

Veronica: Can Oupa explain to me how a little seed becomes a big pumpkin?

Buks: No.

Veronica: You said to me once it was a miracle.

Buks: That's right.

Veronica: You give it water and skoffel out the weeds and it just grows. Isn't that so?

Buks: Yes, that is so.

Veronica: I think it is like that with me and my singing, Oupa. I also can't tell you how it happens. All I know is that when I sing, I'm alive. My singing is my life. I must look after it the way Oupa looks after his vegetables. I know that if I stay here in the valley it will die. Does Oupa understand now?

Buks: No… but that doesn't matter. I'm frightened for you.

Veronica: I'm not.

Buks: It's a bad world out there, Veronica. Ja. Look at what happened to your mother.

Veronica: It won't happen to me, Oupa. You have made me strong. All that you have taught me has made me strong. Will you give me your blessing, Oupa?

Buks: Come here.
She does.
God bless you, my child.

Veronica: I love you, Oupa. (*She leaves, singing.*)

> *You're breaking my heart*
> *Valley that I love.*
> *You're breaking my heart*
> *When I say Goodbye.*
>
> *You gave me a start*
> *Valley that I love*
> *But now we must part*
> *'Cause I'm on my way.*

I'll sing all your songs
Valley that I love
So that people will know
How beautiful you are

The dream I've got
Is leading me away
But Valley that I love
I'll come back one day.

Author: So you're going to do it?

Veronica: Yes.

Author: Johannesburg?

Veronica: Yes. The School Principal is giving me a lift to Bellevue. Then I catch the train.

Author: Are you excited?

Veronica: Yes! But I'm also a little frightened. And sad. Are my eyes red?

Author: A little.

Veronica: I had a big cry when I said goodbye to my Oupa. So did he.

Author: So then don't go.

Veronica: No!

Author: Come on, Veronica. Think of your poor Oupa. He's only got a few years left. Make them happy ones. Go back and tell him that you've changed your mind…

Veronica: No, I can't do that! It isn't something I can change my mind about. I have to go.

Author: You make it sound like an order… 'Go To Johannesburg Veronica Jonkers… And Sing!'

Veronica: Yes! Don't laugh at me. This is what it feels like.

Author: I know. I wasn't laughing at you, I was laughing at myself.

Veronica: Then you understand?

Author: Oh yes.

Veronica: My Oupa didn't. I tried to explain it to him but he didn't understand.

Author: I would have been surprised if he had. You are all he's got left in the world. How can he understand losing that?

Veronica: He's not losing me! I told him I'm going to write to him every week. And the School Principal promised he will read my letters to him. And I'll come back to visit him whenever I can.

Author: And did that cheer him up?

Veronica: No.

Author: I always had a feeling that you would do it, you know.

Veronica: I don't believe you.

Author: No. It's true. The very first time I saw you dreaming on your apple box I had a feeling that one day you would be saying goodbye to the valley.

Veronica: Then why did you make it so hard for me? Always laughing and teasing me and trying to stop me? You're still doing it.

Author: I was testing you.

Veronica: Testing me?

Author: Yes.

Veronica: Like in the tests at school?

Author: Sort of.

Veronica: And did I pass?

Author: Oh yes. You're strong. I think you've got what it takes. But I must be honest with you, there's a selfish part of me that wanted you to fail that test.

Veronica: Why?

Author: A lot of reasons.

Veronica: Such as?

Author: Like your Oupa, I don't want to see you go. It means the Valley is changing and that selfish part of me doesn't want that to happen. It wants it to stay the unspoilt, innocent little world it was when I first discovered it. On all the late night walks that are left in my life, I want to find little Veronica Jonkers dreaming on her apple box outside Mrs Jooste's house. You see the truth is that I am not as brave about change as I would like to be. It involves letting go of things and I've discovered that that is a lot harder than I thought it was.

And then on top of all that, I am also jealous.

Veronica: Of what?

Author: You. Your youth. Your dreams. The future belongs to you now. There was a time when it was mine, when I dreamt about it the way you do, but not anymore. I've just about used up all of the 'Glorious Future' that I once had. But it isn't something you give up easily. I'm trying to hold onto it the way your Oupa wanted to hold on to you.

Veronica: (*Shaking her head*) You old men!

Author: That's right. And take my advice… Be careful of us!

Veronica: It's time for me to go.

Author: Good luck.

They salute each other.

The other arm, Veronica!

Veronica: Thank you. (*She starts to leave.*)

Author: Wait! Can you hear it?

Veronica: What?

Author: Listen. 'Veronica. Veronica. We want Veronica!'

Veronica: Now I'm excited again. (*She leaves the stage.*)

GLOSSARY

Skoffel: A skoffel is a piece of farming equipment used to rake soil – used here as a verb.

A. Reading

Rate this text for 'readability'. Write the word/phrase of your choice into your copy.

VERY EASY ☐   **EASY** ☐   **OKAY** ☐   **HARD** ☐   **VERY HARD** ☐

B. Literacy Questions

1. Why is Veronica leaving the valley?
2. Explain how Veronica's grandfather feels about her decision.
3. How does Veronica try to console her grandfather?
4. Do you think that Buks will reply to Veronica's letters? Explain your answer.
5. How did Author test Veronica?
6. List three reasons why Author didn't want her to go.
7. What do you think are the main themes in this drama?
8. Are these themes a part of our lives too? Explain your answer.

Proofread your answers and correct any mistakes.

C. Writing

Continue the story. Write a few more sentences, using the format above. Think about Buks and how he feels or what might happen next.

ACE this task!

D. Oral Language

Act out this scene. Take turns being the characters, choose a director/producer, and think about props and costumes you might need.

Lovers at Versailles *by Bernard Farrell*

In *Lovers at Versailles,* two sisters are at a nightclub. Anna is the older sister; Isobel is five years younger. Isobel has a boyfriend, Tony. He has gone to the bar to get drinks. Anna doesn't have a boyfriend and Isobel is trying to help her to meet someone. It's dark and shadowy in the nightclub.

2nd male: (*from the shadows* Enjoying it Isobel?

Isobel: Fabulous. Did you see Tony anywhere?

2nd male: Is he here?

Isobel: Went to the bar. If you see him, tell him we're nursing an empty bottle here.

2nd male: Will do. (*Goes*)

Isobel: By the way, this is my…

Anna: (*Angrily*) Don't!

Isobel: He's gone anyway. And who'd blame him – that face of yours would scatter a herd of elephants.

Anna: Thank you!

Isobel: I'm only saying it for your own good. You're nearly thirty, Anna.

Anna: Why don't you put it on a placard over my head?

Isobel: I'm just saying, I'm five years younger and already I have Tony… (*Suddenly*) Oh God, don't look, but there's that peculiar fella again, eyeing me up.

Anna: (*Peering*) Where?

Isobel: I said don't look!

Anna: I can't see anyone. Will I get Tony?

Isobel: And leave me on my own! God he's coming over.

Anna: Maybe we should just go?

Isobel: (*Anxiously*) Too late. Don't leave me. No matter what happens, you stay there. Do you hear me? Do you, do you?!

Anna: Yes! Yes! Yes! God.

David comes into the pool of light. He is, in this memory, aged thirty. He is a big man, but gentle and ill at ease.

David: (*To Anna*) Hello.

Isobel: (*Coldly*) I'm sorry – my boyfriend is with me – getting us drinks – back any moment now.

David: Oh, right. (*To Anna*) Hello, I hope you don't mind, but I've been looking at you, wondering if we met before. My name is David. (*Extends his hand*)

Anna: (*Taken off guard*) What? Oh, how do you do?

(*Shakes hands briefly*) I'm Annabelle.

David: Annabelle? That's a lovely name.

Anna: Thank you. And this is my sister, Isobel.

David: (*Amused*) Isobel?

Isobel: (*Coldly*) Hi.

David: Annabelle and Isobel?

Anna: (*Lightly*) Yes, and our mother's full name is Clarabelle.

Isobel: (*Angrily*) For God's sake!

David: (*Relaxing*) And don't tell me – your father's name is Jingle Bell?

Anna: (*Amused*) No, actually he's Stephen.

David: So you two and your mother are the only belles in the house?

Anna: (*Merrily*) Yes – except for the one on the front door.

David: Oh, very good.

Isobel: God!

David: (*To Anna*) And I really do know you from somewhere. Don't worry, it'll come to me.

An awkward silence. But David stays.

Anna: And do you like this place?

Isobel: (*Through her teeth*) Will you let him go!

David: Here? Oh yes, it's good, great – and really great furniture. They've spent money in here. Have you noticed the tables?

Anna: The tables? No.

David: That's pure teak and, if you look carefully, all those joints are perfectly dovetailed, not a screw to be seen anywhere.

Anna: (*Looking at the table*) Really?

David: And have you noticed the dance floor? Every inch of that floor is pure maple-wood, all in interlocking, five-inch, dovetailed panels, and the full unit internally supported and balanced. That's great craftsmanship, that floor.

Anna: You're not a carpenter are you?

Isobel:	(*Quietly*) Or a lunatic.
David:	Right first time, Annabelle – following in my father's footsteps.
Anna:	He makes tables and floors, does he?
David:	No, no. Don't laugh – he actually specialises in making coffins.
Isobel:	Jesus Christ!
Anna:	(*Seriously*) Does he really? Coffins?
David:	Oh yes. I help him out, but eventually I want to move into more general carpentry. I love the business. Since I was that high, I was always carving things out of wood. At present I'm carving a snow goose, as an ornament.
Anna:	Oh, lovely.
David:	Just in my spare time – get me away from the coffins for a while. And now I have you!
Anna:	Pardon?
David:	You work in that grocery shop – Sullivan's. That's where I've seen you.
Anna:	Oh yes, that's our father's shop.
David:	Oh, is he the oul'fel… the man that's always with you?
Anna:	Yes, that's daddy.
David:	And do you work there too, Isobel?
Isobel:	(*Coldly*) No, I don't.
Anna:	Isobel is a dental receptionist.
Isobel:	Dental assistant!
David:	Oh, right. Teeth. Great.

Another awkward silence. But David stays. The music now is Sinatra singing 'Strangers in the Night'.

Anna:	I love that – 'Strangers in the Night'.
David:	(*Enthusiastic*) Are you serious? That's my favourite song of all time.
Anna:	(*Enthusiastic*) Really? Honestly?
David:	Yes! It's actually my party piece. Any time I'm asked to sing, that's what I sing.
Anna:	(*Listening*) It's brilliant.
David:	I do the 'Do-be-do-be-do' bit and everything.
Isobel:	Christ! (*Then, calls*) Tony? Tony? Over here, Toe.

Tony comes into the light. He holds a drink. He is well-dressed, fit and confident and, in this memory, aged twenty-three.

Tony:	(*To Isobel*) You OK, sweetheart?
Isobel:	Darling, where's our drinks?
Tony:	(*Kissing Isobel*) OK, getting them now, don't panic.

Isobel:	(*Coolly*) But it's been ten minutes since…
Tony:	(*More passionate*) I got, ya know, distracted.
Isobel:	(*Embarrassed*) Tony! We have company!
Tony:	(*Still kissing*) Anna doesn't mind.
Isobel:	And! (*Indicates David standing nearby*)
Tony:	(*Stops*) Oh, hello. Thought you were, ya know, just standing there.
David:	No, I'm talking too.
Anna:	Tony, this is David.
Tony:	How ya. And you're, ya know, with Anna, are you?
David and Anna:	(*Together*) No, no!
Isobel:	No, no! He just came over… and stayed. He makes coffins.
Tony:	Pardon?
David:	No, my father does. I just help.
Tony:	Coffins? For dead people?
Anna:	(*Colder*) Yes, Tony, he's a carpenter. It's what carpenters do!
Tony:	Oh right. (*Little joke*) Long as you're not here looking for business.
David:	(*Seriously*) No, no, I came over because I recognised Annabelle from the shop.
Tony:	Who? Oh, Anna. Right.
David:	Are you connected with the shop, Tony?
Tony:	Me?
Isobel:	You don't know who Tony is?
Tony:	(*Proudly*) Ever go to see the Hoops playing?
Anna:	Tony plays football, David – for Shamrock Rovers.
David:	Oh, sorry. I don't actually…
Tony:	(*Annoyed*) It's OK – no sweat.
Isobel:	God, he really doesn't know who Tony is!
David:	I'm sorry, I've no interest in…
Isobel:	You didn't read in the papers that Tony is going for a trial at Leeds?
David:	A trial? Why, what's he done?
Tony:	Jaysus, I'll get the drinks.
David:	Oh, in football? Sorry.
Tony:	You staying here, David, or going?
David:	Oh, if it's OK, I'll stay – but I'll get these…
Tony:	No, no, you're all right… (*Going*)

David:	No, I'd like to…
Tony:	Just tell me what you want.
David:	I'll help you back with them then…
Tony:	Right. (*To Anna and Isobel, as he goes*) If I'm not back in five minutes, check for my body in the morgue!

Tony and David leave the pool of light.

GLOSSARY

Placard: A large notice or sign put up in a public place or carried by people.

Teak: A hard wood used for making furniture.

Dovetailed: Fitted together easily.

Interlocking: Joined together by means of parts that fit into other parts.

 # A. Reading

Rate this text for 'readability'. Write the word/phrase of your choice into your copy.

VERY EASY ☐   **EASY** ☐   **OKAY** ☐   **HARD** ☐   **VERY HARD** ☐

 # B. Literacy Questions

1. Where is the scene set or located?
2. Describe this setting as you imagine it to be.
3. What would you need if you were dramatising this scene to make it look realistic? What kind of lighting, furniture or props would you need for it? Write the list of items.
4. Imagine you are auditioning for a part in this play. Which of the four characters above would you like to be? Explain the reasons for your choice.
5. Which of the characters would you not like to be? Why?

Proofread your answers and correct any mistakes.

 # C. Writing

What do you think happens next? Write out the next scene. Use the same format as above. Make the next scene unpredictable and interesting but not too far-fetched!

ACE this task! Remember to brainstorm.

 # D. Oral Language

In groups, choose roles and act out the scene.

Elements of a Drama Scene

To write a drama scene, you need to do the following:

- Choose a **setting** (time and place)
- Decide on the issue or problem (the **plot**)
- Invent the **characters**
- Write out the **dialogue** and **stage directions**
- If it were the last scene of the play you would need to come up with a resolution/ending. It doesn't have to be a perfect or happy ending. You can choose a happy or sad ending or a 'compromise' ending.

For example, these are the elements in Athol Fugard's drama, *Valley Song*:

- **Setting:** A farm in rural South Africa in the 1990s
- **Plot:** Veronica wants to leave her grandfather and live in the city
- **Characters:** Veronica, her grandfather and a character called Author
- **Dialogue:** First between Veronica and Buks and then Veronica and Author
- **Stage directions:** *(She leaves, singing)*, *(Shaking her head)*, etc.

A. Writing

In your copy, fill in the following list for *Lovers at Versailles* by Bernard Farrell. Use the above example as a guide.

- Setting:
- Plot:
- Characters:
- Dialogue:
- Stage directions:
- How do you imagine the scene will end?
- How do you imagine the story will end for each of the characters?

STAGE DOOR ←

B. Creative Writing – Write a Drama Scene

In pairs or groups, try to write a drama scene in your **PORTFOLIO**.

- Think about an issue or problem, e.g. an argument between a parent and a teenager over going to the disco, over shopping, over unsuitable friends. Or it could be three teenagers who are arguing over an issue. Give yourselves three to five minutes to dramatise this issue.
- Think about the characters (two or three characters will suit for a first attempt at creating a drama scene).
- When and where is the scene happening?
- What is being said?
- What actions do the characters do during their dialogue: *(throws cup)*, *(storms out)*, *(cries softly)*?
- How will it end?

ACE this task!

Watershed *by G.P. Gallivan*

In *Watershed,* Steve and Kate Dowling have been married for 19 years and are still in love, but Kate is going through a difficult time and there is tension in the house. They have two daughters; one aged 16, the other aged 17. The scene opens with Steve and the two girls offstage, while Kate is on stage in the drawing room (sitting room).

Steve: (*Off, angrily*) Well, since I've already promised you, you can go for this once.

Girls: (*Off*) Thanks, Dad.

Steve: (*Off*) But if ever you dare to speak to your mother like that again…

Kate: (*Angrily, shouting*) I only told them to tidy their rooms!

Girls: (*Off*) But we already have!

Kate: Everything stuffed in the wardrobe. You've only got to open the door, and it's all over the place.

Girls: (*Off*) Honestly, you just can't satisfy her…

Steve: (*Off, angrily*) And you don't call your mother *her*!

Girls: (*Off*) Anything we do is wrong.

Steve: (*Off*) That's enough out of you two. You'd better go before I change my mind.

Kate: I'd keep them in Steve.

Girls: (*Off, hurriedly*) We're going…

Kate: They should be taught a lesson.

Steve: Goodnight.

Girls: (*Off*) We'll be home by tea tomorrow.

Kate: You'd better be!

Steve: (*Off*) Go on then, enjoy yourselves.

Front door closes, Kate reacts in a tense, taut fashion. After a few moments, enter Steve, almost tentatively.

Steve: I'm sorry, love.

Kate: They've had their way again.

Steve: We're rid of them for a night.

Kate: (*Ignoring last remark*) You never take any notice of me.

Steve: Ah for heaven's sake…

Kate: They wind you around their little fingers.

Steve: Be reasonable Kate.

Kate: I'm too damned reasonable… that's my trouble.

Steve: (*Placatingly*) Oh, I know what they are…

Kate: You don't. How could you? You're not here half the time.

Steve: Two stepped-up aggravating little brats, but we've still got to make the effort.

Kate: (*Sharply*) You think I don't?

Steve: Of course you do… but they're so bloody aggravating they bring out the worst in both of us. But we've got to be careful that we don't react too violently and drive them away from us.

Kate: (*Defensively*) *Those* two?

Steve: Well, it *is* a danger.

Kate: You always take their side – and they have no regard – none at all for me.

Steve: That's not true either.

Kate: I've done everything I can for those girls…

Steve: Of course you have. They just don't understand.

Kate: (*Derisively*) Too young, I suppose?

Steve: Young people are always thoughtless.

Kate: They're not the only ones.

Steve: (*Angrily*) Stop needling.

Kate: At seventeen and sixteen…

Steve: It's still too young.

Kate: I was working at their age, but they're not supposed to wash a cup… Expect me to wait on them hand and foot…

Steve: (*Angrily*) And you *do*, I suppose.

Kate: I would if I was fool enough. *You'd* like me to.

Steve: I'm not going to argue.

Kate: Because you can't deny it. (*Derisively*) Too young!

Steve: (*Suddenly losing control*) All right, they *are* too young… too young to have to put up with –

Kate: (*Furiously*) My tantrums?

Steve: Yes your bloody tantrums! The family has been torn apart for the last ten months…

Kate: And it's all my fault…

Steve: Well, I'm damned sure it hasn't been mine. (*Suddenly quieting down, miserably.*) I'm sorry Kate… It's your health.

Kate: (*Quietly*) My nerves, you mean.

Steve: Yes.

Kate: (*Angrily*) Well I… (*Stops, suddenly tearful.*) Oh Steve, what am I to do?

A. Reading

Rate this text for 'readability'. Write the word/phrase of your choice into your copy.

VERY EASY ☐　　　**EASY** ☐　　　**OKAY** ☐　　　**HARD** ☐　　　**VERY HARD** ☐

B. Literacy Questions

1. Use a dictionary to find the meaning of the following stage directions: *tentatively, placatingly, derisively*. Now put each one in a sentence.

2. Describe in detail the setting or location of this scene as you imagine it to be.

3. What are Kate and Steve arguing about?

Proofread your answers and correct any mistakes.

C. Creative Writing – Write the Next Scene

Think about the two sisters. Invent names and personalities for them. Write the next scene for them after they leave the house. Use the scriptwriting format. Think about the following:

- Where are they going?
- Who are they meeting?
- Where will they stay the night?
- How will they get to and from their destination?
- What events will happen?
- Will they be home on time?
- What kind of welcome will they get when they return?
- What will they say about their experiences?
- What might have happened while they were away?

ACE this task!

Waiting for Godot *by Samuel Beckett*

The characters Estragon and Vladimir are near a tree waiting for Godot.

Listening

1. Listen to the extract before you read the script – it's more effective if you simply listen.

- Jot down your impressions of what you hear.
- What kind of characters are Estragon and Vladimir? What class in society do you think they belong to? What problem do they have in this scene?

2. Listen to the same extract read with different accents.

- Having listened to the extract in a different accent, has your impression of the characters changed?
- What do you think of them now?
- What relevance or importance is attached to accents?

Act 1

Estragon moves to centre, halts with his back to the auditorium

Estragon: Charming spot. (*He turns, advances to the front, halts facing the auditorium*) Inspiring prospects. (*He turns to Vladimir*) Let's go.

Vladimir: We can't.

Estragon: Why not?

Vladimir: We're waiting for Godot.

Estragon: (*Despairingly*) Ah! (*He pauses*) You're sure it was here?

Vladimir: What?

Estragon: That we were to wait.

Vladimir: He said by the tree.

They look at the tree.

Do you see any others?

Estragon: What is it?

Vladimir: I don't know. A willow.

Estragon: Where are the leaves?

Vladimir: It must be dead.

Estragon: No more weeping.

Vladimir: Or perhaps it's not the season.

Estragon: Looks to me like a bush.

Vladimir: A shrub.

Estragon: A bush.

Vladimir: A… What are you insinuating? That we've come to the wrong place?

Estragon: He should be here?

Vladimir: He didn't say for sure he'd come.

Estragon: And if he doesn't come?

Vladimir: We'll come back tomorrow.

Estragon: And then the day after tomorrow.

Vladimir: Possibly.

Estragon: And so on.

Vladimir: The point is—

Estragon: Until he comes.

Vladimir: You're merciless.

Estragon: We came here yesterday.

Vladimir: Ah no, there you're mistaken.

Estragon: What did we do yesterday?

Vladimir: What did we do yesterday?

Estragon: Yes.

Vladimir: Why… (*Angrily*) Nothing is certain when you're about.

Estragon: In my opinion we were here.

Vladimir: (*Looking around*) You recognise the place?

Estragon: I didn't say that.

Vladimir: Well?

Estragon: That makes no difference.

Vladimir: All the same… that tree… (*He turns towards the auditorium*)… that bog.

Estragon: You're sure it was this evening?

Vladimir: What?

Estragon: That we were to wait.

Vladimir: He said Saturday. (*He pauses*) I think.

Estragon: You think.

Vladimir: I must have made a note of it. (*He fumbles in his pockets, bursting with miscellaneous rubbish*)

Estragon: (*Very insidiously*) But what Saturday? And is it Saturday? Is it not rather Sunday? (*He pauses*) Or Monday? (*He pauses*) Or Friday?

Vladimir: (*Looking wildly about him, as though the date was inscribed in the landscape*) It's not possible!

Estragon: Or Thursday?

Vladimir: What'll we do?

Estragon: If he came yesterday and we weren't here you may be sure he won't come again today.

Vladimir: But you say we were here yesterday.

Estragon: I may be mistaken. (*He pauses*) Let's stop talking for a minute, do you mind?

Vladimir: (*Feebly*) All right.

GLOSSARY

Inspiring prospects: Feels like something good will happen.
Insinuating: Saying something, but in an indirect way.
Miscellaneous: Various kinds of things.
Insidiously: In a sly way, but meaning to do harm.
Inscribed: Carved onto.

A. Reading

Rate this text for 'readability'. Write the word/phrase of your choice into your copy.

VERY EASY ☐   **EASY** ☐   **OKAY** ☐   **HARD** ☐   **VERY HARD** ☐

B. Oral Language

In pairs, act out the above scene. Use your own accents or experiment with different accents.

C. Writing

Imagine you are Godot. Write a postcard to Estragon and Vladimir.

- Explain why you have kept them waiting.
- Apologise.
- Make a new arrangement to meet them at a specific time and place.
- Remember to use the tone used in the above extract in order to make your response fit the extract.

ACE this task! Remember RAFT.

Short Stories

A **short story** is a story that is much shorter and less complex than a novel. These pieces of fiction use the same **descriptive writing style** and **features of writing** discussed in Chapter 2. They vary in length; some are very brief (a couple of pages), others are longer (10 or 20 pages). Each one is a glimpse at a character or a snatch of action at a particular time.

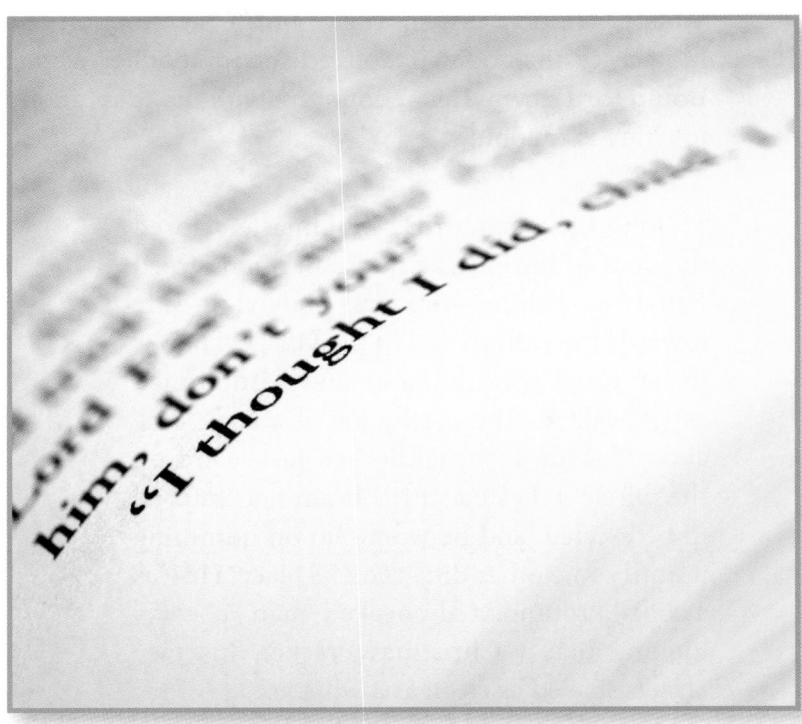

Writers often put a collection of their short stories into one book. Each story is usually a separate story, unconnected to the others in the collection. You can dip in and out of a collection of short stories, reading the different, unconnected stories whenever you want. There's no compulsion to continue reading the entire book, as you might do with a novel.

Features of Short Stories

Short stories use the same features that we have seen for novels and dramas:

- Setting
- Plot (conflict/action)
- Characters
- Resolution/ending
- As with a novel, a short story is written in first or third person narration and uses a descriptive style of writing.

Key moments are important in all stories, whether the stories are told as novels, short stories, dramas or films. A key moment is simply an important event or incident that happens in the story, for example when a character is suddenly shocked or surprised, when someone dies, when a secret is revealed, when the truth is blurted out, or when an accident happens.

The key moments have an impact on the characters. They help the characters to develop and they help the story to continue. They maintain the reader's interest too – if nothing much happened, the reader would get bored.

 ## Reading

Read the following examples of short stories and try to pick out the key moments in them as you read them.

Master Melody *by Sigerson Clifford*

'Master Melody' is a short story from a collection entitled *Irish Short Stories*. Master Melody is an eccentric, retired school teacher who is sad to see his old school building being torn down. His encounters with the teaching Inspectors are funny, while his final journey is touching.

John Melody, retired schoolmaster, closed the door of his lodging house in Main Street, Ballytwig, behind him and walked briskly towards the eastern end of the village. He was in his usual good humour and he hummed as he walked. The catchy air of a song, one about leaving Donegal he had just heard on the wireless, nested in his brain and refused to be evicted, and he would go on humming it until some other ditty took its place. He was a small, rotund, red-cheeked man, cheery-looking like a Christmas cracker, his face always shaved as clean as a whistle.

The street was bare except for a black-and-tan beagle, and a brown horse anchored to the electric-light pole outside Canty's pub. When he came by the animal he lifted his hat courteously and said 'Good evening, Horse.' The horse jingled his head harness as though in reply and the Master chuckled. He liked animals and, with the exception of Bill Carroll's bull, which once made him swim the river with his clothes on, they liked him.

He always saluted horses, no matter how important the person in his company at the time. When he landed in Ballytwig forty-odd years ago, the villagers had stared in amazement at this idiosyncrasy of his and wondered if he was really a schoolmaster. They expected their teachers to have dignity, which meant wearing a stern, unsmiling face and not lifting your hat to a horse. The Master ignored the pained and puzzled expressions, and beamed upon the good citizens like a rich American uncle. Then they found him shaping successful scholars from the rude clay that was their sons, and they decided that he was a genius, and as such entitled to be something out of the ordinary in what he said or did.

There was the evening he walked from the school with the Inspector who had come to sit in judgement upon him. Mike Donnelly's horse stood under a rail of turf outside the Emporium. He saw the Master coming and threw up his head in greeting. The Master lifted his hat and said, 'Good evening, Tom.' The Inspector blinked and looked hard at him. He was a grim man with the weight of the world, the stars and the planets on his narrow shoulders, and when they'd come to button the coffin about him nobody would mourn his passing and only the inscription over his grave would remember him until the moss covered it.

'Do you usually salute horses in public, Melody?' he had asked, the thin lips making a ruler of his mouth.

'Only when they salute me,' the Master answered gravely. 'Some of them can be quite snobbish, you know. Just like humans.'

The horse neighed behind them.

'Old Tom is vexed with me. I usually have a square of sugar for him. You don't happen to have a lump in your pocket, Inspector?'

'Certainly not,' snapped the Inspector.

He turned the corner to his hotel, and the Master went in his own door, chuckling merrily. He got out his diary and wrote the events of the day.

'Inspector Dancy called. A sour, ill-humoured body. He wouldn't talk to a pig. What does he get from life?'

In the hotel the Inspector penned his report to the Department.

'Mister Melody has his pupils in excellent shape, but the man himself strikes me as being mental. He completely lacks dignity and holds conversations with horses on the village streets.'

The Master's evening walk always took him past the old school, down Pat Dannigh's Height and on to the Three Eye Bridge, where he usually stopped to light up his pipe and study the life that flowed over and under the grey humpy arches. The brown trout splashing in the pools, and the small eels wriggling across the stones, swallows stunting under the tent of the sky, brown rabbits slipping through the briars, had always given him a measure of comfort and now that he was alone and lonely he turned to them for consolation. He had never married, his school was shuttered and deserted, his pupils had grown, scattered and married, and were sending their sons to the Brothers. His school among the hazels now served as a windbreak for cattle when the storms blew in from the sea.

As he drew near the school he heard Dick Sullivan's voice raised in a come-all-ye behind the screen of hazel bushes, and the rattle of a hammer upon slates. He slipped through the broken gate and looked up. Dick was straddling the roof, stripping the slates and letting them slide down to the grass. The Master felt himself grow cold as he watched.

'Richard!' he called out after a while. Sullivan stopped working and waved to him.

'Hello, Master,' he greeted him.

'What are you doing to our old school, Richard?'

'I'm taking it home with me, Master. I bought the stones to build a cow-house. 'Twill remind me of old times every time I milk the cows in it. I hope the cows will learn easier than I did anyway. Wisha, do you remember, Master, the composition I did for the Inspector?'

The Master remembered, smiling as he did so, in spite of the pain in his mind. Dancy had ordered the pupils to write an essay on a walk in the country, to test their powers of observation. Afterwards he read some of them to the school as examples of clear writing and clearer observation. Before he read Dick's, which he kept like good wine for the last, he described it as a classic which should not on any account be plagiarised. It was short and sweet and no nonsense.

'"A Walk in the Country". I went for a walk yesterday evening around Mulvey's Mill. I saw nobody and nobody saw me. Richard Sullivan.'

The Master continued towards the river, his brain numbed by the sacrilege of his school's destruction. To him it was not an inanimate thing with a coat of whitewash and a helmet of slate. It was a boy in a gansey, who threw away his shoes when May pinned the stars to the hawthorn, and ran over the long buttercupped grass among the hazel trees. It had a voice that chanted the death of Master Tommy Rook, or King Bruce and the Spider, or shrilled into battle with Kelly of Killane when Mrs Casey came once a week for the music-hour. It had an untidy thatch hair and a forehead that worried itself into corrugated-iron wrinkles over the speed of trains per hour and the profit or loss on shiploads of tea from Ceylon. It was half a century of boys. His boys.

The following evening on his way to the river he slipped through the broken gate again. The roof was stripped and the rafters were naked and lean in the cold air. Dick Sullivan stood smoking and talking to Timmy the Boots from Donegan's Hotel. Timmy had been one of his favourite pupils at school and his devoted ally afterwards. No Inspector could steal a march on him with Timmy meeting the trains and ready to hop on his bicycle and burn up the half-mile to the school while you'd be winking.

'There's a strange man with a small brown case after coming on the 11 o'clock, Master. He's not a commercial so, maybe, he's from the Department.'

'Thank you, Timmy. Now that we are forewarned you can rest assured the Department will have sufficient reason to think highly of scholarship in Ballytwig.'

Only once did an Inspector catch him napping, but that wasn't Timmy's fault. It was the time the heatwave flattened Ballytwig, which was so used to rain that it nearly died of thirst and too much sunshine after a week of it. The boys turned listlessly in their desks and wiped the perspiration from their freckles. The Master went to open the window wider and saw the sandbanks one hundred yards away, brown and wet and beautiful, possessed by gulls and oystercatchers. He turned to the pupils and announced with mock gravity:

'I am now going to the sandbanks for a swim. You can have the choice of coming with me or staying in your desks.'

They were already in the sea when he arrived, the skilful twisting and turning like otters, the beginners splashing and shouting in the shallows. He slipped into his bathing costume and the sand squeezed itself soft and hot between his toes.

'Is the water warm, boys!' he called out.

'You could hatch a goose's egg in it, Master,' declared Dick Sullivan, who made up in the spoken word all he lacked in the written.

After his swim he sat in the sun, watching them enjoying themselves as though they had been locked away in some dark cave for twelve months. A few years and they would nearly all be scattered, he thought, in London or Boston or Melbourne, pining for the sea on the brown sand, and the majesty of the mountains. They would.

'Master!'

Dick was beside him whispering urgently.

'Yes, Richard?'

'There's a strange man after leaving the school and he's coming this way. Maybe he's an Inspector. He has the brown bag anyway.'

The Master looked over his shoulder and saw the stranger crossing the fields. He pursed his lips and sighed.

'Richard, I fear we are undone. Swim away, my boy, and enjoy yourselves while I have a word with him.'

The stranger towered over the Master like a lighthouse. He had blue eyes that twinkled and the mouth under the grey moustache was humorous. He was Inspector O'Toole, he said, and Dancy was in hospital suffering from the bubonic plague or some such ailment, and he was doing the Dancy rounds. The devil is as droll as myself, thought the Master, and he began to complain of the heatwave and the boys wilting like cut flowers in their desks, so he thought it wiser to freshen them up a bit before one of them died on his hands.

'You took a leaf from the copybook of Ancient Greece,' smiled the Inspector.

'Yes, Inspector, I believe the Greeks have a word for it,' said the Master.

'The Department has one, too, Mister Melody, but we won't give them the chance to use it. I think I'll join you in a swim. I have a costume in my case.'

Afterwards the Inspector gathered the boys about him and flung questions at them while the Master stood aside, silently praying that the angel of inspiration would settle his wings over them for that day at least. And, indeed, the water that entered their ears must have cleansed their brains, for they spoke out as though the answers were written on the sand in front of them.

That evening while Mrs Sweeney was making his tea, the Master took out his diary.

'On very rare occasions,' he wrote, 'a man is born into this world and all the bells of heaven ring out loud and clear to announce his birth. Such a man is Inspector O'Toole.'

The Inspector wrote his report in his motor car, lifting his head now and again to watch the sun setting behind the western islands.

'… In a mad, bad world, it is refreshing to meet a man of Mr Melody's splendid sanity. His pupils are the most intelligent I have met in my travels. I was struck also by their cleanliness, and I must be pardoned for thinking that he may have heard of my coming and had them all washed especially for me.'

Every evening the Master walked out the road and watched the school shrinking like a sixpenny shirt. The spring was going from his step now and he was so busy with his thoughts that he failed to return the salutations from the people he met on the way. The Master is failing, they told each other, and you'd swear a few weeks ago that he'd live to be as old as a bush in a fairy fort.

He spent the day before Christmas Eve in bed, and he wouldn't have done it if Mrs Sweeney hadn't bullied him into resting. He had lodged under her roof so long now she became alarmed at the thought of losing him, and these men who were never a day sick in their lives were always the quickest to go in the heel of the hunt. Never having known illness, they hadn't the wits to fight it when it came.

On Christmas Eve he heard the door close behind Mrs Sweeney as she went to meet her two daughters, with civil service jobs in Dublin, who were arriving on the six o'clock train. He got out of bed and dressed himself, and went into the street. The shops were still wide awake and brisk with selling, and a mournful ballad ribboned out of a public house to make the night lonesome.

He went out the road slowly, leaning on his stick, until he came to the broken gate. He groped in and looked for his school. There was nothing at all left of it now except the moonlit black squares that next spring's grass would wipe off the slate for good.

A great tiredness enveloped him and he sat down on a big stone inside the gate. The candles were burning in the mountainy windows across the estuary and, as he watched them, they began to advance and retire like dancers. And then, suddenly, they were quenched.

Dick Sullivan with his horse and cart came singing out of the village. He passed by the gate where the Master was huddled. He saw nobody. And nobody saw him.

GLOSSARY

Wireless: Radio.

Saluted: Waved hello.

Idiosyncrasy: Unusual characteristic.

Vexed: Annoyed.

Plagiarised: Copied from someone else without giving them the credit.

Sacrilege: Against religious teaching.

Inanimate: Non-living thing.

Listlessly: In a tired way.

Gravity: Seriousness.

Droll: Funny.

Sixpenny shirt: A cheap, poor quality, cotton shirt which shrinks when washed.

Heel of the hunt: At the end or the closing stages of something.

Ribboned out: Flowed out.

A. Reading

1. Rate this text for 'readability'. Write the word/phrase of your choice in your copy.

   VERY EASY ☐   **EASY** ☐   **OKAY** ☐   **HARD** ☐   **VERY HARD** ☐

2. Copy the following headings into your copy and fill in the appropriate words from the text of 'Master Melody'.

Gist words (words which I half figured out)	Words I didn't understand at all

B. Literacy Questions

1. Do you think that Master Melody liked animals? Find two points to support your answer.
2. Compare the two inspectors, Mr Dancy and Mr O'Toole; think about their actions and what they say.
3. List as many similes as you can find in the story (similes use 'like' or 'as').
4. From the evidence in the story, what kind of place is Ballytwig?
5. Find two examples of personification in the story and explain them.
6. List four examples of old-fashioned sayings (idioms).

Proofread your answers and correct any mistakes.

C. Oral Language

In pairs or groups, discuss the ending of the story.

The Secret Life of Walter Mitty *by James Thurber*

This is James Thurber's most famous short story. It first appeared in *The New Yorker* magazine in 1939. It has been adapted to screenplay twice; in 1947 and 2013.

"We're going through!" The Commander's voice was like thin ice breaking. He wore his full-dress uniform, with the heavily braided white cap pulled down rakishly over one cold grey eye. "We can't make it, sir. It's spoiling for a hurricane, if you ask me." "I'm not asking you, Lieutenant Berg," said the Commander. "Throw on the power lights! Rev her up to 8,500! We're going through!" The pounding of the cylinders increased: ta-pocketa-pocketa-pocketa-*pocketa-pocketa*. The Commander stared at the ice forming on the pilot window. He walked over and twisted a row of complicated dials. "Switch on No. 8 auxiliary!" he shouted. "Switch on No. 8 auxiliary!" repeated Lieutenant Berg. "Full strength in No. 3 turret!" shouted the Commander. "Full strength in No. 3 turret!" The crew, bending to their various tasks in the huge, hurtling eight-engined Navy hydroplane, looked at each other and grinned. "The Old Man'll get us through," they said to one another. "The Old Man ain't afraid of Hell!" ...

"Not so fast! You're driving too fast!" said Mrs. Mitty. "What are you driving so fast for?"

"Hmm?" said Walter Mitty. He looked at his wife, in the seat beside him, with shocked astonishment. She seemed grossly unfamiliar, like a strange woman who had yelled at him in a crowd. "You were up to fifty-five," she said. "You know I don't like to go more than forty. You were up to fifty-five." Walter Mitty drove on toward Waterbury in silence, the roaring of the SN202 through the worst storm in twenty years of Navy flying fading in the remote, intimate airways of his mind. "You're tensed up again," said Mrs. Mitty. "It's one of your days. I wish you'd let Dr. Renshaw look you over."

Walter Mitty stopped the car in front of the building where his wife went to have her hair done. "Remember to get those overshoes while I'm having my hair done," she said. "I don't need overshoes," said Mitty. She put her mirror back into her bag. "We've been all through that," she said, getting out of the car. "You're not a young man any longer." He raced the engine a little." Why don't you wear your gloves? Have you lost your gloves?" Walter Mitty reached in a pocket and brought out the gloves. He put them on, but after she had turned and gone into the building and he had driven on to a red light, he took them off again. "Pick it up, brother!" snapped a cop as the lights changed, and Mitty hastily pulled on his gloves and lurched ahead. He drove around the streets aimlessly for a time, and then he drove past the hospital on his way to the parking lot.

... "It's the millionaire banker, Wellington McMillan," said the pretty nurse. "Yes?" said Walter Mitty, removing his gloves slowly. "Who has the case?" "Dr. Renshaw and Dr. Benbow, but there are two specialists here, Dr. Remington from New York and Mr. Pritchard-Mitford from London. He flew over." A door opened down a long, cool corridor and Dr. Renshaw came out. He looked distraught and haggard. "Hello, Mitty," he said. "We're having the devil's own time with McMillan, the millionaire banker and close personal friend of Roosevelt. Obstreosis of the ductal tract. Tertiary. Wish you'd take a look at him."

"Glad to," said Mitty.

In the operating room there were whispered introductions: "Dr. Remington, Dr. Mitty. Mr. Pritchard-Mitford, Dr. Mitty." "I've read your book on streptothricosis," said Pritchard-Mitford, shaking hands. "A brilliant performance, sir." "Thank you," said Walter Mitty. "Didn't know you were in the States, Mitty," grumbled Remington. "Coals to Newcastle, bringing

Mitford and me up here for a tertiary." "You are very kind, said Mitty. A huge, complicated machine, connected to the operating table, with many tubes and wires, began at this moment to go pocketa-pocketa-pocketa." The new anaesthetiser is giving way!" shouted an interne. "There is no one in the East who knows how to fix it!" "Quiet, man!" said Mitty, in a low, cool voice. He sprang to the machine, which was now going pocketa-pocketa-queep-pocketa-queep. He began fingering delicately a row of glistening dials. "Give me a fountain pen!" he snapped. Someone handed him a fountain pen. He pulled a faulty piston out of the machine and inserted the pen in its place. "That will hold for ten minutes," he said. "Get on with the operation." A nurse hurried over and whispered to Renshaw, and Mitty saw the man turn pale. "Coreopsis has set in," said Renshaw nervously. "If you would take over, Mitty?" Mitty looked at him and at the craven figure of Benbow, who drank, and at the grave, uncertain faces of the two great specialists. "If you wish," he said. They slipped a white gown on him; he adjusted a mask and drew on thin gloves; nurses handed him shining . . .

"Back it up, Mac! Look out for that Buick!" Walter Mitty jammed on the brakes. "Wrong lane, Mac," said the parking lot attendant, looking at Mitty closely. "Gee. Yeh," muttered Mitty. He began cautiously to back out of the lane marked "Exit Only." "Leave her sit there," said the attendant. "I'll pull her away." Mitty got out of the car. "Hey, better leave the key." "Oh," said Mitty, handing the man the ignition key. The attendant vaulted into the car, backed it up with insolent skill, and put it where it belonged.

They're so damn cocky, thought Walter Mitty, walking along Main Street; they think they know everything. Once he had tried to take his chains off, outside New Milford, and he had got them wound around the axles. A man had had to come out in a wrecking car and unwind them, a young, grinning garageman. Since then Mrs. Mitty always made him drive to a garage to have the chains taken off. The next time, he thought, I'll wear my right arm in a sling; they won't grin at me then. I'll have my right arm in a sling and they'll see I couldn't possibly take the chains off myself. He kicked at the slush on the sidewalk. "Overshoes," he said to himself, and he began looking for a shoe store.

When he came out into the street again, with the overshoes in a box under his arm, Walter Mitty began to wonder what the other thing was his wife had told him to get. She had told him, twice, before they set out from their house for Waterbury. In a way he hated these weekly trips to town - he was always getting something wrong. Kleenex, he thought, Squibb's, razor blades? No. Toothpaste, toothbrush, bicarbonate, carborundum, initiative and referendum? He gave it up. But she would remember it. "Where's the what's-its-name?" she would ask. "Don't tell me you forgot the what's-its-name." A newsboy went by shouting something about the Waterbury trial. ... "Perhaps this will refresh your memory." The District Attorney suddenly thrust a heavy automatic at the quiet figure on the witness stand. "Have you ever seen this before?" Walter Mitty took the gun and examined it expertly. "This is my Webley-Vickers 50.80," he said calmly. An excited buzz ran around the courtroom. The Judge rapped for order. "You are a crack shot with any sort of firearms, I believe?" said the District Attorney, insinuatingly. "Objection!" shouted Mitty's attorney. "We have shown that the defendant could not have fired the shot. We have shown that he wore his right arm in a sling on the night of the fourteenth of July." Walter Mitty raised his hand briefly and the bickering attorneys were stilled. "With any known make of gun," he said evenly, "I could have killed Gregory Fitzhurst at three hundred feet *with my left hand*." Pandemonium broke loose in the courtroom. A woman's scream rose above the bedlam and suddenly a lovely, dark-haired girl was in Walter Mitty's arms. The District Attorney struck at her savagely. Without rising from his chair, Mitty let the man have it on the point of the chin. "You miserable cur!"...

"Puppy biscuit," said Walter Mitty. He stopped walking and the buildings of Waterbury rose up out of the misty courtroom and surrounded him again. A woman who was passing laughed. "He said 'Puppy Biscuit,'" she said to her companion. "That man said 'Puppy biscuit' to himself." Walter Mitty hurried on. He went into an A. & P., not the first one he came to but a smaller one farther up the street. "I want some biscuit for small, young dogs," he said to the clerk. "Any special brand, sir?" The greatest pistol shot in the world thought a moment. "It says 'Puppies Bark for It' on the box," said Walter Mitty.

His wife would be through at the hairdresser's in fifteen minutes, Mitty saw in looking at his watch, unless they had trouble drying it; sometimes they had trouble drying it. She didn't like to get to the hotel first; she would want him to be there waiting for her as usual. He found a big leather chair in the lobby, facing a window, and he put the overshoes and the puppy biscuit on the floor beside it. He picked up an old copy of Liberty and sank down into the chair. "Can Germany Conquer the World Through the Air?" Walter Mitty looked at the pictures of bombing planes and of ruined streets.

. . . "The cannonading has got the wind up in young Raleigh, sir," said the sergeant. Captain Mitty looked up at him through tousled hair. "Get him to bed," he said wearily. "With the others. I'll fly alone." "But you can't, sir," said the sergeant anxiously. "It takes two men to handle that bomber and the Archies are pounding hell out of the air. Von Richtman's circus is between here and Saulier." "Somebody's got to get that ammunition dump," said Mitty. "I'm going over. Spot of brandy?" He poured a drink for the sergeant and one for himself. War thundered and whined around the dugout and battered at the door. There was a rending of wood and splinters flew through the room. "A bit of a near thing," said Captain Mitty carelessly. "The box barrage is closing in," said the sergeant, "We only live once, Sergeant," said Mitty, with his faint, fleeting smile. "Or do we?" He poured another brandy and tossed it off. "I never see a man could hold his brandy like you, sir," said the sergeant. "Begging your pardon, sir." Captain Mitty stood up and strapped on his huge Webley-Vickers automatic. "It's forty kilometres through hell, sir," said the sergeant. Mitty finished one last brandy. "After all," he said softly, "what isn't?" The pounding of the cannon increased; there was the rat-tat-tatting of machine guns, and from somewhere came the menacing pocketa-pocketa-pocketa of the new flame-throwers. Walter Mitty walked to the door of the dugout humming 'Aupres de Ma Blonde.' He turned and waved to the sergeant. "Cheerio!" he said ...

Something struck his shoulder. "I've been looking all over this hotel for you," said Mrs. Mitty. "Why do you have to hide in this old chair? How did you expect me to find you?" "Things close in," said Walter Mitty vaguely. "What?" Mrs. Mitty said. "Did you get the what's its-name? The puppy biscuit? What's in that box?" "Overshoes," said Mitty. "Couldn't you have put them on in the store?" "I was thinking," said Walter Mitty. "Does it ever occur to you that I am sometimes thinking?" She looked at him. "I'm going to take your temperature when I get you home," she said.

They went out through the revolving doors that made a faintly derisive whistling sound when you pushed them. It was two blocks to the parking lot. At the drugstore on the corner she said, "Wait here for me. I forgot something. I won't be a minute." She was more than a minute. Walter Mitty lighted a cigarette. It began to rain, rain with sleet in it. He stood up against the wall of the drugstore, smoking . . . He put his shoulders back and his heels together. "To hell with the handkerchief," said Walter Mitty scornfully. He took one last drag on his cigarette and snapped it away. Then, with that faint, fleeting smile playing about his lips, he faced the firing squad; erect and motionless, proud and disdainful, Walter Mitty the Undefeated, inscrutable to the last.

A. Reading

1. Rate this text for 'readability'. Write the word/phrase of your choice into your copy.

VERY EASY ☐   EASY ☐   OKAY ☐   HARD ☐   VERY HARD ☐

2. Copy the following headings into your copy and fill in the appropriate words from the text of 'The Secret Life of Walter Mitty'.

Gist words (words which I half figured out)	Words I didn't understand at all

 ## B. Literacy Questions

1. What kind of a character is Walter Mitty? Use evidence from the story to support your answer.
2. Is the opening paragraph of the story set in Walter's real world or in his imaginary, fictional world?
3. Explain the setting of the opening paragraph. Where is it? What is happening?
4. What do you think happens that causes Walter to be transported from his real life world to his imaginary, fictional world?

Proofread your answers and correct any mistakes.

 ## C. Pairwork

Copy the diagram below into your copy and fill in the details for each of Walter's five transformations. The first one is done for you, complete the remaining four.

Real World
Driving to town to do weekly tasks: hairdressers/ shopping

The Trigger
The driving and the speed triggers him to go to his imaginary world

Fiction World
Flying a Navy Hydroplane in icy, dangerous conditions

 ## D. Writing

Imagine that it is Walter's wife who has a vivid imagination. Describe a transformation that she might have in the hairdressers.

The Wild Duck's Nest *by Michael McLaverty*

This short story is from McLaverty's first collection of short stories, *The Game Cock and Other Stories*, published in 1947.

The sun was setting, spilling gold light on the low western hills of Rathlin Island. A small boy walked jauntily along a hoof-printed path that wriggled between the folds of these hills and opened out into a crater-like valley on the cliff-top. Presently he stopped as if remembering something, then suddenly he left the path, and began running up one of the hills. When he reached the top he was out of breath and stood watching streaks of light radiating from golden-edged clouds, the scene reminding him of a picture he had seen of the Transfiguration. A short distance below him was the cow standing at the edge of a reedy lake.

Colm ran down to meet her waving his stick in the air, and the wind rumbling in his ears made him give an exultant whoop which splashed upon the hills in a shower of echoed sound. A flock of gulls lying on the short grass near the lake rose up languidly, drifting like blown snowflakes over the rim of the cliff.

The lake faced west and was fed by a stream, the drainings of the semi-circling hills. One side was open to the winds from the sea and in winter a little outlet trickled over the cliffs making a black vein in their grey sides. The boy lifted stones and began throwing them into the lake, weaving web after web on its calm surface. Then he skimmed the water with flat stones, some of them jumping the surface and coming to rest on the other side. He was delighted with himself and after listening to his echoing shouts of delight he ran to fetch his cow. Gently he tapped her on the side and reluctantly she went towards the brown-mudded path that led out of the valley. The boy was about to throw a final stone into the lake when a bird flew low over his head, its neck a-strain, and its orange-coloured legs clear in the soft light.

It was a wild duck. It circled the lake twice, thrice, coming lower each time and then with a nervous flapping of wings it skidded along the surface, its legs breaking the water into a series of silvery arcs. Its wings closed, it lit silently, gave a slight shiver, and began pecking indifferently at the water.

Colm, with dilated eyes, eagerly watched it making for the farther end of the lake. It meandered between tall bulrushes, its body black and solid as stone against the greying water.

Then as if it had sunk it was gone. The boy ran stealthily along the bank looking away from the lake, pretending indifference.

When he came opposite to where he had last seen the bird he stopped and peered through the sighing reeds whose shadows streaked the water in a maze of black strokes. In front of him was a soddy islet guarded by the spears of sedge and separated from the bank by a narrow channel of water. The water wasn't too deep - he could wade across with care.

Rolling up his short trousers he began to wade, his arms outstretched, and his legs brown and stunted in the mountain water. As he drew near the islet, his feet sank in the cold mud and bubbles winked up at him. He went more carefully and nervously. Then one trouser leg fell and dipped into the water; the boy dropped his hands to roll it up, he unbalanced, made a splashing sound, and the bird arose with a squawk and whirred away over the cliffs. For a moment the boy stood frightened.

Then he clambered on to the wet-soaked sod of land, which was spattered with seagulls' feathers and bits of wind-blown rushes.

Into each hummock he looked, pulling back the long grass.

At last he came on the nest, facing seawards. Two flat rocks dimpled the face of the water and between them was a neck of land matted with coarse grass containing the nest. It was untidily built of dried rushes, straw and feathers, and in it lay one solitary egg. Colm was delighted. He looked around and saw no one.

The nest was his. He lifted the egg, smooth and green as the sky, with a faint tinge of yellow like the reflected light from a buttercup; and then he felt he had done wrong. He put it back. He knew he shouldn't have touched it and he wondered would the bird forsake the nest. A vague sadness stole over him and he felt in his heart he had sinned. Carefully smoothing out his footprints he hurriedly left the islet and ran after his cow. The sun had now set and the cold shiver of evening enveloped him, chilling his body and saddening his mind.

In the morning he was up and away to school. He took the grass rut that edged the road for it was softer on the bare feet.

His house was the last on the western headland and after a mile or so he was joined by Paddy McFall; both boys, dressed in similar hand-knitted blue jerseys and grey trousers, carried homemade school bags. Colm was full of the nest and as soon as he joined his companion he said eagerly: "Paddy, I've a nest—a wild duck's with one egg."

"And how do you know it's a wild duck's? " asked Paddy, slightly jealous.

"Sure I saw her with my own two eyes, her brown speckled back with a crow's patch on it, and her yellow legs—."

"Where is it?" interrupted Paddy, in a challenging tone.

"I'm not going to tell you, for you'd rob it!"

"Aach! I suppose it's a tame duck's you have or maybe an old gull's."

Colm put out his tongue at him. "A lot you know!" he said,

"for a gull's egg has spots and this one is greenish-white, for I had it in my hand."

And then the words he didn't want to hear rushed from

Paddy in a mocking chant, "You had it in your hand! ... She'll forsake it! She'll forsake it! She'll forsake it!" he said, skipping along the road before him.

Colm felt as if he would choke or cry with vexation.

His mind told him that Paddy was right, but somehow he couldn't give in to it and he replied: "She'll not forsake it! She'll not! I know she'll not!"

But in school his faith wavered. Through the windows he could see moving sheets of rain— rain that dribbled down the panes filling his mind with thoughts of the lake creased and chilled by wind; the nest sodden and black with wetness; and the egg cold as a cave stone. He shivered from the thoughts and fidgeted with the inkwell cover, sliding it backwards and forwards mechanically.

The mischievous look had gone from his eyes and the school day dragged on interminably. But at last they were out in the rain, Colm rushing home as fast as he could.

He was no time at all at his dinner of potatoes and salted fish until he was out in the valley now smoky with drifts of slanting rain. Opposite the islet he entered the water. The wind was blowing into his face, rustling noisily the rushes heavy with the dust of rain. A moss-cheeper, swaying on a reed like a mouse, filled the air with light cries of loneliness.

The boy reached the islet, his heart thumping with excitement, wondering did the bird forsake. He went slowly, quietly, on to the strip of land that led to the nest. He rose on his toes, looking over the ledge to see if he could see her. And then every muscle tautened. She was on, her shoulders hunched up, and her bill lying on her breast as if she were asleep. Colm's heart hammered wildly in his ears. She hadn't forsaken. He was about to turn stealthily away. Something happened. The bird moved, her neck straightened, twitching nervously from side to side.

The boy's head swam with lightness. He stood transfixed. The wild duck with a panicky flapping, rose heavily, and flew off towards the sea . . . A guilty silence enveloped the boy . . . He turned to go away, hesitated, and glanced back at the bare nest; it'd be no harm to have a look. Timidly he approached it, standing straight, and gazing over the edge. There in the nest lay two eggs. He drew in his breath with delight, splashed quickly from the island, and ran off whistling in the rain.

 # A. Reading

1. Rate this text for 'readability'. Write the word/phrase of your choice into your copy.

   VERY EASY ☐ **EASY** ☐ **OKAY** ☐ **HARD** ☐ **VERY HARD** ☐

2. Copy the following headings into your copy and fill in the appropriate words from the text of 'The Wild Duck's Nest'.

Gist words (words which I half figured out)	Words I didn't understand at all

 # B. Literacy Questions

1. Do you think that Colm likes nature? Explain your answer. Use two pieces of evidence from the story to support your point.

2. What do you think 'she'll forsake it' means, in the story above?

3. While in school, and after school, Colm felt a sense of urgency to return to the nest. What words/phrases show us this feeling?

4. Why does Colm feel happy at the end of the story?

Proofread your answers and correct any mistakes.

 # C. Creative Writing – Write the Next Part of the Story

Imagine you are Colm. You have left the nest, happy and homeward bound. You bump into Paddy. Write out the conversation/dialogue between yourself and Paddy. Use the format and layout used in the drama extracts.

ACE this task!

Janey Mary *by James Plunkett*

This short story is from the collection, *The Trusted and the Maimed*, published in 1945.

When Janey Mary turned the corner into Nicholas Street that morning, she leaned wearily against a shop-front to rest. Her small head was bowed and the hair which was so nondescript and unclean covered her face. Her small hands gripped one another for warmth across the faded bodice of her frock. Around the corner lay Canning Cottages with their tiny, frost-gleaming gardens, and gates that were noisy and freezing to touch. She had tried each of them in turn. Her timid knock was well known to the people who lived in Canning Cottages. That morning some of them said: "It's that little 'Carthy one, never mind opening. Twice in the last week she's been around—it's too much of a good thing." Those who did answer her had been dour. They poked cross and harassed faces around half-open doors. Tell her mammy, they said, it's at school she should have her, and not out worrying poor people the likes of them. They had the mouths of their own to feed and the bellies of their own to fill, and God knows that took doing.

The school was in Nicholas Street and children with satchels were already passing. Occasionally Janey Mary could see a few paper books peeping from an open flap, and beside them a child's lunch and a bottle of milk. In the schoolroom was a scrawled and incomprehensible blackboard, and rows of staring faces which sniggered when Janey Mary was stupid in her answers.

Sometimes Father Benedict would visit the school. He asked questions in Catechism and gave the children sweets. He was a huge man who had more intuition than intellect, more genuine affection for children than for learning. One day he found Janey Mary sitting by herself in the back desk. She felt him, giant-like above her, bending over her. Some wrapped sweets were put on her desk.

"And what's your name, little girl?"

"Janey Mary 'Carthy, Father."

"I'm Father Benedict of the Augustinians. Where do you live?" Father Benedict had pushed his way and shoved his way until he was sitting in the desk beside her. Quite suddenly Janey Mary had felt safe and warm. She said easily, "I lives in Canning Cottages."

He talked to her while the teacher continued self-consciously with her lesson.

"So, your daddy works in the meat factory?"

"No, Father, my daddy's dead."

Father Benedict nodded and patted her shoulder. "You and I must be better friends, Janey," he said. "We must tell your mammy to send you to school more often."

"Yes, Father."

"Because we must see more of one another, mustn't we?"

"Yes, Father."

"Would you always come?"

"I'd like to come, Father."

Father Benedict had talked with her for some time like that, the pair of them crushed clumsily in the desk and their heads close together. When he was leaving he gave her more sweets.

Later the teacher took them from her as a punishment and gave them out again as little prizes for neatness.

She thought of Father Benedict until an old beggar who was passing said to her: "Are you whingin', child? Is there anything up with you?"

She lifted her head and looked stupidly at him, her mouth open and her eyes quite dry. He was a humpbacked man with broken boots and a bulbous nose. The street about him was a moving forest of feet; the stolid tread of workmen and the pious shuffle of middle-aged women on their way from Mass.

"You look a bit shook, kid," he said. "Are you after taking a turn?"

"No, mister," she said, wondering "I'm only going for to look for bread at St. Nicholas's. My mammy told me."

"Your mammy left it a bit late. They'll be going in for to pray." As though awakened by his words, the bell of the Augustinian Friary rang three times. It rang out with long, resounding strokes across the quivering street, and people paused to uncover their heads and to bless themselves.

Janey Mary looked up quickly. The steeple of the church rose clear and gleaming above the tall houses, and the golden slimness of its cross raced swiftly against the blue and gold of the sky.

Her mother had said: "Look till you find, my lady, and you won't lose your labour. This is the day of the Blessed Bread and if you get it nowhere else they'll be giving it out at St. Nicholas's."

She turned suddenly and ran quickly up the length of the street. But when she reached the priory the doors were closed and the waiting queue had broken into small knots. She stopped uncertainly and stared for some time.

The priests, the people said, had gone in to pray. They would be back in an hour.

She was glad to turn homewards. She was tired and her bare feet moved reluctantly on the ice-cold pavement. Johnny might have been given some bread on his round with the sticks, or her mother might have had some hidden away. Her mother sometimes did that so that Janey Mary would try very hard to get some.

Picking her way amongst the debris-littered wasteland upon which houses had once stood, she watched her shadow bobbing and growing with the uneven rippling of the ground. The light of the wintry sun rested wanly on everything and the sky was dizzily blue and fluffed a little with white cloud. There were rust-eaten tin-cans lying neglected on the waste, and fragments of coloured delf which she could have gathered to play chaneys had she had the time. The children often went there to play shop; they marked out their pitches with a file of pebbles in the form of an open square. When Janey Mary stood in one of the squares for a moment she was no longer Janey Mary. The wasteland became a busy street and the tracery of pebbles glittering stores. Her face would grow grave. It was that serene gravity of a child at play. But when she stepped out of the magic square she was again Janey Mary, a Janey Mary who was cold and hungry and whose mother was waiting impatiently for bread that had not been found.

"There was none," she said, looking up at her mother's face. "Nobody would give it and the man said the priests wouldn't be back for an hour." She looked around hopefully as she spoke, but there were only a few crumbs on the table. They littered its grease-fouled and flower-patterned covering. An enamel jug stood in the centre and about it the slopped ugliness of used cups. Now that she was home she realised how endless the morning's trudging had been. She realised how every door had been closed against her. Her mother's voice rose.

"Then you can do without. Are you after looking at all, you little trollop? Two hours to go the length of the street and around to the holy priests, and us all in a wakeness with the hunger. And Johnny going out with the sticks and him famished but for the little bit I had left away. Are you after looking at all?"

The enamel of the jug was broken in three places. The breaks were spidery, like the blobs of ink which used to fall so dishearteningly on her copy-books. Down the side of each cup clung the yellow residue of dribbled tea. The whole table shifted suddenly and went back again, and her mother's voice seemed far away. Janey Mary wanted to sit down.

"Gallivanting," her mother said, "off gallivanting with your pals. I'll gallivant you. But you can go back again. There's nothing in the house. Back with you to the priests' house and wait like any Christian for what's going. And take the bag with you. You don't do a hand's turn till you do that."

Janey Mary stood with her hands clasped in front of her and looked up at her mother. The thought of going back again filled her with misery.

"I asked," she said. "I asked everywhere."

"Then you can ask again," said her mother. "You can ask till you find," and swung away. Janey Mary went wearily to the corner to fetch the bag. The kitchen trembled and became dark when she bent to pick it up. As she went out of the door her mother said:

"Put a bit of hurry on yourself and don't be slingeing. It's certain you'll never die with the beating of your heart. The world and its wife would get something and mine'd be left."

Once more she was out in the ancient crookedness of streets, picking her way amidst the trundling of wheels and the countless feet. Tiny and lost beneath the steepness of houses, she went slowly, her bare feet dragging and dirty. At this hour the shops in Nicholas Street were crowded with women who haggled over halfpennies. White-coated assistants leaned quickly over marble-topped counters with heads cocked to one side and pencils raised in readiness, or dashed from counters to shelves and back again, banging things on the scales and then licking pencil stubs while they frowned over figures. Sometimes Janey Mary used to stand and watch them, but now she went by without interest. When a tram went grinding past her, her lips trembled, and though the rails after it and before it gleamed in the sunlight, it was a pale cold gleaming. There was no friendly heat in the sunlight. There was nothing friendly. There were only trundling trams and the tramp of feet, and once again the slim cross on the spire of St. Nicholas's.

On the Feast of the Blessed Bread it was the custom of the priests to erect a wooden counter on the high steps before the door of the priory. Here two of the brothers stood to watch the forming of the queue. Janey Mary looked hard through the veil which blurred occasionally in front of her eyes, but could catch no sign of Father Benedict. No bread had yet appeared though the queue was growing. She took her place and kept close to the wall. In near the wall she found it easier to hold her position. It was very cold at first, but after a while more people came and the air grew warmer. They came, as she had known they would, with baskets and shawls, with torn shopping bags and ragged coats, and gathered thickly about her. There were men there too, old pensioners and men who had not worked for years.

"There won't be much going," they said. "There was a shocking crowd here this morning."

"Take your bloody hour," they said. "Who d'you think you're pushing?"

"Aisy, aisy, mind the chisler."

They talked like that for a long time. At first they argued furiously with one another. But later they became dour with impatience. They shuffled uncomfortably. They spat frequently and heaved long sighs.

After a while it became frightening to be in there so close to the wall, to be so small that everyone towered over you. Janey Mary felt weak and wanted to get out. When she glanced sideways or ahead of her she could see nothing but tightly packed bodies, and when she looked down there were feet, but no ground. She tried to look upwards, but could not. An hour passed before Father Benedict appeared on the steps.

"Father Benedict, God bless him," they said. "It'll be coming soon when he's here."

Janey Mary was lifted clear off the ground by the movement of the crowd and lost her place. Now she was behind a stoop-backed man with a threadbare coat and heavily nailed boots.

His collar was flaked and greasy with dandruff and his coat was foul smelling, but it was the boots which held Janey Mary's attention. They clattered unsteadily on the pavement very close to her bare feet. There were diamond-shaped nails in double rings about the heels of them. She bent to keep her eyes fixed on the boots and wriggled to avoid them. Her attention became fixed on them. To a man near her she said, "I want to get out, mister, let me get out," but even if he had heard her he could not have helped her now. She tried to attract attention, but they had forgotten her. They kept telling one another over and over again what each of them already knew.

"It's coming," they said, pressing forward, "it's coming." And after a while the murmuring changed and the queue surged.

"Look," they shouted,"it's here."

Janey Mary was lifted once more. Once more her feet were clear of the ground and her breathing stifled by the pressure of those around her. She was in danger now and clawed whimpering at the dandruff-flaked collar. Through a whirl of arms and shoulders she had a view of Father Benedict, his broad shoulders tall and firm above the press of bodies. She tried to call out to him.

"The chisler," someone said, noticing. "For God's sake quit pushing. Look at the chisler." A man threw out his hand to grip her, but a movement of the crowd twisted him suddenly aside.

She saw his hand grabbing futilely to her left. As the crowd parted she began to slip.

"Father Benedict," she called faintly, "Father Benedict."

Then the man in front stumbled and the nailed boots crushed heavily on her feet.

When her eyes opened again she was on the sofa in the visitors' parlour. Father Benedict and one of the lay brothers were bending over her. Someone had put a rug about her. An electric fire glowed warmly against the opposite wall, and over it hung a gold-framed picture of the Sacred Heart. Her feet felt numb and heavy and the picture swam before her eyes. But it was warm in the parlour and the morning's searching was over. Then she remembered the bread and her mother's words. She moved suddenly, but when she tried to speak her ears were filled with noise. The lay brother had turned to Father Benedict.

"You were very quick," he was saying. "Is she badly hurt?"

Father Benedict, answering him, said in a strange voice:

"Only her feet … You can see the print of the nails …"

A. Reading

1. Rate this text for 'readability'. Write the word/phrase of your choice into your copy.

   VERY EASY ☐   **EASY** ☐   **OKAY** ☐   **HARD** ☐   **VERY HARD** ☐

2. Copy the following headings into your copy and fill in the appropriate words from the text of 'Janey Mary'.

Gist words (words which I half figured out)	Words I didn't understand at all

B. Literacy Questions

1. What problems does Janey Mary face at home?
2. What problems does she face at school?
3. What was the tradition carried out by the priests on the day of the Blessing of the Bread?
4. List all the characters in the story who are i) mean to Janey Mary and ii) kind to her.
5. In your opinion, is Janey Mary a strong or a weak character? Find evidence in the story to support your view.
6. The story is written very descriptively with great detail. Find two examples of description which impressed you.
7. Is there anything which you found good and positive in the story? Explain your answer.

Proofread your answers and correct any mistakes.

C. Visual Literacy/Drawing

Draw the following scenes as you imagine them in your head from the description given; you may need to read the story again in order to put in correct details and colour.

1. Canning Cottages (a row of small terraced cottages)
2. Janey Mary (a small girl)
3. The street which is described as a 'debris-littered wasteland'
4. The visitor's parlour in St. Nicholas's Church

Watch the short film of this story by Paul Brady of Little Step Productions (http://www.janey-mary.com/film.html) and compare the story to the film.

D. Research

James Plunkett also wrote *Strumpet City*, which was chosen for the 2013 Dublin: One City, One Book. This initiative encourages everyone to read a book connected with the capital city during the month of April every year. Find out what the Dublin: One City, One Book is for this year and why it was chosen.

Films

The scriptwriting format we saw in the Drama section is used for films too. When writing a script for something that will be shown on a screen, it is called **screenwriting**. The **screenplay** is written by a **screenwriter** or a group of screenwriters. They write the dialogue and the action (how the characters will act: their movements, gestures, facial expressions, etc.).

The screenwriter can have an original idea, or they might use a novel, short story or drama as the basis for the screenplay of the film. Changing from one type of story to another can change the way in which the story is told, and it can also change the impact that a story has. Remember you had a discussion in Chapter 2 about which you prefer 'the book or the film'?

As in drama, the story in a film is told both visually and aurally. You watch, listen and become absorbed in the world of the film. It is all presented to you, whereas when you read a story in a book, you have to imagine and visualise that world yourself.

The **producer** is responsible for making sure that those making the film have the resources they need while keeping to the budget. The 'author' of a film is usually considered to be the **director** as he or she is responsible for the way the story is told. He or she directs the action.

In a film, the director controls the **viewpoint** and the **perspective**, so unknown to the viewer they are being led to think in a certain way.

Books to Films

Once a novel is chosen to be made into a film, it now has a different audience and a different medium of telling the story. On average, films are 90–120 minutes long (**feature-length**), so the story in an average novel of 200 pages has to be told visually and aurally in two hours or under.

The original story is edited. Parts of the plot may change, bits can be added to the original story or parts can be left out. Characters change too. Sometimes the viewer likes the changes made; other times they are disappointed with them.

Writing

Choose a book that was made into a film. Think about the differences and changes made. Fill in the table below in your copy.

BOOKS TO FILM: CHANGES MADE TO THE BOOK

Title of book: _____

Characters added	
Characters left out	
Order of events changed	
Storyline changed	
Other changes that I liked or disliked	

Film Genres

As with books, there are many types, or genres, of film and people have particular favourites. What genres do you like?

- **Adventure/action:** Fast-paced action stories (*The Bourne Ultimatum*, *The Fast and the Furious*).
- **Animation:** These films are created using methods other than live-action. They can be created using a series of illustrations or using computer graphics, and many of the ones made today fall into the family friendly genre as well (*Toy Story*, *Up*, *Frozen)*.
- **Classic:** These are generally old films that are excellent and are loved from generation to generation (*Some Like It Hot*, *Citizen Kane*, *Casablanca*, *Chitty Chitty Bang Bang*).
- **Comedy:** The characters in a comedy do and say things that are funny and amuse the audience (*Anchorman: The Legend of Ron Burgundy*, *Muppets Most Wanted*).
- **Detective:** In these films detectives investigate crimes (often murder) using their special talents (*Sherlock Holmes, Murder on the Orient Express*).
- **Drama:** A film drama shows real situations and the development of realistic characters, usually showing their emotions (*The King's Speech, Philomena)*.
- **Epic drama:** Epics are long films telling a long story, maybe with history or war in the plot (*Gone with the Wind, Lawrence of Arabia)*.
- **Family friendly:** These are films that the whole family can watch as the content is appropriate for younger viewers, yet interesting enough for the adults (*Shrek*, *E.T.*).
- **Film noir:** These are stylish crime thrillers created in the 1940s and 1950s in black and white (*The Third Man*, *The Maltese Falcon)*.
- **History:** These are films based on historical events and famous people (*Gandhi*, *JFK*, *Hotel Rwanda)*.
- **Psychological thriller:** Psychological thrillers or horror movies are full of tension and suspense and they focus on the mental state of the characters (*Black Swan*, *Psycho)*.
- **Romance:** The plots of these movies revolve around central love stories between the characters, *(The Notebook, Love Story)*.
- **Science fiction/Fantasy:** Stories set in other imagined worlds or in situations not true of the world we live in now (*Star Wars*, *E.T.*, *Alice in Wonderland)*.
- **Western:** Stories from the 1860s onwards in America – the 'Wild West' (*Butch Cassidy and the Sundance Kid*, *True Grit)*.

Look up Halliwell's Film Guide if you want to find out a film's genre.

Pairwork

1. Read the list of films below and, working in pairs, try to place each film into its genre.

We saw in Chapter 2 that novels can fall into more than one genre, and the same can be said for films. Place them where you think they are best suited. If you feel you need to add genres to the list, then do that.

First, place the ones you know, and then research the ones that you don't know – check Halliwell's Film Guide, search online or ask your friends or parents if they have seen them.

Beautiful Creatures	I Married a Monster	Pitch Perfect	The Lord of the Rings
Bridge to Terabithia	In America	Princess: A Modern Fairytale	The Man from Laramie
Brief Encounter	Life is Beautiful	She's the Man	The Pursuit of Happyness
Captain Phillips	Madagascar	Spiderman	The Simpsons Movie
Despicable Me	Monsters Inc	Spy Kids	The Truman Show
Gravity	Mr. Bean's Holiday	The Birds	Turbo
Grown-ups 2	Mulan	The Blind Side	Wreck-It Ralph
The Hunger Games	My Girl	The Hobbit	
I Am Sam	Philomena		

2. Write a list of your favourite films. Swap lists with a partner and discuss them.

3. Compile a list of the class group's Top 10 favourite films.

Features of Film-making

Meaning can be created in a film using different techniques:

- Opening scene
- Lighting
- Camera shots and angles
- Camera movement
- Soundtrack
- Voiceovers

Opening Scene

The opening scene is very important in a film as it does some or all of the following:

- Presents the setting/location
- Introduces the main characters
- Sets a mood or tone
- Captures the interest of the viewer
- Sets the expectations of the viewer
- Gives background information

The opening scene can be set in the present, the past or the future.

A. Oral Language

Look at the opening scenes in a few films (ask your teacher if you can bring in 12-rated films) and discuss the following.

1. How do films use openings to draw the audience into the story?
2. How do films use openings to set up certain expectations on the part of the viewer?

Lighting

Lighting is a very important aspect for shaping meaning in films. What kind of atmosphere is created in a room lit by candles? Have you ever heard of mood lighting? A room that is brightly lit by neon lights might seem to be sterile, and a shadowy room might be eerie or scary. The lighting technicians in a film crew have the task of creating lighting to suit the mood and atmosphere of each scene in a film.

Camera Shots and Angles

A **camera shot** is the amount of space that is seen in one shot or 'frame'. Camera shots are used to show different aspects of a film's setting, characters and themes.

- **Extreme long-shot:** Gives a good idea of the general location.
- **Long shot:** Gives the viewer a more specific idea of setting.
- **Full shot:** Contains a complete view of the characters.
- **Close up:** Helps the viewer to understand the character's emotions.
- **Extreme close-up:** Creates an intense feeling as it focuses on one part of a character's face or an object – used a lot in horror films.

Camera angles are used to position the viewer so that they can understand the relationships between the characters.

- **High angle:** The camera is looking down on the character, can make them look vulnerable.
- **Low-angle:** The camera is looking up at the character, can make them look powerful.
- **Eye-level:** This is the most commonly used and puts the audience at the same level as the characters.

When analysing a film, you should always think about the different camera shots and angles and why they are being used.

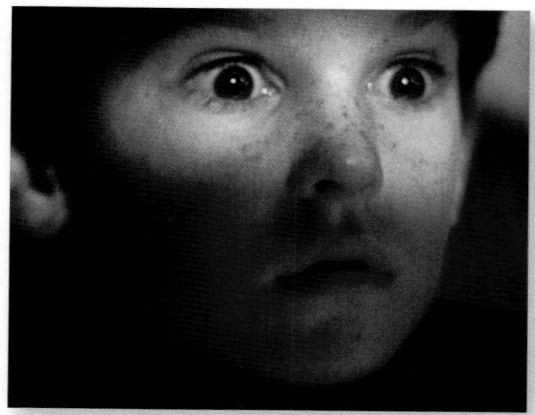

E.T. – the Extra-Terrestrial

The Blair Witch Project

Titanic

Jurassic Park

The Return of the Magnificent Seven

Terminator 2: Judgment Day

Superman

Independence Day

B. Visual Literacy

Can you say what camera shot/angle has been used in each of the film stills on p. 256 opposite? In each case say why you think that shot/angle was used?

Camera Movement

Camera movement is often used to 'follow' the action. It is also used to show the setting in different ways.

- **Crane shot:** The camera is put on a crane and lifted upwards – often used at the end of a film.
- **Tracking shot:** The camera moves on tracks to follow the action or character,
- **Panning:** The camera moves from one side to the next in a wide sweeping way to give the viewer a panoramic view of the setting.

Cinematography is the name given to the combination of the techniques described above. We use the term cinematography to group all of these together; for example, we might say 'The cinematography in that film was exceptional'.

Visual Literacy

Watch all or a part of a film and notice the cinematography. The 1941 film *Citizen Kane* was nominated for an Academy Award for Cinematography and is considered by some to be one of the best films ever made.

Soundtrack

Music is a powerful tool in films. A film's soundtrack affects the mood and atmosphere and has an impact on the viewer/audience.

Listening

For homework or classwork, make a list of the songs in *Shrek* or any other film of your choice. Which ones are sad? Which ones are happy and uplifting?

Voiceover

A **voiceover** is when a voice narrates a piece of the story. The listener/viewer hears the voice, but there is no image of the speaker. A voiceover may be used in the opening scene, closing scene or any scene. The voice gives important information to the audience.

Voiceovers are used a lot in advertising on radio and television, as well as in films.

A. Pairwork

In pairs, write a ten-second voiceover to match the opening shots of a film that the teacher has shown your class.

B. Oral Language

1. Speak your voiceover from task A above. If possible record it and replay it.
2. Create your own voiceover for a trailer (ad) for your favourite film.

Short Films

Short films are shorter than the average feature-length film. They can be any length, from a two-minute film uploaded on YouTube to a 10-, 20- or 30-minute film on TV, or even longer.

Short films can easily be shown in one class period. They can be powerful, generating discussion on a wide range of themes. YouTube is a good resource for short films.

A. Research

1. See what short films you can find on www.irishfilm.ie/shorts or on YouTube.

2. Check out Údar on YouTube for great short films in Irish.

B. Creative Project – Design a Film Poster

In your **PORTFOLIO**, design a poster for any film you like, new or old. Use the following list to brainstorm before you start to draw.

- Title of film
- Text promoting it
- Colour scheme
- Main image
- Background image
- Font styles
- Font sizes
- Symbols
- Other features

ACE this task! Remember RAFT.

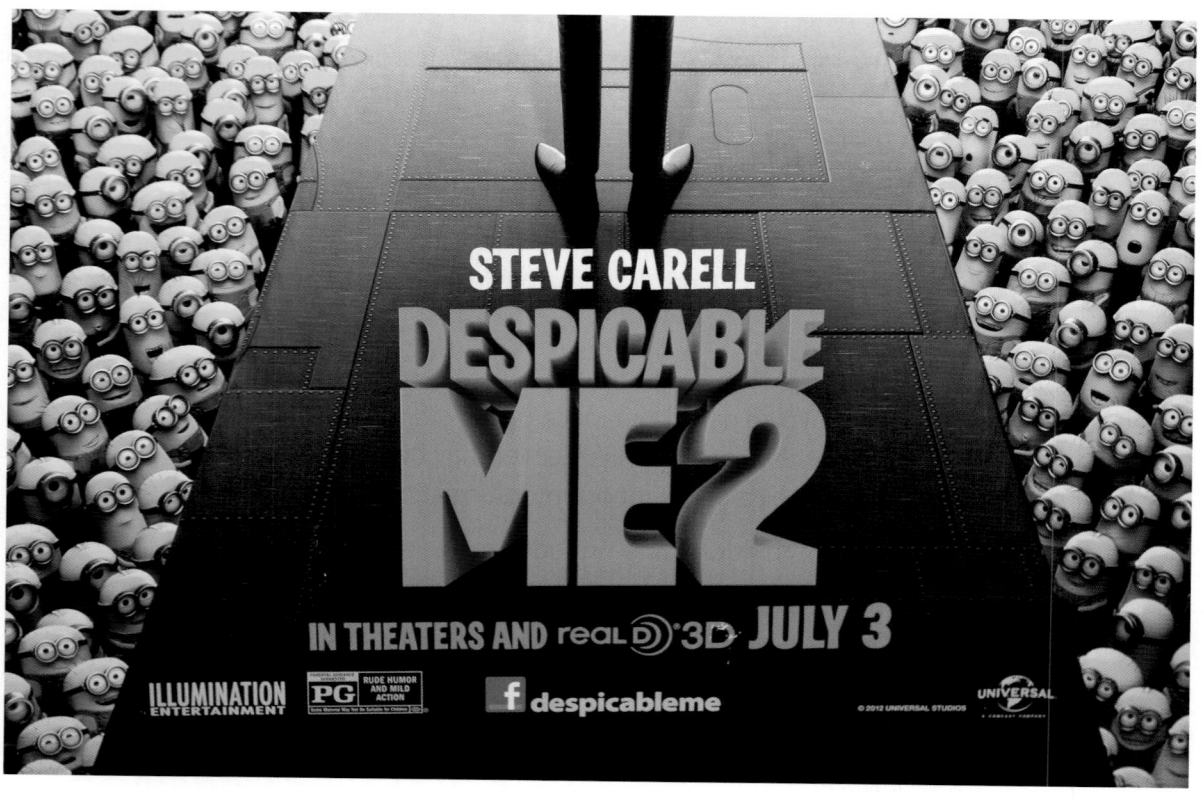

Focus on Fairy-tales

In general there are good and bad characters in films – the **heroes** and **villains**. The audience usually likes the heroic, good characters and hopes that the evil ones will be defeated. Let's look at fairy-tales as a good example of where heroes meet villains. Usually these stories have conflict and problems and then happy endings.

A fairy-tale is a short story set in a magical place or a fantasy land with characters such as goblins, elves, fairies, giants, witches, trolls, dwarves, gnomes and mermaids. Fairy-tales have evolved from stories that are centuries old. They take place not in an actual time but 'once upon a time'. Humble heroes battle the bad guys, impress the beautiful girl and they marry so it all ends 'happily ever after'. Elements of the fantastical such as talking animals and magical powers are common features of fairy-tales.

Usually in these tales, the prince will try to meet and marry a beautiful princess and they will live happily ever after. Evil characters, such as a wicked witch or the evil stepmother will put obstacles in their way. The good characters suffer for a while, but finally defeat the bad characters. The message is that good triumphs over evil.

 ## A. Pairwork

1. Read the description above and make a list in your copy of the features/elements of fairy-tales. Here is the first one to get you started:

   - Set in a magical place or fantasy land

2. What fairy-tales did you like or dislike when you were younger? Discuss this with the person beside you. Choose one and fill in the table below in your copy. Some examples have been filled in for you.

Character	Traits and Role	Personality	Problem the Character Has
Prince	The good person The hero: brave, courageous, rescues people	Charming Handsome Admired by all Wealthy Powerful	Deceived by evil characters
Princess	The heroine: beautiful, perfect, wealthy	Kind and good Searching for true love with a prince Wants to live 'happily ever after'	Helpless role She is dependent on others and on fate/ fortune

B. Writing

Think about the following fairy-tales: *Pinocchio, Snow White and the Seven Dwarfs, Sleeping Beauty, The Three Little Pigs, Little Red Riding Hood, The Princess and the Frog.*

Copy the following table and fill in the details for each of the fairy-tales listed above:

Fairy-tale	Good Characters	Bad Characters	Plot
Cinderella	Cinderella Fairy Godmother The Prince	Stepmother Stepsister 1 Stepsister 2	Cinderella is treated like a servant by her evil Stepmother and Stepsisters. The Prince has a ball in search of a bride. Cinderella is helped to go by her fairy godmother. The Prince falls in love with her. She must leave before midnight and loses a glass slipper as she runs out. The girl whose foot fits the slipper will marry the Prince. The Prince finds her and they marry and live happily ever after.

Shrek: A Modern Fairy-tale

Think about the *Shrek* series (*Shrek*, *Shrek 2*, *Shrek the Third*, *Shrek Forever After*) and how the film-makers took the traditional plots of old fairy-tales and nursery rhymes and modernised them. *Shrek* is a modern twist on old stories and rhymes.

Here are summaries of the first two *Shrek* films.

Shrek

Shrek is a grumpy green ogre who loves the privacy of his swamp in the Kingdom of Far Far Away. One day his peace is destroyed when Lord Farquaad sends all the fairy-tale characters in the land to live in his swamp. Shrek tells them that he will go ask Farquaad to send them back. He brings along a talking donkey who is the only fairy-tale creature who knows the way to Duloc.

When Shrek and Donkey get to the palace, they become involved in a tournament organised by Farquaad. He wants to find the most courageous knight so he can send them to rescue Princess Fiona, who lives in a castle guarded by a dragon. Farquaad can only become King if he marries a Princess. He doesn't love Fiona and he doesn't know her secret. A childhood curse means that from sunrise to sunset she is a beautiful girl, but at sunset she turns into an ogre. Shrek beats all the knights in battle. Farquaad says he will take all the fairy-tale creatures out of the swamp if Shrek rescues Princess Fiona from the dragon.

Shrek and Donkey travel to the castle and split up to find Fiona. Donkey meets Dragon and sweet-talks the beast. Dragon takes a liking to him and captures him. Shrek finds Fiona and then rescues Donkey from the dragon, who chases them out of the castle.

On the way back to Duloc, Shrek and Fiona fall in love. Shrek overhears Fiona telling Donkey that she is an 'ugly beast', and Shrek thinks she is talking about him. The next morning, Shrek brings Farquaad to her and he goes back to the privacy of his swamp. He is miserable without Fiona and Donkey convinces him to go to her.

Fiona must marry Farquaad before she turns into an ogre at sunset. Shrek interrupts the wedding just as Farquaad is about the kiss Fiona. The sun sets and Fiona turns into an ogre in front of everyone in the church, causing Shrek to fully understand what he overheard. Farquaad, disgusted by Fiona, orders his knights to kill her. They fight with Shrek. Shrek whistles for Dragon who bursts in and eats Farquaad. Shrek and Fiona kiss. Fiona is bathed in light as her curse is broken, but is surprised that she is still an ogre, as she thought she would become beautiful. Shrek thinks she is beautiful and they marry in the swamp without her parent's knowledge.

Shrek 2

Prince Charming is reading a storybook about Fiona's early life. He is sent by Fiona's parents, the King and Queen, to rescue her from the castle, unaware of the fact that he's too late – Shrek has already rescued and married her! When Prince Charming gets to the castle, a wolf is in Fiona's bed. He informs Charming that Fiona and Shrek are on honeymoon. When time passes, her parents think that she has married Prince Charming. They invite Fiona and her husband to come home to them for a ball in Far Far Away. Shrek thinks it's a bad idea to go, but Fiona convinces him. Gingerbread Man, Pinocchio, the three little pigs and the Big Bad Wolf house-sit for them when they go.

The King and Queen are horrified at Fiona's changed looks and her ogre husband. A huge fight occurs and Fiona storms off. Her Fairy Godmother appears and offers her material goods to make her happy. Fiona refuses these. Shrek thinks that they should leave, but they stay the night. In the middle of the night, Shrek finds a diary in Fiona's room. He reads it and realises that she had wanted to marry the typical, traditional, handsome prince and now he feels inadequate. The next morning, the King apologises to Shrek over the fight and suggests that they go hunting. In the forest, Shrek realises that the King has sent an assassin to kill him: Puss in Boots. Shrek defeats Puss in Boots. Puss is humbled and offers to help Shrek. They go to the Fairy Godmother to get a potion to make Fiona feel happy. The Fairy Godmother refuses to give the potion (because Prince Charming is her son and *he* wants to marry Fiona). Shrek steals a potion. On the way back to the castle, Donkey offers to taste the potion. He tastes it, and then Shrek tastes it. The potion makes them drowsy. They fall asleep. When they awake, Donkey is a handsome stallion and Shrek is a handsome man. Since Shrek drank the potion, it also affected Fiona – she's pretty now.

Back at the castle, Shrek and Fiona try to find each other. The Fairy Godmother locks Shrek in a room. Her son, Prince Charming, finds Fiona and pretends to be Shrek. The King, however, knows the truth. He asks the Fairy Godmother to stop it all. The Fairy Godmother wants to give Fiona a potion to make Fiona love Prince Charming. The Fairy Godmother threatens to take away the King's own 'happy ever after', so having no choice, he agrees. Shrek finds out and tries to stop Charming from stealing Fiona, but Shrek gets arrested. His house-sitters see this on the news and they rush to Shrek's rescue. They ask the Muffin Man to make them a giant gingerbread man. A ball is organised at the castle. The King drinks the love potion instead of giving it to Fiona. Shrek breaks into the castle and ruins the ball. Charming thinks Fiona has taken the love potion. He kisses her but she knocks him out. The Fairy Godmother attacks Shrek and Fiona. In the ensuing battle, the King gets turned into his true form, a Frog Prince, and it is revealed that the Fairy Godmother is Prince Charming's mother. Shrek offers Fiona a chance to stay beautiful forever, but she refuses. She wants to stay an ogre like Shrek. Charming gets arrested. Shrek and Fiona live happily ever after.

 ## A. Oral Language

Compare the *Shrek* films to traditional fairy-tales. What have the film directors done with the traditional fairy-tales in the *Shrek* films?

How have they taken the basic plot and made it modern, exciting, funny and highly entertaining?

B. Creative Project – Write a Story for a Film

Imagine you work for a film company like DreamWorks (the makers of *Shrek*). You and your team of scriptwriters, illustrators, graphic designers, animators and computer experts have been assigned a task:

'Find an old story and rewrite a modern version of it, which will then be turned into a film.' Keep it short and manageable: a three-minute story can tell a lot and have a great impact. Remember the ingredients for a story from Chapter 2:

- **Setting:** a place/location and a time, date/era
- **Characters**
- **Plot** or storyline
- An interesting **beginning**
- Unexpected actions/**events**, twists and turns
- **Suspense** and tension to keep the reader reading
- A thought-provoking (perhaps unpredictable) **ending**
- Also, as the writer/director you will control the **viewpoint** and **perspective** for the reader/viewer.

Consider the following questions:

Step 1: Setting:
- Where is your film set? (Magical world, fantasy world, futuristic world, space, etc.)
- How is this world ruled or governed?

Step 2: Characters and plot
- Are there one or two main characters that the audience will like and support?
- Are there one or two villains who will shock the audience and spoil the good in the story?
- What problems will the characters face? What conflicts will occur? How will they cope?
- Is it a story of good versus evil with heroes and villains?

Step 3: How will the story end?
- Try to figure out your ending early on so you can add in your unexpected twists and misleading clues about characters.

Step 4: Beginning and unexpected events
- How will your beginning catch the reader's attention?
- Where can you put in an unexpected twist to surprise the audience and the characters?
- Think about the unexpected in murder mysteries; what tricks do they use?
  - Is someone related to another character, but this is only revealed much later in the story?
  - Who appears to be the trustworthy friend, but is the villain all along?
  - Who appears to be the villain and the main suspect, but is actually a good person?
- How is coincidence used in the story? Someone just happens to arrive at a location or just turns up at the right time or finds an important clue, etc.
- What clues are genuine and which ones are false to lead you on the wrong trail?

Step 5: Write in a very descriptive way
'The green gargoyle lunged furiously at the headless half-horse, half-boy beast and let out a blood-curdling snarl', etc.

Step 6: Draft and re-draft the story until you are all happy with it.

Step 7: Change the story from prose to dialogue. Rehearse it and act it out.

Step 8: Film the story if you can.

Step 9: Show it to your class.

Remember to ACE this task and have fun!

ASSESSMENT

Complete this assessment in your **PORTFOLIO**.

💬 Oral Assessment

With another student, act out a scene from a drama or film of your choice.

OR

Give a short, informal talk to the class about 1) your favourite film/novel/drama, or 2) your experience of the performing arts (theatre/variety shows/talent shows/concerts, etc.). (Complete the Oral Assessment Checklist in your **PORTFOLIO**.) (10 marks)

Written Assessment

A. Telling a Story

1. Explain *how* Drama tells a story. What elements/features/tools are used in drama to tell the story? (10 marks)

   _____

2. Explain *how* Short Stories tell a story. What elements/features/tools are used by the writer? (10 marks)

   _____

3. Explain *how* Film tells a story. What elements/features/tools are used by the director? (10 marks)

   _____

B. Revision on Writing Styles

Can you match the words from the list below with their features in the table? The first one is done for you.

- Personal Writing
- Songs
- Poems
- Fiction novels/short stories

- Non-literary texts
- Drama
- Writing for Film

Type of Writing	Features
Personal writing	Personal and unique experiences
	First person narration
	Sentences
	Paragraphs
	Biographies, autobiographies, memoirs, diaries and anecdotes
	May exaggerate for humour or emphasis
	Verses
	Descriptive words
	Concise, shorter style than story writing
	Chorus
	Rhythm and rhyme
	Tell stories about themes such as love, loss, etc.

ASSESSMENT

Type of Writing	Features
	Stanzas
	Descriptive words
	Rhythm and rhyme
	Repetition
	Alliteration and assonance
	Sibilance
	Onomatopoeia
	Similes, metaphors and personification
	Sentences
	Paragraphs
	First or third person narration
	Descriptive words
	Many different genres
	Written to entertain
	Informal or formal
	Interviews
	Surveys and questionnaires, instructions and rules, press releases, petitions, memos, reviews, debates, letters and emails, newsletters, blogs, application forms, brochures, pamphlets and leaflets, invitations
	Persuasive writing
	Advertisements
	Documentaries
	Written for a specific purpose
	Acts and scenes
	Dialogue and stage direction
	Costumes, props, sets, narrator, voiceover, lighting and sound
	Written to entertain
	Opening scene
	Lighting
	Camera shots and angles
	Camera movement
	Soundtrack
	Voiceovers

(7 marks)

Peer Assessment – *swap copies and compare your answers; how did you do?*

C. Self Assessment

I did well in _____

The things that I found difficult were _____

The things that I don't fully understand are _____

I would like to improve _____

Appendix I: Reading for Pleasure

Junior Cycle English Text List (2014-17, 2015-18, 2016-19)

Texts for First Year

Novel

Author	Year First Published	Novel Name and Synopsis
Almond, David	1998	**Skellig** A short, gripping novel about a boy who makes a ghostly friend when his family move to a new house. Unbelievable, yet believable. Highly recommended. This will appeal to boys and girls.
Babbitt, Natalie	1975	**Tuck Everlasting** This is an engaging short (139-page) novel set in America in the late 1800s/early 1900s. It tells the story of a sweet farming family who innocently drink from a spring in the woods and now have the power to live forever, never ageing or dying. Their chance encounter with Winnie, a bored young girl longing for excitement, causes problems which must be resolved somehow. The setting and the families are reminiscent of *The Waltons* and *Little House on the Prairie*. It is an easy-to-read, enjoyable page turner. Suited to all abilities.
Carey, Anna	2011	**The Real Rebecca** A typical, teenage tale about school, friends, crushes, a rock band and a battle of the bands competition.
Colfer, Eoin	2007	**Artemis Fowl** This is the start of a series of eight science/fantasy novels, starring teenage criminal mastermind Artemis Fowl. Colfer himself described the series as '*Die Hard* with fairies'.
Doyle, Roddy	2007	**Wilderness** You can almost feel the cold and see the snow in this engaging tale about a family suffering from a parental separation and the arrival of a long-abandoned sister. Courage and bravery set against freezing temperatures and mixed emotions ensure a very good read for all. Mixed appeal also.
Gaiman, Neil	2002	**Coraline** This is a fantasy novella published in 2002 which traces the adventures of young Coraline into other mysterious, frightening worlds. It is a modern version of *Alice in Wonderland*. Very engaging, easy to read and is a real page turner. It is possibly more suited to girls. There is also a film version.

Author	Year First Published	Novel Name and Synopsis
Grisham, John	2010	**Theodore Boone: Half the Man, Twice the Lawyer** Theo is a 13-year-old boy who likes law. Both his parents are lawyers and he loves courtrooms, trials, judges and complex cases. That is until he unwittingly gets dragged into a murder trial and he knows who dunnit! However, he has promised not to tell. How will he cope with this moral dilemma? Will the cold-blooded murderer go free or will justice be served? Full of tension, a typical Grisham thriller.
Henry, April	2010	**Girl, Stolen** Griffin steals a car not realising that there's a 16-year-old girl asleep in the back seat. Neither does he know that his captive, Cheyenne, is blind and that she is the daughter of a wealthy, powerful businessman. What will he do? What can she do when she literally can't see her way out? Taut and thrilling. Published by the New York Times' best-selling author of teenage thrillers.
Hinton, Nigel	1982	**Buddy** Buddy, a young teenager, suffers because his family are poor, he is taunted in school and his dad is a thief. When his mother leaves them, a series of mysterious events occur which Buddy tries to sort out with the help of his two friends, Julius and Charmian. Full of twists and thoroughly engaging.
Landy, Derek	2007	**Skulduggery Pleasant** This is a horror/fantasy/adventure story about the character Skulduggery Pleasant, a sorcerer and detective who appears at the funeral of Stephanie's uncle and saves Stephanie from a mysterious attacker. He then makes her his partner. Can they save the world from the Sceptre of the Ancients?
McKenzie, Sophie	2006	**Girl, Missing** This thriller tells the story of 14-year-old Lauren who thinks that she may be the missing child, Martha Lauren. Lauren was adopted two months after the child's disappearance and their photos are strikingly similar. Lauren and her best friend James set out to investigate. An engaging page-turner.
Morpurgo, Michael	2003	**Private Peaceful** This is a heart-warming yet sad story of two brothers who fall in love with the same girl and who fight in World War I. An excellent read, suited to boys and girls.
Palacio, R. J.	2012	**Wonder** Highly recommended. This is a very convincing story of a boy named August, who is completely different to his peers due to his facial abnormalities. He is home-schooled until he is ten. Then he starts going to school and he recounts his experiences, both good and bad. Well worth reading and will appeal to girls and boys.

Author	Year First Published	Novel Name and Synopsis
Paulsen, Gary	1993	**Nightjohn** This is a story about slavery, set on the Waller plantation in the 1850s and 1860s. Freed black man, John, returns to slavery and teaches Sarny, the 12-year-old girl who narrates the story, how to read. They must learn in secret in the dead of night since reading is forbidden. The penalty for reading is dismemberment and when John is caught, his middle toes are cut off. Will he make it to freedom, and what will happen to Sarny? A sequel called *Sarny, A Life Remembered* was published in 1998.
Pullman, Philip	2004	**The Scarecrow and his Servant** This award-winning novel tells the story of a scarecrow who is struck by lightning and who comes alive. He sets out on a quest to reach Spring Valley, with an orphan called Jack whom he has hired as a servant. Very enjoyable and suited to all.
Sachar, Louis	1989	**The Boy Who Lost his Face** David tries to get in with the cool gang so he helps to steal a cane from an old lady. She threatens him and he believes she is a witch who has put a curse on him because from that day onwards, misfortune befalls him. Full of surprising twists and an unexpected ending.
Shan, Darren	2000	**Cirque Du Freak** This is the first book in the 12-part series of fantasy/horror stories about a boy and vampires. In this book, Darren and his friend Steve are two ordinary schoolboys who go to a freak show. After the weird show, Steve confronts Mr Crepsley because he thinks he is a vampire. Darren eavesdrops on the conversation and discovers something disturbing!
Taylor, Theodore	1969	**The Cay** This is the popular story of a racist white boy named Phillip, who is rescued from the ocean by an old West Indian man named Timothy. A friendship develops between them as they are both stranded on an island.
Tolkien, J. R. R.	1937	**The Hobbit** This fantasy novel follows the quest of the hobbit Bilbo Baggins to win treasure guarded by the dragon Smaug. He meets many weird creatures on his journey, which culminates in the Battle of Five Armies.
Trinity Comprehensive Writing Group	2013	**In Pieces** Second Year students in Trinity Comprehensive School, Ballymun, wrote this novel with author Kevin McDermott. It tells the story of Alan, whose life has been going to pieces since his mam died. With support from his friend Mary, he wards off hassle from an enemy and discovers he has a special gift which sees him embark on a ghostly journey. This changes his life forever.

Texts for Second and Third Years

Novel

Author	Year First Published	Novel Name and Synopsis
Blackman, Malorie	2001	**Noughts and Crosses** Callum is a Nought. Sephy is a Cross. Noughts and Crosses live in a hostile world and are forbidden to mix. But Callum and Sephy fall in love and are desperate to remain together. Thrilling and absorbing.
Boyne, John	2009	**The Dare** Twelve-year-old Danny Delaney is looking forward to the summer holidays. However, his life is suddenly changed when his mother has a car accident. She knocks down a small boy who is rushed to hospital and is in a coma. Narrated from Danny's viewpoint, this is a moving story, well worth reading.
Brontë, Charlotte	1847	**Jane Eyre** This classic story charts Jane Eyre's life from when she is a ten-year-old orphan, living with the cruel Reed family. She then goes to Lowood school and qualifies as a governess. This takes her to Thornfield Hall where she falls in love with the enigmatic Mr Rochester. Mysterious events unfold after Jane agrees to marry Rochester and she flees the house in the middle of the night. A gripping 400-page read.
Cather, Willa	1918	**My Ántonia** This is the final and most successful novel in a trilogy about migrant families living in hardship in the prairies on their journey to Nebraska. It is preceded by *O Pioneers* and *The Song of the Lark*. Jim is the narrator while Ántonia is the eldest daughter of the Shimerda family. They meet on the train to Black Hawk, Nebraska and there is an instant connection. Jim's parents have died so he is going to live with his grandparents. The novel documents the hardships of these people's lives, particularly the women, and it is an emotional read.
Connolly, John	2006	**The Book of Lost Things** Connolly merges reality and fantasy as 12-year-old David mourns and pines for his dead mother. His family fall apart, he retreats to his attic bedroom and seeks comfort in his books. But what happens when the books begin whispering to him?
Crossan, Sarah	2012	**The Weight of Water** This is a coming-of-age story about Kasienka and her mother who migrate to England. Kasienka not only has to cope with prejudice and bullying in school and finding her first love, but also with accepting the new life which her dad has.

Author	Year First Published	Novel Name and Synopsis
Gleitzman, Morris	2005	**Once** Morris Gleitzman has written a number of books based on the holocaust and his research of people's diaries, letters and stories during 1939-1945. He has written *Once, Then* and *Now* based on his research. *Once* is about a Jewish boy named Felix who hides in the cellar of an orphanage when the Nazis are on the rampage. It is based on the true story of a Jewish doctor who protected and tried to save orphans from the holocaust.
Hinton, S. E.	1967	**The Outsiders** This is a story about peer pressure, rebellion and identity. Two rival teenage groups clash in this compelling story. Wide appeal. There is a 1983 film version by Francis Ford Coppola.
Johnston, Jennifer	1977	**Shadows on our Skin** Shortlisted for the Booker Prize in 1997, this book, set in Derry, explores the difficulties of growing up during 'The Troubles'. Joe Langan leads a monotonous life having to go straight home after school every day for fear of being shot by the British soldiers patrolling the streets. His mother is the main breadwinner while he must help care for his aged alcoholic father. Joe writes poetry during Maths class and his friendship with a lonely young schoolteacher, Kathleen Doherty, changes his world.
Kiernan, Celine	2011	**Into the Grey** Winner of the CBI Book of the Year in 2012, this is a chilling ghost story with an historical backdrop. The plot centres on twins Pat and Dom, and a mysterious goblin-boy. Strained and poignant family relationships, a granny losing her memory, an unexpected fire, and other mysterious events combine to make this a compelling read.
Lee, Harper	1960	**To Kill a Mockingbird** This is a classic American novel set in Alabama in the 1930s. Atticus, a white lawyer, takes on the case of black man Tom who is accused of raping a white woman. Atticus is a widower with two children, Scout, a girl of six, and Jem, her older brother. They befriend Dill and wonder about the mysterious 'Boo' Radley who lives alone and never leaves his house. This is an intriguing tale suited to good readers.
Mitchell, Jane	2009	**Chalkline** Rafiq, like any other young boy, goes to school, goes home, does homework and plays football. But one day, he is snatched by the militant army, brought to live in the mountains and trained to become a soldier. Set in Kashmir, Rafiq's story is based on the reality of children in war-torn regions being abducted and trained as soldiers. It is a harrowing and honest read, highlighting a real human rights issue.

Author	Year First Published	Novel Name and Synopsis
Mulligan, Andy	**2010**	**Trash** Raphael and his friends are poor. They search through trash in dumpsites in order to survive. When Raphael finds a small, leather bag one day, it signifies hope, but then a desperate chase ensues. Raphael and his friends are hounded by the police. Who gets the best deal in the end?
Ness, Patrick	**2008**	**The Knife of Never Letting Go** This is the first intriguing book in a trilogy (*The Ask and the Answer* and *Monsters of Men* follow). Todd Hewitt lives in Prentisstown, a town with no women or girls. As a result of a virus, all the men are able to hear each other's thoughts. However, one day Todd hears a pool of silence in the marshes, and he discovers a girl. Todd decides that he must flee with her. Compelling. Winner of the Guardian Children's Fiction Prize 2008.
Nicholson, William	**2000**	**The Wind Singer** This is the first book in the Wind on Fire trilogy. (*Slaves of the Mastery* and *Firesong* follow). Three children set out on a quest from Aramanth, the walled city ruled by meritocracy (toil, work, grind to succeed). It is an entertaining fantasy which won the 2000 Nestle Smarties Book Prize.
Orwell, George	**1945**	**Animal Farm** A classic story about the 1917 revolution in Russia narrated using the metaphor of animals on a farm.
Portis, Charles	**1968**	**True Grit** This is a classic Western novel told from the viewpoint of 14-year-old Mattie Ross who ventures into Indian country in pursuit of the coward who killed and robbed her father. Portis is one of America's finest comic writers. The novel was made into a film starring John Wayne.
Steinbeck, John	**1937**	**Of Mice and Men** Another great classic tale of survival in the 1930s during the depression in America. Friendship, love and loyalty are tested during George and Lennie's tough experiences throughout the novel.
Swindells, Robert	**1993**	**Stone Cold** Set in London, this is an exciting thriller narrated by homeless teenager Link and his would-be killer, Shelter. Shelter is a psycho on the loose, an ex-soldier whose mission is to clean up the streets.

Drama

Screenwriter/ Playwright	Drama
Breen, John	**Alone it Stands** This is an historical comedy recounting Munster's 1978 victory in Thomond Park over the All Blacks from New Zealand.
Friel, Brian	**Lovers (Winners and Losers)** Written in 1967, the play is told in two parts: part one is Winners and part two is Losers. Winners is about teenagers Mag and Joe who are in love but who lose everyone's respect when Mag becomes pregnant and they are not married. Losers is about an older couple, Hanna and Andy, who have problems in their relationship but cannot divorce.
Gogol, Nikolai	**The Government Inspector** Originally published in 1836, this play, set in Imperial Russia is a comedy of errors focussing on and mocking greed and corruption in human nature.
Haddon, Mark (adapted for stage by Simon Stephens)	**The Curious Incident of the Dog in the Night-Time** Based on the 2003 novel and adapted for the stage, this is a detective story told from Christopher Boone's viewpoint. Chris has Asperger's syndrome so we get a different, inspiring and humorous view of the teenager's dilemmas.
Hill, Susan (adapted for stage by Stephen Mallatratt)	**The Woman in Black** Written in 1983, this frightening ghost story was later adapted by Stephen Mallatratt for the stage and was the second longest running play in the West End. The Woman in Black haunts her native village in revenge for the death of her child.
Laurents, Arthur	**West Side Story** Inspired by Shakespeare's tragic drama Romeo and Juliet it tells the story of two rival gangs in 1950s' New York. The Jets are Polish migrants and the Sharks are Puerto Rican. Tony (a member of the Jets) falls in love with Maria (a member of the Sharks). The musical was performed in 1957 in Broadway and was an instant and enduring success, winning numerous awards.
Morpurgo, Michael (adapted for stage by Nick Stafford)	**War Horse** This is the musical based on the novel written in 1982, about a horse called Joey who is sold to the British cavalry and sent to the front in World War I. His young owner, Albert, sets out on a dangerous mission to find Joey and bring him home. Widely acclaimed.
O'Casey, Seán	**The Shadow of a Gunman** Set in 1920 (written in 1923) during the War of Independence, it tells the story of poet Donal Davoren who is mistakenly labelled as an IRA assassin. This is the first play in a trilogy, the sequels being *Juno and the Paycock* (1924) and *The Plough and the Stars* (1926).

Screenwriter/ Playwright	Drama
Rose, Reginald	**Twelve Angry Men** Set in 1954, this is a tense courtroom drama about a man accused of murdering his father. Twelve men on the jury almost find him guilty but one juror sows the seed of 'reasonable doubt'. If the accused man is found guilty, the penalty is death.
Russell, Willy	**Blood Brothers** Written in 1983 as a story and a musical, the musical became an instant hit, and like *West Side Story*, is still being performed widely. It is based on the *The Corsican Brothers*, a story by Alexandre Dumas, about two conjoined brothers, who, after separation, still felt each other's pain. In *Blood Brothers*, Edward and Mickey are separated at birth but become friends, not realising their connection. The musical has won numerous awards and it ran for 24 years in the West End.
Shakespeare, William	**A Midsummer Night's Dream** **Henry IV Part 1** **Much Ado About Nothing** **The Merchant of Venice** **Romeo and Juliet**
Shaw, George Bernard	**Pygmalion (My Fair Lady)** Published in 1912, this is the charming story of cockney flower seller Eliza Doolittle who is transformed into an upper class lady by Henry Higgins, an elocution teacher and professor of phonetics.
Wilde, Oscar	**The Importance of Being Earnest** First performed in 1895, this is an hilarious comedy of errors satirising the upper class British society of that time.

Film

Director	Film
Benigni, Roberto	**Life is Beautiful** An award-winning film made in Italy in 1997, weaving together humour, pathos, love, war and childhood fun and innocence. It is a truly beautiful film.
Caro, Niki	**Whale Rider** In this 2002 film set in New Zealand, Kahu, a 12-year-old Maori girl wants to become the chief of the tribe, a role reserved for men. Traditions and relationships are challenged in this moving story.
Chadha, Gurinder	**Bend It Like Beckham** A lighthearted 2002 film about a football-mad teenage Indian girl who is a tomboy.
Jennings, Garth	**Son of Rambow** A 2007 film set in the 1980s. It is a coming-of-age story about two boys; Will the model child and Lee the bold child, who join forces to try to make an amateur film.
Laughton, Charles	**The Night of the Hunter** A fantastic black and white thriller, made in 1955, starring Robert Mitchum as a preacher who hates women. He marries them and then kills them. Tense but enjoyable and not at all gruesome.
Linklater, Richard	**School of Rock** A 2003 musical comedy which will appeal to all. A starving rock singer pretends to be a teacher in a posh school. Funny and extremely enjoyable.
Miyazaki, Hayao	**Spirited Away** A 2001 Japanese animated film about a sullen ten year old girl who moves house only to find that she moves worlds too. She leaves the human world and enters the spirit world.
Sheridan, Jim	**In America** A 2002 semi-autobiographical screenplay by Jim Sheridan, this film focuses on a family who migrate to New York and encounter various struggles.
Spielberg, Stephen	**E.T. (The Extra Terrestrial)** This is a 1982 science fiction film telling the story of an alien, E.T. who is stranded on Earth and is befriended by a boy named Elliott.
Zeitlin, Benh	**Beasts of the Southern Wild** An American fantasy drama film not for the faint-hearted. This is a tale of poverty, hardship, broken relationships and the power of nature.

More Classic Fiction – Keep Reading!

Author	Book
Alcott, Louisa May	*Little Women*
Barrie, J. M.	*Peter Pan*
Baum, L. Frank	*The Wonderful Wizard of Oz*
Carroll, Lewis	*Alice's Adventures in Wonderland*
Crompton, Richmal	*Just William*
Dickens, Charles	*A Christmas Carol*
Dickens, Charles	*Oliver Twist*
Eliot, George	*Silas Marner*
Grahame, Kenneth	*The Wind in the Willows*
Handford, S. A.	*Aesop's Fables* (translated)
Hodgson Burnett, Frances	*The Secret Garden*
Lewis, C. S.	*The Chronicles of Narnia*
London, Jack	*The Call of the Wild*
Montgomery, L. M.	*Anne of Green Gables*
Nesbit, E.	*The Railway Children*
Norton, Mary	*The Borrowers*
Pearce, Philippa	*Tom's Midnight Garden*
Peyton, K. M.	*Flambards*
Sewell, Anna	*Black Beauty*
Shelley, Mary	*Frankenstein*
Spyri, Johanna	*Heidi*
Stevenson, Robert Louis	*Kidnapped*
Stevenson, Robert Louis	*Treasure Island*
Tolkien, J. R. R.	*The Lord of the Rings*
Twain, Mark	*The Adventures of Tom Sawyer*
Twain, Mark	*The Adventures of Huckleberry Finn*
Wyss, Johann	*The Swiss Family Robinson*

Appendix II

Suggestions for a Thematic Approach

Theme	Drama	Link	Short Story	Poem
Change	Valley Song	Leaving	Master Melody	The Nomad Torn in Two
Imagination/ Inspiration/ Escape	Waiting for Godot	Dreamers Fantastical worlds	Walter Mitty	The Lake Isle of Innisfree The Song of Wandering Aengus The Door
Love/ Romance	Lovers at Versailles	Love Concern Care	Janey Mary The Wild Duck's Nest	My luve is like a red, red rose Torn in Two The Chess-Board
Nature	Waiting for Godot	Natural world; is it kinder, more noble than the human world?	The Wild Duck's Nest	I wander'd lonely as a cloud Stopping by Woods on a Snowy Evening Silver Frogs Spy in the Sky Blackberry-Picking
Powerlessness	Waiting for Godot	Vulnerability Powerlessness	Janey Mary	Leisure Encounter Boy at the Window Blackberry-Picking Spy in the Sky
Reality/ Truth	Watershed	Arguments Struggle	Janey Mary	Woman Work Dover Beach
Reality/ Truth	Watershed	Childhood	Janey Mary	Mud Between the Toes Golden Stockings Blackberry-Picking
Relationships	Watershed	Conflict Struggle	Janey Mary	Warriors
Relationships	Waiting for Godot	Unusual Eccentric	Walter Mitty	The Song of Wandering Aengus
Relationships	Lovers at Versailles	Humour Comedy	Walter Mitty	The Worm The Fiddler of Dooney Dancing on the Table

Other Themes to consider:

Memories	Childhood	Christmas	Conflict
Love/Romance	Youth	Mystery	Humour

Great Expectations 1: permission acknowledgements

The publisher and author gratefully acknowledge the following for granting permission to reproduce the following copyrighted works.

The publisher and author gratefully acknowledge the following for granting permission to reproduce the following photographs.

Nelson Mandela: *The Long Walk to Freedom* cover (Little Brown, 1995). Reproduced by permission of the publisher • John Hayes: *The Bull* cover (Simon and Schuster, 2013). Reproduced by permission of the publisher • BOY – TALES OF A CHILDHOOD by Roald Dahl (Puffin Books, 2013). Cover reproduced with permission from Penguin Books Ltd • Katie Taylor: *Journey to Olympic Gold* cover (Gill & Macmillan, 2012). Reproduced by permission of the publisher • Katie Taylor playing football: ©INPHO/Andrew Paton • Brian O'Driscoll: © Allstar Picture Library / Alamy • rugby ball: bigstockphoto.com/sportsphotographer.eu • THE SECRET DIARY OF ADRIAN MOLE AGED 13 3/4 by Sue Townsend (Puffin Books, 2009). Cover reproduced with permission from Penguin Books Ltd • Evelyn Waugh: © Lebrecht Music and Arts Photo Library / Alamy • Kilruddery House: © Design Pics Inc. - RM Content / Alamy • *Hilda Murrell's Nature Diaries* cover, reprinted by permission of HarperCollins Publishers Ltd © 1987, Hilda Murrell • servant girl: © Amoret Tanner / Alamy • © Old Visuals / Alamy • Michael D. Higgins: © Doreen Kennedy / Alamy • Harry Potter book cover: © razorpix / Alamy • R J. Palacio: *Wonder* cover published by Bodley Head (2013). Reprinted by permission of The Random House Group Limited • Sarah Moore Fitzgerald: *Back to Blackbrick* cover (The Orion Publishing Group, London, 2013), reprinted by permission of the publisher • Seamus Heaney: © Jeff Morgan 15 / Alamy • *Life of Pi* film poster: © AF archive / Alamy • Jacqueline Wilson: *The Dare Game* cover, published by Corgi Yearling. Reprinted by permission of The Random House Group Limited • Enid Blyton cover: © Antiques & Collectables / Alamy • *The Hobbit* cover, reprinted by permission of HarperCollins Publishers Ltd © The J.R.R. Tolkien Estate Limited 1937, 1965 • Cover illustration of *Eva's Holiday* by Judi Curtin published by The O'Brien Press Ltd, Copyright © 2011 • THE FAULT IN OUR STARS by John Green (Penguin Books, 2012, 2013). Cover reproduced with permission from Penguin Books Ltd • Cover illustration of *Fugitives* by Aubrey Flegg published by The O'Brien Press Ltd, Copyright © 2010 • Cover illustration of *Star Dancer* by Morgan Llywelyn published by The O'Brien Press Ltd, Copyright © 1995 • Cover illustration of *Rebecca Rocks* by Anna Carty published by The O'Brien Press Ltd, Copyright © 2013 • *Hunger Games* cover: © Ben Molyneux / Alamy • Twilight series covers: © Ben Molyneux / Alamy • OLIVER TWIST by Charles Dickens (Penguin Books, 2003). Cover reproduced with permission from Penguin Books Ltd • Little Women cover © Antiques & Collectables / Alamy • WUTHERING HEIGHTS by Emily Brontë (Penguin Books, 2003). Cover reproduced with permission from Penguin Books Ltd • GREAT EXPECTATIONS by Charles Dickens (Penguin Books, 2004). Cover reproduced with permission from Penguin Books Ltd • LES MISERABLES by Victor Hugo (Penguin Books, 1982). Cover reproduced with permission from Penguin Books Ltd • *Harry Potter and the Deathly Hallows* film poster: © Photos 12 / Alamy • *Eclipse* film poster: © AF archive / Alamy • Hogwarts Castle train: © Islandstock / Alamy • Harry Potter film still: © Pictorial Press Ltd / Alamy • Hunger Games trilogy covers: © Ben Molyneux / Alamy • The Magician's Nephew cover: THE LION, THE WITCH AND THE WARDROBE by C.S. Lewis copyright © C.S. Lewis Pte. Ltd. 1950. Jacket art by David Weisner © copyright CS Lewis Pte Ltd 2007. Reprinted by permission • *Great Expectations* film still: © Moviestore collection Ltd / Alamy • *Just William* cover: © Pictorial Press Ltd / Alamy • One Direction: © ZUMA Press, Inc. / Alamy • Rihanna: Everett Collection / Shutterstock.com • Taylor Swift: Helga Esteb / Shutterstock.com • The Beatles: © Pictorial Press Ltd / Alamy • Rolling Stones: © RIA Novosti / Alamy • David Bowie: © ZUMA Press, Inc. / Alamy • One Direction: Featureflash / Shutterstock.com • Passenger: © EXImages / Alamy • Robert Frost: Library of Congress. New York World-Telegram & Sun Collection • W.B. Yeats: © Pictorial Press Ltd / Alamy • The Song of Wandering Aengus: Gianna Ragagnin (Morgaine le Fee) • Seamus Heaney: © jeremy sutton-hibbert / Alamy • Evelyn Cosgrave: photograph reproduced by kind permission of poet • Dermot Bolger: photograph reproduced by kind permission of author • Film review: © Clynt Garnham Publishing / Alamy • *How I Live Now* film still: © Moviestore collection Ltd / Alamy • Nintendo 3DS: © ZUMA Press, Inc. / Alamy • health leaflets: © Jack Sullivan / Alamy • Northern Ireland tourist leaflets: © Stephen Barnes/Northern Ireland / Alamy • Michael Palin: © Stephen Barnes/Arts and Culture / Alamy • Ernest Hemingway's house: © Peter Horree / Alamy • Kilkee Bay: © Arco Images GmbH / Alamy • Coole Park: © Picade LLC / Alamy • Aer Lingus logo: © Peter Probst / Alamy • Ad: © Jeff Morgan 01 / Alamy • Irish broadsheet newspapers: © Radharc Images / Alamy • Irish tabloid newspapers: © Radharc Images / Alamy • Cheryl Cole: Featureflash / Shutterstock.com • Adnan Januzaj: © Aflo Co. Ltd. / Alamy • JFK shot newspapers: © Richard Levine / Alamy • *Waiting for Godot* theatre still: © keith morris / Alamy • *Sherlock Holmes* film poster: © AF archive / Alamy • *Beautiful Creatures* film poster: © AF archive / Alamy • *The Hunger Games* film poster: © Pictorial Press Ltd / Alamy • *Shrek* film poster: © AF archive / Alamy • *Monsters Inc* film poster: © AF archive / Alamy • *E.T. – the Extra-Terrestrial film still*: © Pictorial Press Ltd / Alamy • *The Blair Witch Project film still*: © Photos 12 / Alamy • *Titanic* film still: © Pictorial Press Ltd / Alamy • *Jurassic Park* film still: © AF archive / Alamy • *The Return of the Magnificent Seven film still*: © AF archive / Alamy • *Terminator 2: Judgment Day film still*: © AF archive / Alamy • *Superman* film still: © AF archive / Alamy • *Independence Day* film still: © AF archive / Alamy • *Despicable Me 2* film poster: Getty Images • Cinderella: © Lebrecht Music and Arts Photo Library / Alamy • illustrations on pages 6, 28, 73, 86, 157, 219, 221, 224, 229 and 236 by Emily Skinner of GCI • All other photographs are from Glowimages, Alamy, Bigstock and Shutterstock